# Cultural Intelligence for Stone-Age Brains

# Cultural Intelligence for Stone-Age Brains

## How to work with Danes and beyond

DENNIS NØRMARK

TRANSLATED BY PAUL BRUMMIT

GYLDENDAL BUSINESS

Cultural Intelligence for Stone-Age Brains
*How to work with Danes and beyond*
Dennis Nørmark
© 2013 Gyldendal A/S

Cover and illustrations in the book: Sarah Egbert Eiersholt
Typesetting: Stuntfire/Søren Roed Schack
Printing: Livonia Print
Translated from Danish by Paul Brummit

ISBN: 978-87-02-14993-7

1st edition, 1st printing

Printed in Latvia

Gyldendal Business
Klareboderne 3
1001 Copenhagen K, Denmark
Tel: +45 33 75 55 55
www.GyldendalBusiness.dk

# Chapter Overview

Foreword

Introduction – a realistic book about cultural challenges · 11
    Why have I written this book? · 16
    Principles in this book · 17
    What is the big problem in Denmark? · 18
    Structure · 19
    About this edition · 19


Part 1  Cultural Consciousness · 21

1   When cultures collide · 22
    How is someone anthropological? · 23
    The story of the North West Passage · 24
    The methodology of culture relativism · 26
    The situation in a cultural nutshell · 27
    What does a handshake mean? · 27
    Culture as a "headwind" · 28
    Put words to your culture · 32
    Why is it so important?  · 33
    Crocodiles gone astray · 34
    Global stone-age men · 36
    A question of trust · 36
    Social capital · 38
    Norms, morals and ethics · 41
    The spiral of mistrust · 44
    The battle with the stone-age brain · 48

2   Cultural Intelligence · 50
    The art of preparation · 51
    Cultural intelligence as a skill · 52
    The rules follow the location · 53
    Who has to budge? · 55
    The art of choosing your battles · 58
    What is tolerance? · 63
    To sum up · 64

3   Cultural Understanding · 66

The difference between *knowing* and *understanding* the rules · 67
Bachelors and front teeth  · 68
When there is no real reason why we do what we do · 70
Why? Because! · 71

4   Why do Danes do what they do? · 73

Differences that make a difference · 74
How Danish is that? · 101


Part 2  Mapping – where are we different? · 103

5   Can countries be compared? · 104

The difference that makes a difference · 106
The countries chosen · 107

6   Some are more equal than others… · 108

What values do they have? · 109
Who's who? · 111
Problems for egalitarian-oriented people in hierarchical cultures · 114
Problems for hierarchical-oriented people in an egalitarian culture · 117

7   Those we know, and those we don't know so well  · 122

How knowingly do we communicate? – High or low context? · 123
Why do we have to sing so much karaoke? · 125
Trust – again · 126
People are everything, paper is nothing · 128
Don't get too close! · 129
When social relationships mustn't pay · 134
Who is what? · 135

8   For my sake, or the group's? · 146

More than the sum of its parts? · 147
The whole or the part? · 149
The special way of thinking in Asia · 152
Dirty Harry · 154
Universal rules versus special rules · 155
Why do people in the East lie? · 157
Generosity · 160
Who is what? · 161

9   How much change is allowed? · 168

When "usually" will not die out · 169
Who is what? · 171

10  Gorilla or mother hen? · 179

Why "feminine" and "masculine"? · 181
Who is what? · 183
Gender differences are good and natural – versus gender differences should be limited · 185

11  May I show my feelings? · 194

A question of volume · 196
Self-control versus commitment · 197

12  Is time a limited resource? (tomorrow) · 204

When time goes in circles and doesn't move forward · 206
Who is who? · 211


Part 3  Bridging differences · 218

13  Use cultural knowledge in the right way · 219

What are stereotypes? · 220
Why stereotypes? · 222
The best protection against stereotypes is *real* knowledge · 223
Control your expectations · 226

14  How to choose your cultural battles · 227

Surroundings create people · 227
Where do I belong? · 228
We are definitely *not* like the others · 230
Who am I? · 231
Inner differences are often greater than national differences · 232
Management and leadership across borders · 233
Diversity leadership – in a good and a bad way · 234
Cultural openness and consciousness rather than diversity planning · 237
Your rules or mine? · 237
Where should you draw the limits of diversity? · 238
Moving from culture as an essence to culture as a process · 241
The three box principle · 242
There is an elephant in the room and its name is "Culture" · 247

15  What everyone should know about cultural encounters with the Danes · 252

Trust is good but control is better · 253
A delicate balance · 254
Danish management – when the manager is not the expert · 257
Lead by challenging – lead by rewarding · 260

Drop the formalities · 263
Being reserved and the careful approach · 264
Meetings without decisions – talk without action · 266
The language problem · 269
Moral self-overvaluation and German-Danes · 272
And everything else: · 274

16  Communications and negotiation · 279

It takes (at least) two to communicate · 279
Pakistani prunes · 281
What was it all about? · 282
What could have been done? · 283
The art of asking the right questions · 285
Not a question of clear messages but clear contexts · 287

17  Informants – nothing beats local knowledge · 291

The informant · 291
Who are your informants? · 291
What can informants help you with? · 292
Choosing your informant · 293
How to look after an informant · 294

18  What have I learned and how do I move on from here? · 297

You are going to be a colleague of or manage people who come to
Danish culture · 298
You are going to work in a culturally diverse environment · 299
You are to be sent abroad · 299
Remember the weaknesses of the stone-age brain: · 300

Bibliography · 301

About Living Institute · 318

Thanks to the informants · 319

# Foreword

My colleagues and I have spent the last several years researching cultural intelligence and global leadership. Our driving question is: "What's the difference between those who can successfully adapt to different cultures and those who can't?" We've gathered data from more than 60 different countries around the world and we've found some recurring characteristics of those who can be described as culturally intelligent. Cultural intelligence, or CQ, is the capability to be effective across any cultural context. It's hard to overstate how important cultural intelligence is for anyone who wants to succeed in today's increasingly globalised world.

But cultural intelligence has little benefit if it merely remains as a grandiose, overarching idea. It has to be applied to specific contexts. That's one of many reasons why I'm so excited about having Dennis Nørmark's new book available in English. It's a riveting picture of what cultural intelligence looks like in the Danish context.

I've had the privilege of interacting with anthropologists and cross-cultural trainers all over the globe. But it's rare to find an individual like Dennis who is steeped in a rigorous understanding of anthropological insights but who can simultaneously share practical tips for how to utilise that understanding in the real world. This was one of the first things I noticed about Dennis when I met him—his conversation is filled with the kinds of epiphanies and reflections that endear me to other thoughtful researchers; but he can also communicate in ways that are relevant, compelling, and practical.

Furthermore, unlike many intercultural experts, Dennis doesn't worship at the holy grail of culture. He starts right off by telling us that our interactions are with fellow human beings, *not* with cultures. And my favorite line from the first chapter: "Some people are just idiots!" Thank you Dennis! Sometimes those of us in the cross-cultural space try so hard to attribute every behavior and incident to cultural differences and that isn't always the case. Most importantly, Dennis provides English readers with a much-needed resource for being culturally intelligent in the Danish context (and beyond!).

I hope you enjoy this book as much as I did. Not only did it improve my understanding of Danish and Scandinavian culture, it helped me think further about how cultural intelligence applies to other contexts. As I work with companies and governments around the world, I look forward to pointing them to this book.

Enjoy your journey with one of the stone age's greatest minds!

David Livermore, PhD
Author and thought leader on cultural intelligence

# Introduction

## – a realistic book about cultural challenges

"Despite popular beliefs to the contrary, the single greatest barrier to business success is the one erected by culture". That quote comes from the American anthropologist Edward T. Hall, who throughout his professional life tried to understand what culture is and what it does to us.

His conclusion is not particularly politically correct, but it is true. Because despite the popular assumption that a multi-cultural and diverse workplace is mostly a source of inspiration and creative solutions, things go very wrong when people don't know how to tackle cultural challenges, which if not addressed greatly exceed the benefits. That means they never get to learn how to tap this diverse source of new development and creativity. I will go as far as to say that the key to your country's future success as a society, in business and as a nation lies in solving the barriers in cross-cultural encounters by recognising them and dealing with them – so that we can reap all the benefits.

So it is also this book's fundamental position that cross-cultural encounters actually create more problems than they solve – but that that doesn't need to be the case. Not because culture in itself creates problems, because humans would be no more intelligent than a chimpanzee if we lacked the *ability* to create culture. The problems occur when there are *several different* cultures in play at the same time or in the same place. We need to deal with such situations openly and honestly.

We didn't have that sort of problem when in the distant past, we were only walking around the African Savannah together with our "own" people: in other words people from our own group. The situation nowadays is quite different. That is why this book is called *Cultural Intelligence for Stone-Age Brains* because while we may not necessarily *believe* we are still in the Stone Age, our brains definitely are. They are in fact fighting a daily battle to keep up with our ambitions to be modern, global, open to change and – last but not least – *culturally intelligent*. The biological evolution of our brains has in fact gone at a much slower pace than our cultural evolution. In other words, we have been equipped with brains which are thinking just like they did in the past. That is why today we have so much difficulty thinking beyond our differences and *how to work with Danes and beyond* – which is the book's subtitle. Whether we meet them at home in Denmark or abroad.

I also ought to emphasise that it is Danish brains in particular which belong to the Stone Age because it is my assertion that as regards culture, Danes are more challenged than most other Western peoples. That is due to having been allowed to a great extent to continue their "stone age existence" – meaning an isolated existence without very much external cultural input. That is not just an off-the-cuff assertion but also an observation where I have research and statistics on my side. I will expand on that later, but it is clear to anyone who digs into the facts that Danes are not particularly used to having to exercise "cultural skills" and that they never really have been. A primarily homogeneous "family" of around 5 ½ million people is not the most suitable place to be culturally challenged. In the last survey of Danes' general "skills" prepared by the Education Ministry, researchers reached the conclusion that only 5% of Danes have highly developed cultural skills. What the Education Ministry's definition means is that very few Danes have experience with other cultures or are good at working together with and understanding people with different cultural backgrounds than their own. At the same time, a whole 66% of Danes are decidedly bad at it, when their "insight into and ability to understand everyday cultural complexity and ability to communicate without prejudice with people from other cultures" is measured. Taken together, these are abilities which are about being culturally skilled and culturally intelligent.

So perhaps it is not so strange that many people who have contact with Danish culture at work can feel that Danes are somewhat of a handful. For the same reason, I decided quite early on to have my book translated into English. The original Danish version contained a couple of chapters about what Danes ought to know about themselves, but I quickly found out that this information was of course of great interest to the many thousands of foreigners working with Danes in Denmark, but who would not be able to understand a book in Danish targeted at Danish readers. Maybe you are either working with Danes in a Danish company, work a lot with Danes in a subsidiary of a Danish company abroad, have a Danish spouse or in some other way need to supplement your knowledge about cultural understanding with a specific focus on Danish culture. Instead of just talking generally about culture, it is always good to have a basis for comparison. So Denmark will in many ways be a kind of baseline throughout this book. But you will also experience Danish culture in comparison to your own culture and hopefully become more aware of why you don't always fully understand the Danes around you.

This version of *Cultural Intelligence for Stone-Age Brains* has therefore been changed a little from the original Danish version, which by definition was addressed to a Danish audience. The book deals to a great extent with the same issues as the original version – how can I improve my handling of cultural diversity at work? It is namely one of the most important skills for working in the 21st century. Both because culture can create so many problems for collaboration and teamwork, but also because there are hidden benefits to reap when you shake things up a bit and work with people who do not think in precisely the same way as each other.

In fact, a research report from the Research and Innovation Agency from 2007 shows that a company can increase its innovative ability by 30% if it hires people with different ethnic and national cultures. However, the survey did not measure all the other complications which cultural diversity brings in the form of communications problems, teamwork difficulties, misunderstandings, psychological strain and misjudgements. These are, however, issues often reported by the companies who seek help from consultancies such as Living Institute, where I myself gained experience as a cultural consultant. So the benefits can definitely be even greater if a company learns to tackle the problems Hall mentions.

Cultural differences can thus be a benefit, but let us nevertheless be honest and admit that *businesses and organisations scarcely work in a culturally diverse environment because they think about the business benefits of cultural diversity, but because contact with people who happen to be from other cultures is necessary.* In other words, pragmatism rather than pure idealism.

It is definitely not necessary to mention to readers of this book that the global society is a reality, meaning that most of us work with people from other countries every day, and that we therefore manage or work with people from other cultures. First and foremost with Danes in Denmark or in a subsidiary of a Danish company, but maybe also with Indian programmers sitting thousands of miles away, but who nevertheless have daily contact with you or your colleagues. And if not that, we travel abroad to sell to or buy from people who can't be treated in the same way as we treat our "own". We can no longer avoid other cultures, so neither can we avoid dealing with the skills required of us as a consequence.

We therefore have to deal with culture. Not only because cultural diversity is an *advantage*, but also because it is a *reality*. What we can do is get a realistic picture of the cultural challenges and then learn to minimise the problems so that we can harvest the fruits of intercultural collaboration.

This necessity is starting to sink in with companies, organisations and the public sector. In a survey undertaken by the Economist Intelligence Unit in 2012 of 572 senior managers from around the world, 51% expressed that differences in cultural traditions between the countries they worked in were the most important reason for misunderstandings. 49% felt that they had lost money as a direct consequence of those misunderstandings. In the same survey, an overwhelming majority stated that the current crisis needs to be met with more – not less – globalisation. So there is no way to avoid improving how we handle differences.

But there is no reason why it should be so difficult and cost so much money. In the 1980s, Dr Carol Kovach from UCLA under-took a groundbreaking study in how diversity affected a group's ability to work together. The study showed that diversity can affect the group's performance in crucially different directions. There was namely a tendency for both the worst and the best groups to be the most diverse. The homogenous teams were simply mediocre.

This insight has since been shown in studies both in Denmark and abroad. Things can either go really well with cultural diversity or go really badly. It is all about how the diversity is tackled. It is this book's assertion, backed up by the scientific studies, that those organisations which can avoid ending up at the bottom of the curve and instead move themselves to the top end are the winners of the future – and that the key to this movement is something called *cultural intelligence.*

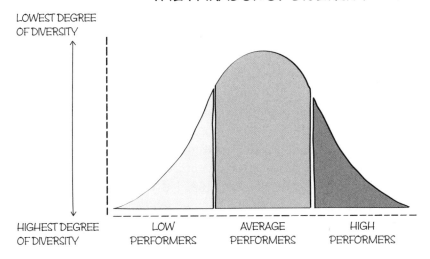

THE PARADOX OF DIVERSITY

LOWEST DEGREE OF DIVERSITY

HIGHEST DEGREE OF DIVERSITY

LOW PERFORMERS

AVERAGE PERFORMERS

HIGH PERFORMERS

It is not enough just to mix different cultures together and then believe that innovation will suddenly occur as if by magic. Or as mobility researcher Sally Khallash writes in her latest book *Send more immigrants, please*: "It's not enough to hire 2 Pakistanis and a Chinese and then sit down and wait for the fireworks".

But I wonder whether there are quite a lot of managers around who secretly hope that that will happen, by doing what Khallash also writes: "just put a few extra brown M&Ms in the packet" and then just carry on as before?

If only it was that easy – but it isn't. New insight and a change in behaviour across *the whole organisation* is needed if cultural diversity is to be tackled.

Any modern organisation should therefore ask itself: are we doing enough so that the unavoidable diversity that we are striving for does not end up becoming a problem, but instead becomes the key to our success? If you know that you are not doing enough yet, then you should read on.

## Why have I written this book?

My reason for writing this book is that I am an anthropologist. I have also given cultural training to managers, staff, Danes sent abroad as expats and expats living here in Denmark since 2007. I have done that as head of training and chief consultant in Living Institute, which has advised some of the country's largest international companies about the subject since 2004. The book is thus a collection of knowledge about culture and people I have dedicated myself to, partly as an anthropologist and partly in my practical work with thousands of people. The book will therefore have professional references and also anecdotes as examples. In essence, it is a handbook but it is built on a solid knowledge of research and practice.

I have written the book in as easy and as down to earth language as possible. For the same reason it definitely does not include all the long and complicated definitions needed to satisfy an academic reader. I have chosen to write a book which can be used by people tackling practical challenges every day – not a book to impress my colleagues. It is a book which tries to say things as they are, about a subject where, in my experience, far too many people tread lightly and wrap their own lack of an opinion in abstracts and unspecific clichés.

- - - - - - - - - - - - - - - - - - - - - - - - - - - - - - - - - - - - - - - - - - -

This is how culture is defined in this book:
Culture is a common set of interpretations shared by a group and which dictates the group's expectations of other people's behaviour and norms. It is a network of meanings structured by central values which are regarded as significant and correct by the members of the culture. The values have shown themselves to be useful and constructive in that culture's meetings with the surrounding social and ecological reality.

- - - - - - - - - - - - - - - - - - - - - - - - - - - - - - - - - - - - - - - - - - -

## Principles in this book

Culture is a sensitive subject and people invest a great deal of themselves in cultural issues. So it is therefore appropriate for me as the author of the book to briefly explain where I stand in a number of significant questions. The reader can then choose whether he or she can agree with these principles or whether he or she wants to challenge them.

*We shouldn't have respect for the culture – we should have respect for individuals.*

Culture is just an instrument which people use to interpret the world around them, to organise their interactions with other people and base their identity on.

That means that cultures can and should change if people make new discoveries about their reality, or new challenges or needs appear. So the view of culture which I present the reader with is a dynamic view, not a static one. We are obliged to challenge culture, change culture and ask questions about culture, and that goes for one's own culture more than any other. But we need to know what the preconditions are. They can seem very abstract, but in reality it is a very specific problem for companies and organisations, where we don't realise how much we can challenge people about their culture. My principle is that we can definitely challenge people about their culture, but that we should know *when* and *how* to do so. Those are the sorts of questions this book tries to answer.

It is important to understand that everyone deserves dignity and respect. And anyone who believes that you can't talk logically and sensibly with people, "because they have a different culture", then that is the same as treating them like children – impervious to sense and reason. That would be treating them wrong for the simple reason that:

*People have more things in common with each other than they have differences which divide them.*

That means that we mustn't put too much emphasis on culture, because in reality the cultural differences are simply hiding a core of something which is surprisingly similar. We are often blinded by the differences without being able to see everything we have in common. So culture should not be a universal explanation we can use for everything – and neither are cultural differences an excuse which can be used in any situation because:

*Sometimes people are just idiots.*

"Idiots" come in all shapes and sizes. "Idiots" are really just a fact of life. They can be found everywhere, but funnily enough most people around the world are aware of what characterises an "idiot". The things we value in other people are often strikingly similar: keeping one's word, showing care and attention, teamwork, and trying to be liked. We can have different ways of showing these, and that is where the challenge is. But everyone agrees that those are the rules. Unless you are faced with an "idiot". The problem is how to distinguish "idiots" from "cultural differences", and that is the ability this book would like to pass on to its readers.

My fundamental point is therefore that it is OK to challenge culture – both your own and others'. Culture is in fact just the tip of the iceberg, with most of what is below the surface being what we have in common with others. So it is possible to find a mutual understanding between everyone in the world who is *not* an idiot. And fortunately, they are in the majority!

## What is the big problem in Denmark?

In my work as a consultant I have observed the following weaknesses in Danish organisations, workplaces and companies, although I am sure that Danes are not the only ones to face these challenges:

- People don't fight their fear of the unknown. We ought to be able to talk about culture and challenge culture. We must be able to identify whatever is different and problematic, laugh a little at the differences and consider changing something – not least about ourselves. We need to get better at explaining, listening, expressing our own astonishment in a decent way and asking the right questions.
- We lack knowledge about *other people*. When people behave differently, how much of that difference is due to their culture, and how much to their own personality? When can they "do something about it", so to speak, and when is it "their upbringing"? What can I expect from a German, a Spaniard, a Chinese, an Indian, and so forth? Which differences make a difference?
- To a great extent we lack knowledge about "ourselves". For Danes, everything Danish is "normal", and you will certainly feel the same about your own culture. That is why as a rule, people have

limited knowledge of how peculiar they appear to people with a different cultural background from their own. This aspect is normally grossly underprioritised in books and courses about cultural understanding (because we know who we are well enough). So we will focus in particular on one culture in this book, but will also look at how you can better reflect on your own.

- We don't know which battles to choose, and which not to. Where can you set the limits for what to put up with and why? When is culture an "acceptable excuse" and when is it not? We often fumble in the dark here, and the rule seems to be: if in doubt, ignore it and hope it will go away. Except that's exactly what doesn't happen.

- We don't understand our own reaction patterns. Why do we often react so strongly to cultural differences, and is what we think even especially rational? We lack fundamental knowledge of what psychological mechanisms are in play when we are offended, insulted and surprised by "other people". We don't get to know our stone age brains better, so that we can stop them coming to damaging and completely wrong conclusions.

It is these aspects that this book will try to strengthen by giving the reader a language for what he or she sees; tools to deal with problems and knowledge of how people think in other cultures, how you yourself think and how we can bridge the cultural gap.

## Structure

This book has three parts: *Cultural Understanding, Mapping and Bridge Building*. The division is quite classic for theoretical cultural understanding: first of all we get a handle on the term and phenomenon of culture, learn where it occurs and how. Then we look at Danish culture and map out a lot of other differences in other cultures. We should thus end up better equipped with knowledge and self-understanding to work out how we can get on together.

## About this edition

*Cultural Intelligence for Stone-Age Brains* was first published by Det Andersenske Forlag in 2011. This edition, as well as being written for a non-Danish speaking audience working in Denmark or with

Danes, is also an updated and more compact book than the first edition. Developments in this area are very fast, both in the real business world and in research. In addition, I have also learned more myself, become more knowledgeable about the subject and received useful input from the many – and fortunately enthusiastic – readers of the book. For the same reason, I have taken the opportunity to update the book all the way through for this edition.

The examples will typically be about Danes meeting others, retained from the original edition because this book is also about giving an impression of what characterises Danish culture. So instead of being about Pakistanis meeting Chinese and so on, they are all about meetings of cultures where one of the cultures is Danish. The whole idea is to open this culture up, and also to give some insight into all other possible cultures than that of Danes.

# Part 1

## Cultural Consciousness

In the first part, I will try to give you, the reader, some basic tools to help you become a "junior anthropologist". In other words, an expert in what culture is, and what culture does. I will elaborate on the definition and the value of cultural understanding, or cultural intelligence, and we will look at what we can do from a cognitive and practical point of view to improve how we deal with cultural differences.

Finally, we will look at the value of cultural self-understanding: Using Danish culture as a starting point, we will learn about what particular characteristics this culture has, and you as reader will get to dig a little deeper into the particular behaviour of the Danes.

# 1

## When cultures collide

As mentioned, I am writing this book as an anthropologist. Few people know much about this profession, as it is a discipline which has not always been very forthcoming about itself.

In short, anthropologists deal with the many different ways it is possible to be human on this planet. The many different ways a society can be organised, what beliefs people have and what particular norms and values to live by.

As a rule, anthropologists investigate all this by going on long trips to conduct research into the people they want to study. These are known as field trips and consist of anthropologists living among the people whose culture they want to understand. For example, they can go off to live with a tribe in Africa, sharing their food, hearing their stories and living with them under the same roof. It can often be very time-consuming work, partly because the anthropologist himself has to overcome the initial culture shock, build trust and learn the elementary norms before the hosts begin to open up.

Maybe it is because I come from Denmark's second city of Aarhus that I chose to make my first field trip to somewhere as "exotic" as its rival city of Copenhagen, the capital. But regardless of that, that is what I did. I lived with some of the left-wing activist groups who unfortunately have attracted attention because of several violent episodes, the most recent being when the police ended their occupation of the Youth House in Copenhagen.

For a while, these activists were my "tribe". They were the ones I had to learn to understand. Why did they do what they did, and what were their values? I often mention this field work when I am giving cultural training to Danish companies and organisations.

Not because I think they will ever come into contact with these young, left-wing radicals, but because it says something about what culture is. I dare to suggest that this "activist tribe" have some values which are completely different from those of the salesmen, engineers, nurses, human resource managers and directors I have the pleasure to teach. In other words, there are cultural differences even within Danish culture. Differences which can actually be very significant.

But regardless of how strange people are, it is always possible to understand them, something I found out when I was with the activists. That is the fundamental assumption that anthropology as an academic discipline is based on, and which I will attempt to get the reader to understand. It is perfectly possible to understand people without agreeing with them or starting to take on their values.

## How is someone anthropological?

Anthropologists don't understand people such as the activists, the bushmen in the Kalahari Desert or fishermen in the Pacific Ocean just because we are cleverer than other people. Anthropologists understand other cultures because we have been *trained* to do so. This book attempts to pass on that training. It is a craft which can be learned.

What anthropologists say to themselves again and again out in the field, and which can be useful lessons for anyone who wants to act culturally intelligently, are a few phrases I will come back to several times:

- There is a reason people do what they do
- Grasp the natives' point of view
- Keep an open mind but not an empty head
- Seek the known in the foreign and the foreign in the known

The first pieces of advice express a fundamental attitude in anthropology: you must not prejudge or judge the cultures you encounter. Anthropologists investigate people *based on those people's own preconditions*. Which means it is not the anthropologist's task to determine whether what the other people are doing is right or wrong – we simply don't care. When we research, we are scientists and not judges of good taste. We have to understand – not judge or prejudge.

History has shown us that we achieve the most through understanding. One of the best stories to illustrate that is the North West Passage:

## The story of the North West Passage

Before the Panama Canal opened in 1914, there was only one route from the Atlantic to the Pacific – all the way around Cape Horn at the southernmost tip of South America. But everyone knew that there might be an alternative. A sea passage north of Canada through dangerous, frozen waters past Canadian islands in the Arctic Ocean. It was a very attractive route, and when Captain John Franklin sailed from England in 1845 to find it, he was not the first to try. Fortunately, neither was he the last.

Things went really wrong for Franklin and his men. After just over a year in the area, his ships HMS Erebus and HMS Terror were stuck helplessly in the ice at King William's Island. Still a long way from the open waters of the Pacific. And still a very, very long way from home.

Not one of the 129 crew survived. They were stuck for almost two years, and in the final stages the crew wandered around the ice, alone with their supplies of canned food in the biting frost. The only witnesses to their desperate searching are their graves and the small notes they left behind, as well as reports from local Inuits who saw them.

Franklin and his men were completely unsuited to survival in the harsh environment. They had no idea of where and when the sea froze, so the cold was the main reason for their death. But there was another much more surprising thing that contributed to their demise. When some of their still frozen bodies were found over a hundred years later, it became apparent that one of the significant causes of death was in fact the food they had brought with them. The cans they ate from were sealed with lead, and several of the bodies showed visible signs of lead poisoning. The lead in their food slowly attacked their organs, which were already subject to the harsh temperatures.

Sir John Franklin and his men died of ignorance, because the knowledge they had with them wasn't suitable for the place they were in. But the man who finally did find the way through to the Pacific had a quite different approach.

It took him three years. From setting sail in 1903 until 1906, when Norwegian explorer Roald Amundsen was able to send a telegram from Alaska to say that his mission was complete.

Amundsen was a different person than Franklin, and he first and foremost had a different attitude. The Norwegian adventurer had done his homework differently to Franklin. He had gathered knowledge from experts who knew about survival on the ice. The experts were not Norwegian scientists, but local Inuits – Netsilik as they are called. Who else could know how to find food in the harsh climate, how to keep warm, how to build an igloo, what sort of clothes were needed, how to hunt for food and lastly, how to use dogs to pull sleds across the ice? The Inuits had survived there for thousands of years and had adapted to the environment. There were no better masters to teach Amundsen.

Why did Franklin not do the same? Because it simply never occurred to him that he could learn something at all useful from "natives". Whereas Amundsen's solution was culturally intelligent, Franklin's approach was culturally arrogant. But to understand why Franklin was so foolish, you also need to understand Franklin's culture.

Franklin was an Englishman who had grown up with the notion that it was the British who were at the top of the human development ladder. Great Britain was in all respects Great, and that gave the British the firm belief that all wild and primitive peoples in the world ought to drop their foolish ways and become civilised – in other words be like the British. So there was nothing white men could learn from the Inuits. The only learning possible was for the wild, indigenous people to learn from the British. So Franklin turned a deaf ear to the wisdom of the Inuits. In fact, he never even asked them anything.

Maybe they could have taught him how to find, kill and prepare a seal to eat. But Franklin preferred his canned food, which was civilisation's admirable discovery, but whose lead content ultimately sent so many of his men to their graves.

## The methodology of culture relativism

The first anthropologists behaved very similarly to Franklin. They tried to find out how highly developed different cultures were. They wanted to find out how clever the "natives" were. How close were they to becoming "civilised"? Were they still near the bottom of the evolutionary ladder, or were they in the process of attaining the same high level as we ourselves have? No anthropologist thinks like that nowadays. These days, we think more like Amundsen. "There is a reason people do what they do" – and that is "it works for them!"

Other people do things differently than we do, because that is what has given them the best results over the course of time. And when it comes down to it, everyone has fundamentally the same needs: survival, development, having children, being happy, being loved and all the usual things. Which paths we take to those goals depends on where we live, how society is made up and what our history is.

So it's not about judging and rating other people. It's about understanding why they do what they do. That doesn't mean you have to like what you see them doing. We'll come back to that later. *Culture relativism* is about *understanding people in their own environment. It is a method* for analysing and understanding cultures, it is not *ethics*.

Other people may be strange, but their strange behaviour has meaning. Dog sleds are a strange method of transport, and lamps that burn blubber are a strange way of getting light. But not if you live in the Arctic. Later on we will look more closely at how we can understand customs that are quite different from our own, and thus be better prepared for what is new and unknown, avoid frustrations and maybe actually learn to value differences and learn from other people.

One's own culture looks just as strange from the others' perspective. For example, the western tendency to blow one's nose into a pocket handkerchief causes offence in India. They do not understand why westerners value their nasal excretions so much that they wrap them up and keep them in their pocket. In India, they do things fast and simple and empty their noses onto the ground – something westerners think is completely disgusting. But who is right?

Let's start by bringing the cultural misunderstanding from the Arctic into our day-to-day lives and then looking at why our brains have such a hard time thinking more appropriately.

## The situation in a cultural nutshell

Anna offers to shake the hand of a new 28-year old colleague of Pakistani descent, who declines. Anna's hand is left hanging. Thrust out in front of her until she pulls it back. She gets a gut feeling. A knot of unpleasantness. As if she has just smiled at someone who has responded by sticking out their tongue.

But that is nowhere near what has actually happened. On the contrary, the young man has done nothing. And that is where the problem lies.

Anna tries hastily to conclude the conversation and rushes back to her desk. "That was a weird lack of respect", she thinks. "Is it because I'm a woman? So he thinks I don't count?"

## What does a handshake mean?

Anna's analysis of the situation is wrong – or put another way: it is culturally unintelligent. That is because she has interpreted the situation as it appears – from her own Danish perspective. But she won't get very far with that, and the interpretation is quite simply incorrect. It is not in sync with how the young Pakistani sees the world (let's assume he does *not* know how people do things in Denmark).

From his point of view, the world looks different. For him, touching a woman he doesn't know is indecent behaviour. Physically touching a woman you don't know is indecent and insulting, which could in fact be interpreted as an invitation to sex. One honours someone of the opposite sex by *not* touching them.

So Anna shouldn't feel insulted – quite the opposite. Her Pakistani colleague doesn't touch her because he does *not* want to embarrass her. Had she known that this was the Pakistani's cultural background, she would probably have thought differently. But even that is not enough. For her understanding to be properly *culturally intelligent*, Anna needs to do more. She also has to learn to understand why she reacts the way she does. She has to know her own cultural background.

What does a handshake actually mean in her own culture? Take a look at the following phrases which are very Danish but most certainly extend beyond Danish culture:

- "Give Africa a hand"
- "I asked for her hand"
- "Would you shake [hands] on that?"
- "Give me a hand"
- "Let's shake on that – we have a deal"
- "Hand on heart"

What do these expressions say about a culture as regards hands and handshakes? What is the hand a symbol for in all these phrases?

The common denominator is trust, respect, acceptance and help. Hands are something you *give* and *receive*, they are something you *hold out* and something you *expect* to receive in return. Hands are used, for example, in Danish culture to indicate trust and respect. And if you are used to the same thing, you will realise how hurtful it is to offer your hand and not have it taken. You'll most definitely feel it in your gut. Just like Anna did. Rejection and hurt. It is a very strong cultural signal to not take an "outstretched hand" in many cultures, including Denmark.

In other words, it is important for both sides to understand how each side perceives the situation – and not least to understand your own reactions and prior understandings.

But the problem is, that we quite often just don't think about the rules and norms we have in our own culture. Because our culture is "normal" for us. That means that all other cultures are deviant.

## Culture as a "headwind"

Culture is like pedalling against the wind: you only realise you're doing it when you change direction. And you only change direction when you meet someone who plays according to different rules, or when you move to somewhere where your own culture is in the minority.

You don't notice culture when you are among people like you. That is why you get the impression that what you do is *normal*.

If you are sitting on board a ferry, and a stranger across the table gets up to buy his lunch from the cafeteria, would you ask him to get you a coke? Maybe a coke, fries and two hotdogs? Most people would say no. What if you had the exact change? Most people would still say no. It's only acceptable if you have already spoken or know each other.

Given this scenario, Danes on my cultural training courses have on average maintained that a conversation of at least ten to fifteen minutes duration would be needed. After that, it would be OK. With the exception of extenuating circumstances such as a natural disaster. When people find themselves in extraordinary circumstances such as hurricanes or other "catastrophic" events, then suddenly we can all talk about anything at all and help each other out. Just as when it is announced that the train will be delayed even longer, and Danes slowly start to exchange a few words with the people next to them. Now we have something in common! The "catastrophe" is a common frame of reference, and allows us to talk to each other. If there had been a heavy storm on the ferry, the conversation would have been easier, and it would have been more acceptable to ask each other for favours.

But a coke, fries and two hotdogs – without a natural disaster to permit the favour... no, that won't do in Denmark. Think about how that might have been with your country's culture. Would it have been OK? Would it have been OK if you only asked for a coke? Would it have been OK to only talk for one minute before asking? If so, what's the "price" for the two hotdogs? Six minutes more? Or longer?

When should you give back garden tools borrowed from a neighbour? What about a trailer or a tarpaulin? How far into the morning should you say "good morning" to a colleague? When do you just say "hello" instead? How long since you last said "hello" until you can say it again? When do you stop to talk to a colleague in the corridor? Maybe you don't do that unless you're already looking for him, but what about if you meet in the car park? Maybe you will – and you definitely will if you meet him in the supermarket. Won't you? What about on holiday in Thailand?

Maybe you're smiling as you read these useless questions. If you are, it's because talking about these things seems to you to be nonsense. They're not things you think about, they're things you just do. It's something you know. In any event when you're at home in your own culture.

You're right, of course. We know what to do and what not to do when we are at home. But how do we know? We have been brought up to know, some will say. But is that even correct? Have your parents ever told you how to behave if someone on a ferry or on a train asks you to get hotdogs, fries and a coke from the cafeteria or the buffet car?

No, no one has told you. Similarly, there is no detailed instruction manual available about how to greet people when you start a new job. No one hands you a pamphlet with the "Company Greeting Rules", "best regards and hugs from the HR manager". (A hug, by the way, is only if you meet each other abroad or are drunk at an office party).

But if you don't talk about it, how do people learn?

In reality, people don't learn very much from instructions. We learn by doing. Just like you can't teach someone to ride a bicycle just by telling them how and then expecting them to do it straightaway. Culture works in the same way. We seldom *talk* about what we do, because we learn culture through *practicing* it.

Unfortunately, that means that we don't have a lot of experience in teaching people about our own culture. We are quite simply not used to talking about it. The reason is that culture in reality has to be understood as in this model.

A very popular model of culture is the onion model shown below. Culture is in the outer layer: the funny hats, the strange customs and the special products which end up in museums and which are the first thing we see, smell and taste when we are out. That is what we feel when we arrive in a foreign country. We can describe it all and talk about it.

The next layer is all the cultural stuff that is still visible but rarely talked about. It's all the behavioural expectations that we have and that we *assume* other people know, but which we never talk about. It's only when the garden tools have not been returned *half a year after borrowing them* that the owner finds it necessary to say that he had expected to get them back by now. To which the new neighbour quite rightly can answer: "Of course, why didn't you say when you wanted them back?" We already know the answer: "I thought you realised".

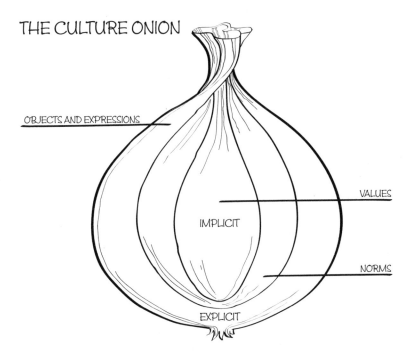

# THE CULTURE ONION

OBJECTS AND EXPRESSIONS

VALUES

IMPLICIT

NORMS

EXPLICIT

That you should stop saying "good morning" at work in Denmark after about 9.30 is something nobody tells you. Just as nobody tells you that if you say good morning later than that, it can imply that people think you are late for work. Danes just know these things. When I once told this to an Englishman in Denmark, he rushed to tell me "That's why my staff always insist they've been here since 9.00, if I say 'good morning' at 11.00!" In England, like almost everywhere else in the world, it is normal to say "good morning" right up until midday, but as he didn't realise this he ended up unintentionally making his staff uncomfortable. No one had told him about this particularly Danish way of greeting. Danes just forget about it. For them, it's just "normal".

The last layer is values. What are the qualities in others we value, are we a society which values the family highest or is it individual responsibility and development instead? Everyone always wants the best, the truth, what is right and honourable – but they do not always agree about what that is. The values are impossible to see and very rarely discussed. That is why they are at the core of the onion, invisibly holding everything together.

## Put words to your culture
It's not because culture is put together in precisely that way that it gives us so many problems. Because we assume that other people know what we do, it surprises us when they don't meet our expectations. We aren't just surprised. It's a gut feeling that what the "other people" are doing is wrong, strange, peculiar or rude.

Because Anna has not thought about the inner core of culture she carries around with her, she doesn't understand her own reaction when her offer to shake hands isn't reciprocated. It's all "the other guy's fault". But "the other guy" is answering in the same way as the neighbour who returned the garden tools too late: "how should I know, no one has ever *told* me".

- - - - - - - - - - - - - - - - - - - - - - - - - - - - - - - - - - - - - - - - - - - -

*"Why didn't you say something earlier?"*
Here's one of my favourite stories I always tell when I give my courses:

A group of Chinese staff joined a Danish company, leading to the discovery that queuing culture in China is quite different from in Denmark.

The Danes thought that the Chinese quite openly jumped right to the front in the canteen queue, emptying a whole dish and not even leaving a symbolic bite behind for anyone else. It was purely and simply "survival of the fittest".

Everyone was very irritated by their behaviour, and the Danes often talked about their "completely unreasonable" ways. But no one said a word to the Chinese.

Finally, after a few weeks, a Danish employee plucked up the courage to say something to one of the Chinese about how the Danes perceived their behaviour in the canteen.

The Chinese employee was dreadfully embarrassed, but also very pleased that this particular Dane had overcome his own shyness to tell them about the cultural codes in the company.

His reponse was simply "why didn't you say something earlier?"

"Because it was embarrassing", the Dane replied.

The Chinese employee said nothing, but it was clear that he was thinking "just how embarrassing do you think it is for us to have been doing this for three weeks!"

------------------------------------------------

We don't explain – we just do. But if we are to become more culturally intelligent, the first step is to *articulate* our culture. We all have to understand that our way of doing things is *normal for us*, that other people *don't know our ways* and that we are not used to *explaining our ways* because we are used to *discovering them*. That means you have to explain something you are not used to explaining. Instead of looking the other way like Anna did, ending the embarrassing encounter and going quickly back to her desk, she is now responsible for passing on her cultural knowledge. Otherwise her Pakistani colleague will end up in the same embarrassing situation again. And most likely again and again and again. To everyone's frustration, and no-one's satisfaction. It is those who *know* who also have the *responsiblity*. There is no other conclusion.

You are almost certainly not used to putting words to your own culture, but when you encounter people from other countries or when you are just at home and come across people who don't know the "rules", you are obliged to do so anyway. You can't do anything else. It's not about talking down to people or explaining every detail, it's about giving (and we get back to that favourite Danish metaphor again here) a helping hand.

## Why is it so important?

Just as Anna was frustrated about not having her offer to shake hands reciprocated, we have all experienced some sort of culture shock. In fact you don't even need to leave the country before you find cultural differences. Someone from Copenhagen going to the west of Jutland will quickly notice that people there talk a lot less than people in Copenhagen. Another good example of tiny cultural differences is celebrating events such as Christmas with one's in-laws. Many people find such events difficult to cope with. Because even though the in-laws appear normal on the surface, you often find out that they are heathens when big religious festival times come round.

The reason is that rituals such as Christmas Eve in Christian cultures are all about re-confirming a common meaning. This is the time when people confirm to each other that they *know* what is important in life. That they know the rules and know how to play by them. They do that year after year (in fact there are tiny variations each time even in the most rigid rituals – we just like ignoring them).

But why can we feel culture shock? Why is it that suddenly, it's unpleasant to be standing on a street in a strange city, where it smells weird, where people speak a language you don't understand a word of and where someone comes along and tells you something you don't understand? Why is it directly physically unpleasant to be somewhere where everything seems wrong and impossible to grasp?

The answer lies buried in our stone-age brains.

## Crocodiles gone astray

Nature is so smart that it re-uses what works. Every animal's brain is basically the same: it regulates the body's balance of energy and fluids, finds food, fleeds from danger, fights and finds a mate. We have those parts of our brains in common even with simple reptiles. A crocodile, for example, doesn't have to do any more than those few tasks from the moment it is born until it dies.

Humans, on the other hand, have to do a whole lot more. But when we encounter situations we haven't seen before, or are unsure about, we react with what can in simple terms be called our "reptilian brain". It is a powerful part of our brain which is in close contact with our nervous system, so we feel the fear and unpleasantness physically as well.

It can be exceedingly difficult for the sensible, analytical part of our brains to cancel out these "primitive" signals from our inner crocodile. That's why we don't always react very sensibly, analytically or rationally to the unknown.

Culture shock pushes us off balance. So it is stressful, and that's why we often end up being aggressive and look for escape routes or maybe, more seldomly, ways to attack. Once our inner crocodile is switched on, it becomes a matter of life and death, so there isn't time for more precise or accurate thoughts. We *feel* an enormous amount, but *think* very little.

So we need to learn how to tame our inner crocodile. We do that with the newest part of our brain, one that we have in common with other mammals and primates (in other words, apes).

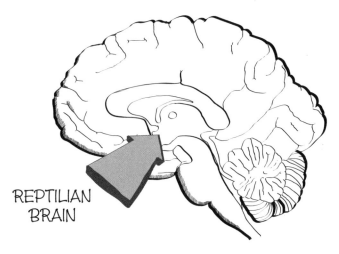

REPTILIAN
BRAIN

This part of our brain is controlled higher up in the brain, in the frontal lobes which are just under the forehead. This is where we learn from experience and restrain impulses (such as when we resist eating sweets, because we know it will affect our weight). This is where we have the opportunity to judge something which is happening, so we can at least decide whether there is a need to attack or flee, or whether it would be better to *learn* something from the situation. Crocodiles never learn anything, because their brains can't cope with that. Humans and other mammals can learn, however.

When we get a strange handshake, or someone shouts at us in a language we don't understand, we can feel the crocodile in us react. The solution is to address what we don't understand, and turn it into something we do.

But why do we get so nervous and uneasy with other cultures? After all, it's not a question of life or death, is it?

No, not any more. But once upon a time in our past it was. In order to understand why we put so much emphasis on culture and other people's behaviour, we need to understand that we are simply not built to live the life we do today. We are built to live on the African Savannah. We are walking around with a crocodile brain within a stone-age brain.

## Global stone-age men

For most of the history of our species, we have lived in Africa. With primitive stone tools, a fear of predators and with hunting and gathering as our primary sources of food. Our brains are built accordingly. Brains that communicate with the other members of the group merely about how to get the next meal. In fact, humans work best together with others. In this we are quite different to crocodiles, even though we still have the reptilian brain's fear instinct intact. We are definitely a social species with a good ability to collaborate, helped well along the way by our very advanced means of communication: language.

And that is something essential. Try to imagine how you could kill a gazelle or an ox armed with nothing more than your bare hands and a few primitive stone weapons…

The people on the African Savannah needed to tell their hunting partners that the following day, they would attack the old gnu with the black patch between its eye when the sun was at its highest point in the sky on the other side of the hill. One of them was to bring two stones and the other a spear. One would attack from above, and the other from the side. First throw the stones, and then when the first hunter gave the signal, the other one should cast the spear.

Very simple, really? No, not at all. It's actually very complicated. Before they could start, they had to agree on lots of things. What do "old" and "black patch" mean, where is the "highest point in the sky", which hill are we talking about, what is a spear and what sort of stones are we talking about? The first hunter is hardly expecting the other to turn up with a handful of gravel. What do "from above", "from the side" mean and what sort of "signal" should be given?

It all requires a very large amount of common knowledge. They had to agree about what words and signals *mean*. The slightest misunderstanding could be fatal. So they had to be sure they understood each other perfectly. If they misunderstood each other too much, it was better to go their separate ways. A misunderstanding when hunting could mean death for both hunters.

## A question of trust

Everyone needs some fundamental things to be in place in order to be able to collaborate with others:

- Predictability
- Minimisation of misunderstandings
- Collective planning

All these things give *trust* – something people in social sciences also call *social capital*. Because it *is* capital. It can be saved up, cashed in and used. If I have high social capital, I have connections to partners whose behaviour I can predict and therefore count on, which is a great help. Unpredictable actions can often turn out to be innovative and exciting, but most often they just get in the way of collaboration. Just think how much you take for granted in day-to-day life – how much do you depend on other people's actions being predictable? If they didn't do what you expect, there would be no electricity coming out of the socket, the phone would not work, the train would not run and the plane would not take off. People as a rule behave amazingly predictably – thank goodness for that.

When we make an appointment for 2 o'clock, or when you are looking for a particular document, or when you order "a table for five" – each time you expect to be understood – because a mountain of problems would occur if that were not the case. So it's good to trust your surroundings.

People who speak differently, don't turn up on time and don't react as you expect, don't earn your trust. You don't need to be from another culture to have your expectations left unmet. Colleagues, friends or family may repeatedly do something unexpected or wrong, so we end up seeing them less and less, we fire them or in some way start to avoid them.

People who do unexpected and strange things create uncertainty. We say "they can't be trusted" or "we don't know where we are with them". We are conservative stone-age people.

People who say hello to everyone they see on the street, talk to themselves or sit on a bench smiling vacantly for no reason are people we steer a wide berth around. We are not attracted by the unexpected, we are repelled by it; even though we say the opposite in job interviews in order to appear more open and interesting. Because our brains are attracted by the known and reward us with a warm feeling when we are around things we recognise. This is called the "Mere Exposure Effect" and is well-documented in psychology.

The reason is that during the stone-age, outsiders were a risk to good collaboration. For the same reason, we are still repelled by behaviour which deviates too much from the norm. It is the body's way of ensuring that we do not go about killing a gnu with the wrong partner. It can be fatal.

When we meet another person, our stone-age brains think "can I kill a gnu or an ox with this person – or is it too risky?" Or in a more feminine version: "can I count on her looking after *my* children while I just step away from the camp fire for a moment?" Fundamentally though, it is the same reaction pattern: when we turn away from other people because we feel strange or uncomfortable about their behaviour, it is just our brains telling us: "don't waste your time on them, they are too dangerous".

It's not very nice, but it is what we are up against. The more we know about it, the more we can do something about it. It's not every time that our stone-age brains are right.

It can be said that we have all had the feeling of not being able to trust a "stranger". We are more sceptical about people who are not like us, and are quite naturally reserved about cultural differences. We all have this in common. These feelings are quite OK, no one needs to be ashamed of them, and no one is better than anyone else in this regard. It is how we *deal with* the feelings, that makes all the difference. This is where we can learn something from each other.

## Social capital

When we meet people from other cultures, our whole body tells us to keep away from them. They will only give us problems. That is very likely the reason why racism and fear of the unknown are so common in all cultures. Being suspicious of people who are not like us, do not talk like us or do not think like us is – unfortunately – one of the most human things there is.

Our bodies are in fact right. It *is* difficult, expensive and in many ways inappropriate to negotiate and work with "*other people*". This book gives countless examples of where things have gone really wrong. But *there is no other way*, because even though we may be cavemen in our brains, the world is global, and we quite simply have to deal with that fact.

That is why cultural training is so essential. Our brains simply cannot tackle the problem without training. Our instincts win over our common sense, if we cannot find out how to "short-circuit" the crocodile and stone-age parts of our brains before we give up and lose the necessary trust.

It's something you likely know from when you are standing by the Eiffel Tower or any other tourist place in the world, and you want a picture of yourself with the tower in the background. The pictures you take with your arm outstretched, the camera pointed back at yourself and the tower behind you are usually pretty poor, so you very likely look around for someone to take the picture for you. Who? Who will get to hold your camera for a few short moments?

When asked, most people say that they look for someone who looks the same. Tourists in the same situation (and preferably fathers with the family in tow). Once again, we are looking for signals that we have the same culture. "Deviations" from our own norm are to be avoided at all cost.

To show that degree of trust, and when abroad, is very Danish by the way. As the former British ambassador to Denmark, Sir James Mellon, once described the Danish national character: "Danes are not a nation in its normal sense, they are a tribe; that is their community strength and the reason for their unshakable trust in each other".

Some researchers believe, that the reason for Denmark (and the rest of Scandinavia) having such high social capital can be found back in Viking times. The Vikings traded over long distances and had to know that a deal was a deal when they came to collect the goods they had been promised the previous year. Another (I think) more likely explanation is that Scandinavian people are so *culturally homogeneous*; that the cultural differences within the countries are so amazingly small because for centuries, immigration has been very limited. Danes lost their colonies of "exotic" people before any of their inhabitants started to move to the colonial power in any signficant numbers. Thus in 1901, apart from Scandinavian and German immigrants, there were only 5,688 foreigners in Denmark out of a population of a little over 2.3 million, and in the previous century net immigration was a modest 20 people a year. Compared to other countries, it might as well be zero.

In other words, Danes have not been "mixed" with very many other people, something which is also noticeable in the genetic makeup. In Denmark, there is not much variation there either. Danes are more genetically similar than most other countries' populations. So they are literally very closely related to each other – or to be very direct we could say that Danes are quite simply one of the most inbred nations – and it is family people have the greatest trust in.

In many ways, Danes are thus used to the people they deal with from day-to-day being very similar to themselves. That makes it all the more challenging for them to have to deal with big cultural differences.

But in fact there is no reason at all for any of us to be particularly sceptical. Because "the others" are just as interested in collaboration as you are yourself. They also want trust, respect, friendliness, help and recognition. The problem is just that you meet "the others" with different forms of greeting, language, gestures and rules than the ones you use for recognising those from your own community. Those are all the strange things we never talk about, and which lie right at the core of the cultural onion. All the assumptions we don't put into words. They are all our *norms*.

If we get closer to each other, we will find out that all these differences are actually purely superficial banalities and formalities. Every time we do something other than what is expected, we show that we are not a member of the "other" tribe.

If we are culturally intelligent, we can get over the problem. Cultural intelligence consists partly of recognising in advance that our behaviour can reduce trust. So the task consists of finding *what exactly we have in common despite the irritating differences*, and that is much more than you would immediately think.

- - - - - - - - - - - - - - - - - - - - - - - - - - - - - - - - - - - - - - - - - - - - -

### A few things that set us apart, but which show we have much more in common

Around twenty years ago, anthropologist Donald E. Brown tried to sum up some of the many things which people all over the world have in common despite cultural differences. The lists includes over 300 well-documented common human characteristcs. Here are just a few of the many things we all do, just in slightly different ways.

| | | |
|---|---|---|
| Correcting injustice | Fear of dying | Language |
| Age terms | Gift giving | Political control |
| Facial recognition | Grammar | Rituals |
| Inheritance rules | Hospitality | Sexual attraction |
| Visual arts | Trade | Gossip |
| Care of children | Hygiene | Care |
| Property ownership | Incest prevention | Taboos |
| Etiquette | Body adornment | Units of time |
| Family | Play | Jokes |
| Beliefs about death | Magic | Weapons |
| Insults | Melody | Marriage |
| Hair styles | Nepotism | Economic inequalities |

## Norms, morals and ethics

Here is a very important point, so pay attention! People generally want to be sociable. They want to be perceived as polite and decent – and they don't want to be made a laughing stock, step out of line or otherwise make a fool of themselves. Our species is a social one, maybe in fact a "hypersocial" one, where we are constantly aware of other people's reactions.

As mentioned earlier, that is because we have to collaborate with each other. It also means that if you perceive the "stranger" as impolite, indecent, amoral or inept, there is a strong likelihood that something has gone wrong in the inter-cultural communication. It is very unlikely that the other person is deliberately doing something that repels you. If they do it deliberately, they are an idiot. He or she is an idiot in your culture and very probably in his or her own culture too. As I mentioned in the introduction, there are idiots of all shapes and sizes in all countries, and they are characterised as being completely indifferent to others from a social point of view. For social animals such as humans, it simply doesn't do to be socially illiterate or deliberately not give a damn about other people. As for all the others, the non-idiots, who have insulted, irritated or hurt you – they have most certainly had no idea what they were doing.

The solution to cultural clashes must therefore be to think culturally intelligently and to consider how the other person sees the world. As a rule, much comes down to misunderstandings, but sometimes our thinking doesn't get that far, because we are short-tempered and promptly react in a stone-age manner. One of the most important pieces of advice to give is therefore *to always test the temperature of the water.* Find out what is happening before you react. Don't *assume* a whole load of things before you have the *knowledge* needed. Otherwise you will react by reaching for the book on your inner shelf that is called "How I must perceive that behaviour, because that is how I would be perceived if I did the same". Remember it is *not* someone like you who you are dealing with. It is *someone else* with different *norms* from your own. It can be said that when it comes to cross-cultural encounters, you have for a moment to tone down the old adage "do unto others as you would have them do unto you". In any event you should *wait* before you do anything. Listen before you speak, and think before you act.

The reason for many cross-cultural clashes is what we call *norms*. This is where we humans differ significantly from each other. In fact differences in norms can be so great, that we can sometimes think that we have nothing in common with someone. We can end up believing that the other person has completely different morals or ethics than we have.

That was the reaction to the Chinese in the above example who pushed their way to the front of the canteen queue. "He just doesn't care about good manners and what we think of him!" – that's what Danes think, and shake their heads. The Chinese have not learned a set of rules for that, because in China they do not regulate norms in the same way as in Denmark. Conversely, a Dane will get nowhere in China, because he will have difficulty understanding why people put so much emphasis on personal relationships. He might in fact drop some of the social events. Maybe he will stay in his hotel room when the others go out. "He doesn't care about anyone else", might be the pre-judgement from the Chinese. Now it's going the other way.

Both parties are of course mistaken. The clash here is of two different sets of norms. Norms which we *believe* say something about the other person's psychological and social makeup. Norms don't do that at all. They say something about the codes developed historically by different societies. They are different codes we use to find out whether the other person is playing according to the same rules as we are. Because having rules in common means that we can go off and hunt ox together.

To understand why, we must have a quick look at two areas where people have a lot in common, but where they often believe that they differ.

### Ethics

Ethics are basically about not hurting others and there is no society in the world where people are allowed to just go around murdering others. We all have a strong resistance to hurting, fighting and killing others. We are fundamentally ethical animals because collaboration is so important for us, which makes murderous deviants dangerous and unpredictable partners we can't count on. What we sometimes (and only when under heavy pressure) do to people outside our group is another thing, but society generally punishes its own violent members. We often punish our own deviants harder than those from outside our own community.

In most cultures, violent offenders are considered to be idiots by the vast majority of people. No one gets any benefit from asocial people who go around murdering others (at least not *within* the group) – somebody like that can't be trusted and as a rule remains socially isolated. It was the ox we were supposed to hunt, not each other.

### Morals

Morals are about socially responsible behaviour and fairness to each other. That means not cheating, stealing or defrauding each other, and that generally we agree about mistrusting those who do. Even chimpanzees have morals, who know who owes what to whom within the group, so it is very likely that humans share the same biologically determined and fundamental sense of fairness. If you give something, you expect to get something in return. This simple moral rule, which the well-known French anthropologist Marcel Mauss discovered in the 1920 and described in his book *The Gift*, has since been confirmed in one society after another. That is why we punish theft and fraud. Those who do not contribute, those who are not generous, those who never invite others to visit but always visit others, those who scrounge – such people are not popular anywhere in the world.

## Norms

Should you go to a funeral in a gaudy, low-cut dress? No, not in most cultures. Should you chomp your food noisily, pass wind at the table or openly and completely uninvited start talking about the hostess's weight? In some cultures you can, in others you can't.

If you are from a culture where you can't, then people call that type of behaviour *insulting* or *inappropriate*. We wouldn't dream of saying the same about ethical or moral transgressions. It is not "inappropriate" to kill someone or steal his car. It is frightful, extremely unfair and in any event illegal. It is not frightful, and seldom illegal, to breach a norm.

Norms are basically about signals. You show that you are part of a group because you use the group's special signals. Norms are a way for our stone-age brains to determine whether someone is in the group or not. If you deviate too much from the group's norms, it can make collaboration risky. So people look for norms about shaking hands, how they dress, how they say good morning at work and how they behave on ferries. Because non-adherence to these norms is a *signal* that there are deeper cultural differences which could make collaboration difficult.

The division between ethics, morals and norms is not sharply defined, but holds in most cases. This means *that we have to be more careful about believing that just because people do not adhere to norms (which of course are often not their norms, but ours), then they will also breach our moral and ethical rules too. The moral and ethical rules are, as mentioned, almost universal.*

## The spiral of mistrust

Differences of norms can thus be misunderstood as differences of morals and ethics. This is where we have to be careful and understand that norms are often banal *signal differences* and thus not very substantial.

It is about being at the forefront of these mechanisms, because the problem is that as soon as things go wrong, they quickly go very wrong indeed.

As I have said, trust is key in cultural conflicts. The less trust, the more you get dragged down into a spiral of mistrust. Along the way there are a number of danger signals which unfortunately get noticed too late:

Mistrust can quickly be fostered by small, insignificant things because within one's own "tribe" it's generally the case that other people mean well, so there is immediate doubt when dealing with someone who is an "outsider". Just a small amount of uncertainty about whether there are shared values or agreement on the same things is enough to start a growing spiral of unrest and suspicion. One wrong word, one cryptic comment, something puzzling – *which you of course never asked about, because you forgot to express your bewilderment.*

## SPIRAL OF DISTRUST

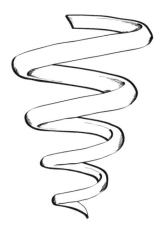

NEGATIVE STORIES

NOBODY WANTS TO CHALLENGE THOSE STORIES

STORIES BECOME "TRUTHS"

YOU STOP SHARING INFORMATION

YOU IGNORE THEIR REQUESTS

THEY BECOME THEIR CULTURE AND NOT PERSONS (THE CHINESE ARE...)

YOU STOP SHARING VITAL INFORMATION

THEY FAIL AND YOU DON'T CARE

TRUST IS GONE

It doesn't take much more, and the downward spiral has begun. Suspicion has been aroused. Next time it's easier to be bewildered, suspicious or even hurt and angry again.

Often, we are much too careful about not articulating surprise, or even an insult, based on a misunderstood culturally tolerant idea that "other people are allowed to insult me". They don't have the same morals and ethics that I have. They're just less polite where they come from.

That sort of idea is very dangerous, because it sets the standard for morals and ethics *lower* among the other people. If you don't expect the *same ethical and moral* standard of other people as you do of yourself and "your own", then you have not given the other people sufficient recognition. You can't expect that they greet, reward, speak, perceive or think like we do. We like to expect that the temperament, the fundamental morals and ethics, will be decent, generous, empathic and responsible. The problem occurs when we think that the other people don't have to "behave as well as we should" in precisely this area. When we set our expectations for their morals and ethics deliberately lower. It is a very misunderstood form of cultural respect and it is a very dangerous path to go down, because if we don't demand decent behaviour from others, then we also end up thinking that we don't need to behave decently to them.

It is important to understand that other people are welcome to have other rules, so that we don't *prejudge* people. But if we don't ask *why* they did what they did, and what happened when we were surprised or insulted, then we will never find out whether the other people were simply using different norms. So we can easily begin to imagine that there really *is* something wrong with them *as people*, and that they are just idiots.

Now we have already come down the spiral a little. We have wondered, and been insulted, and we have no precise idea what happened. "What did you mean with that email?", "why didn't he say goodbye properly"? We don't know if it's serious or nothing to worry about. Should we attach any "meaning" to it? We have not got around to asking, and can easily begin to think the worst…

Now we need to double-check everything and we get nervous when the "other people" speak their own language to each other. "What is it they can't say in a language we can all understand?" We feel a greater need to check up on something and make sure that they understand it too. Now our tolerance for deviations has become decidedly narrower, and we get more and more irritated and less and less willing to yield and forgive.

The worst comes when we start to avoid talking to each other. The communications and information gap gets bigger, and the time between conversations gets longer and longer. The conversations we do have are curt and their content very limited and compact. We only write and talk about work and jobs to be done as briefly and precisely as possible. Then we start to retreat into our own group. We start to exchange stories about the others, the worse the better.

And everything, simply EVERYTHING they do gets interpreted as yet more evidence that they can't do anything right, or that they have a hidden agenda. Now all it needs is for someone to light the fuse, and the whole powder keg will explode.

Sounds familiar? As well as illustrating the situation in many workplaces, unfortunately, and possibly a few marriages, it is very typical for such downward spirals of mistrust to stem from cultural differences. They can occur when a company *outsources* part of its work abroad and those abroad need daily contact with the head office in Denmark. Many times things develop just like the escalation of ethnic conflicts, civil wars and genocide such as in the Balkans or Rwanda. The patterns are frighteningly similar. The really dangerous escalation occurs when two groups begin to wildly dream up things about the other side and *stop communicating* with each other. Then we are well into the us/them attitude which easily leads to people quite simply killing each other (although it usually needs a Slobodan Milosevic or similar tyrant before things get really bloody). In the office, things seem a bit more civilised on the surface, but – hand on heart – how many of us know of someone who obstructs their colleagues' good ideas? That we kill off creative solutions because our own department wants the kudos for doing something else? Thank goodness that comes nowhere close to genocide, but the underlying process is the same.

If you are, or have been in such a spiral, it can generally be useful to consider where things went wrong (so that it doesn't happen again) and then consider what is needed to reverse the downward drift. The code words are:

- Express your doubt and surprise, ask about the meaning of what they are doing instead of grumbling about a strange comment or a weird phrasing in an e-mail (maybe it means something different to what you think it does, or maybe it means nothing at all).
- Explain how you feel if someone's behaviour makes you uneasy, concerned or makes you wonder –
- that requires trust. But trust is something you only receive when you show trust and respectful honesty yourself.
- Make sure that everyone communicates in a common language when others are around.

- When the group starts to exchange stories about the others, challenge this.
- Be aware of all the danger signals listed above, and tell your colleagues about the spiral of mistrust and the danger signals.

There is no need to replay scenes from the former Yugoslavia in the office or let a subsidiary company abroad you only speak to on the phone be the whole office's scapegoat and collective irritant. We have to have respect for spirals of mistrust and now that you know what they look like, you have a responsibility to make sure they don't affect your workplace.

## The battle with the stone-age brain

The psychological reality is that we get on best with our "own people" and find it easier to extend interest, sympathy and trust to people who look like us. In fact, we like to group according to the most trivial factors we have in common. Psychologists have performed masses of experiments with children, young people and old people, and this fact gets proven time after time. Give one group blue shirts and the other red, and they will immediately form two groups and conflicts will then occur between them. Let one bus of scouts arrive half an hour before another, and it won't be long before we have two groups feeding on mistrust and hate for one another before the week is out.

That doesn't mean that we have "natural" hate for one another. The idea that different cultural / ethnic / national groups have an instinctive hate for one another is rubbish. It would be far too expensive if we all went around with an irrational thirst for each other's blood. What on earth would come of that? War is an unimaginable waste of resources with very little gain compared to the gains from collaboration.

In reality, we do not hate each other when it comes to crossing cultural boundaries. Our relationships are more akin to mild indifference. The other people are just not that important to us. It is more difficult to be really interested in their lives beyond the fact that on the surface they may appear to be interesting and arouse our curiosity. In the long run we prefer our own type.

So it is not because of any ill will that we quickly forget "other people's" accidents, natural disasters or civil wars once we switch the TV off. We forget because people who are not like us just don't foster our emotions in the same way – their world is simply not important to us.

But that has to end. Other people's worlds *are* important because we talk, trade and live together with them and we share offices, canteens and the water cooler with them at work. Furthermore, some of the challenges we face are global, so we have to work with *other people*. A greater understanding of the baggage our stone-age brains carry around in the form of inappropriate ideas would help us a lot. So we can understand that the differences in norms hide deep similarlities which our stone-age brains don't immediately notice, because they are so busy looking for differences.

As Shylock the Jew said in Shakespeare's *Merchant of Venice*, Act III, Scene 1:

*I am a Jew. Hath not a Jew eyes? Hath not a Jew hands, organs,
dimensions, senses, affections, passions? Fed with
the same food, hurt with the same weapons, subject
to the same diseases, healed by the same means,
warmed and cooled by the same winter and summer, as
a Christian is? If you prick us, do we not bleed?
If you tickle us, do we not laugh? If you poison
us, do we not die? And if you wrong us, shall we not revenge?*

In order to become better at seeing all the similarities *and* understand all the differences, we have to train our cultural intelligence. We need to learn about what separates us so that we can take it into account and so that in time we can better understand, prepare ourselves and act according to what we know about "the other people". That is what the rest of this book is about.

# 2

# Cultural Intelligence

Richard Gere is standing on the stage with his colleague, the beautiful Shilpa Shetty. Dressed in a casual checked shirt, jeans and white t-shirt, he takes her hand and kisses it. We are at a benefit event for AIDS. The American actor is playing the role of a flirting, idolising man opposite a beautiful woman. A role he has played several times, and which if he were at home in America would not have attracted any special attention at such an event.

The good-natured larking-about and innocent, flirty behaviour is a very familiar part of every Oscar-type ceremony. Over-dramatically, Richard Gere then takes the young actress, tips her back theatrically and kisses her. She grins broadly in an "aren't you a fool, Richard" type manner and the scene is over within seconds – but two worlds have just crashed head-on. It's just that Richard Gere doesn't realise that. He wasn't prepared for that. But over the following days, there are street protests, crowds shouting and orders to arrest both him and Shilpa Shetty issued in two Indian states. An innocent kiss and a hug had become a national scandal.

Most people will have realised that the event took place outside Richard Gere's home territory. A place where other norms apply, and where what he did was very quickly seen as a breach of morals. In this case, it took place in New Delhi in India. Richard Gere's gesture was quite innocent, but no one there understood that, even though he obviously didn't mean to offend anyone. He was not *aware* that he had behaved like an idiot.

There was not a lot of understanding for Richard Gere from the Indian audience, just as Richard Gere showed no understanding for the rule of thumb of "when in Rome, do as the Romans". That is what we will look at in this chapter. When you are in another place, you must as a minimum find out about how that country's "norms" differ from those you are used to. For everyone's sake. In Chapters 7 to 13 we will look more closely at some of the other areas where we as humans differ from each other. Because it is possible to determine *which differences make a difference* and thus orient and prepare yourself in advance.

## The art of preparation

Preparation is part of what we in this book call cultural intelligence. A phenomenon which author Elisabeth Plum defined as "the ability to act appropriately in situations where cultural differences have meaning, and the ability to make oneself understood and establish constructive collaboration across those differences". This preparation consists of:

- Specific preparation, *mapping* of the current cultural differences for this area in particular (see Chapters 7-13), which can also involve specific practical rules of behaviour (dress, programme, food etc.), local information or other sources of knowledge which can be consulted beforehand (Chapter 18).
- Mental preparation, special *attention* and *vigilance* where you learn to think that there *can* be a number of differences here, and that what you see is not necessarily the same as when you are at home.

In the above example, Richard Gere should have prepared himself for Indian culture, because then he would have known that men and women in India do not go hand in hand, hug or kiss each other in public. It is a lack of respect for those at the event to make such an affront to public decency in that way. At first glance it can seem strange, but in reality the reaction of the Indians was not much different from what people in most western cultures distance themselves from as regards doing things in public which they really only ought to do at home in the privacy of their own bedrooms. There are limits to how much intimacy people want to see their fellow citizens display at a bus stop or on a park bench. We can say that the Indians' prudishness limit is lower than other peoples', but we *all* have our limits.

Preparing for something is not the same as *expecting* something. I will deal with the latter later in the book, but in short we can say that preparation is about taking account of differences. Before you act, you have to be sure that your assumptions are correct. All cultures have exceptions. Even in India, there are couples who like Gere and Shetty don't stick to the rules (in general, this is more widespread in India's lower classes / castes). So it is important always to observe before you act. You can use the good old English expression *dip your toes in the water*. For example, before a meeting in a Middle-East country, you can be given a lot of information about strict dress-codes, and that it is expected that you over-dress for the occasion. In this case, it is good to follow some rules. Choose smart trousers, a tie and a jacket – or skirt and jacket – and let the first impression decide what to do after that (or whether you should also have a Rolex watch, gold-edged business cards or whether other sorts of bling are required to show respect during the next visit).

In other words, dipping your toes in the water means waiting before reacting. If a Dane starts talking about a dress code (read: headscarf) with a Muslim woman over the phone, before he has even met her at the job interview, then he has created *expectations* rather than *prepared* himself. It could be that the headscarf is not large enough to create problems in the job, or that the woman doesn't even wear a headscarf. But if you have *prepared*, then you will know what to say *if* the headscarf becomes an issue at all, or whether it is even relevant. If you expect something so strongly in advance, you have already decided that culture comes before the individual.

## Cultural intelligence as a skill

Researchers, such as those at Michigan State University, have described and scientifically validated that there is a skill called Cultural Intelligence. Pioneers such as Soon Ang, Christopher Earley, Linn Van Dyne and David Livermore have found that the skill can actually be measured, and that it is similar to other intelligence skills such as emotional intelligence (EQ) and general intelligence (IQ). It is not part of one's personality to have a high cultural intelligence (or CQ), so it is something which can be improved through training.

Research clearly shows that people with a measured high CQ simply achieve better results when they are outside their cultural comfort zone, which is a strong indicator for it being more than just talk. Cultural intelligence exists, and cultural intelligence works. With increasing globalisation, it is just a question of time before CQ screening becomes a regular part of a job interview, before it is done prior to a company sending an employee abroad as an expat and in fact is just included in general day-to-day management.

But what is it that culturally intelligent people can do? Overall, they have four sub-skills. They feel motivated and self-assured in intercultural situations, they have knowledge of themselves and other cultures, the ability to use this knowledge in their planning and they behave according to which culture they are in. It is these skills which are at play in the situations and circumstances I will describe below.

## The rules follow the location

An important thing that culturally intelligent people have an eye for is that rules have a tendency to be linked to a territory. That is in fact a phenomenon I dare to call universal. In any event, I have never come across the opposite in anthropological texts; that cultures always adapt to guests and suspend their own practice as long as outsiders are present. According to models by evolution psychologists, this is also precisely the behaviour to be expected of "stone-age brains".

The German author Hans Magnus Enzensberger has also noticed the phenomenon and described it in a short metaphorical story about a train compartment, where the new arrivals in the compartment respect that they are in "foreign" territory and thus adapt. Until someone even newer arrives. Then suddenly they become one of the "old ones" in the compartment, who can command respect and recognition from the new passengers.

---

Two passengers in a train compartment. We know nothing of their history, their origins or their objectives. They have made themselves at home, commandeered the table, the coat hooks and the overhead rack. Newspapers, coats and bags are strewn over the empty seats.

The door opens, and two new passengers enter. Their arrival is met with derision. There is a noticeable unwillingness to make room, clear the vacant seats and share the overhead rack. The two original passengers behave as if they own the compartment, even though they don't even know each other. They behave as a group in their approach to the newcomers. It is their territory which is being questioned. Anyone coming in is seen as someone forcing their way in.

Their self-perception is that of natives making demands on the whole space for themselves.

From Hans Magnus Enzensberger's *The Great Migration*

----------------------------------------

As humans, this is usually second nature for us, and most of us remember it when we are abroad. Other people's rules are the *basis* for what we ourselves must do, but it being a basis does not mean that we have to copy them in everything we do. In fact, pure mimicry can quickly start to look like parody.

A Danish course participant once told about when he was in an American airport, where suddenly and without warning, the American national anthem was played. Everyone stood up and put their right hand on their heart – but what was he to do? He stood up like the others, but left out the bit with the hand on his heart. He respected that he was on their territory and that it was basically a good idea to show respect and not stand out. But putting his hand on his heart was an unnecessary thing to do. Not all Americans do it, and so there is no reason to be "more Catholic than the Pope", as we say. In fact, it can seem to be a direct parody, and "selling out" of one's own culture may seem unpleasant to many. If you have no cultural backbone, and take on the colour of your surroundings just like a chamaeleon, can you even be trusted?

As a rule, it flatters other people and makes them happy if you try to follow their conventions, and the saying "when in Rome, do as the Romans" could usefully be expanded to "unless you do as the Romans, then get out of Rome!" Many of us think it is fun to introduce foreigners to the norms, greetings and small rituals of our culture, and we think it is fun when they make a mess of it, but at least they try. But if they get too enthusiastic about our culture and start singing our national anthem out loud at a sports event, then we laugh at them. "Sorry, but who are you trying to fool here?" is perhaps what we think.

## Who has to budge?

In cross-cultural encounters, there are a number of strategies which can be used when you suddenly find that the "rules of play" are different. But not everyone is equal when it comes to being culturally intelligent.

1: The chamaeleon strategy – I will blend in to my surroundings and do as the others do
2: The gorilla strategy – I will immediately show the others how I do things and define the rules right from the outset
3: The reading signals strategy – I will pause for a moment, look around at what other people do, find out where I deviate, make it clear to them what I am used to doing and find a way to agree on a compromise or either follow my rules or theirs.

To be a pure chamaeleon is irresponsible and over time you cannot carry on simply mimicking all the others and compromising your core being. The gorilla strategy is also seldom workable as it merely introduces rules that are not obvious to the others (gorillas think that explanations are not worth the effort). Gorillas take responsibility well enough, but on the other hand show absolutely no humility or receptiveness.

It doesn't take much to work out that personally, I believe that combining the chamaeleon and the gorilla into the reading signals strategy is the best way forward. I do that because cultural collaboration is about finding a way where:

- We agree that there are various different norms, but that those norms must not get in the way of the collaboration underway.
- The norms are the basis, but have no special value other than steering collaboration in a group of like-minded people – the norms as such have in principle no strong practical value (quite the opposite).
- Everyone is in principle willing to budge, but simple rules such as "who was here first" and "rules are linked to location" create a *basis* for the cultural negotiations.

- Emphasis is on the shared task, and the interest that each individual has in completing that task – the rational, pragmatic arguments rather than the gorilla's "we're doing it that way because I say so" or "this is good, because I/we've always done it that way."

We will go deeper into cultural negotations in the section on bridge building. Instead, we will now look more closely at the big question of how far you can or must go when it comes to adapting to others. We're getting into an area with lots of emotions and lots of politics, but it's essential to look at the big question too: how much of my own cultural being do I want to let go of in order to get closer to the others?

### What can I allow, and where are my limits?
"Rules are linked to location", or "when in Rome..." are excellent rules of thumb, but what if I am presented with behaviour that I am passionately opposed to? Is it just a question of norms, or is my own opposition to others' customs and usage just an over-reaction to something superficial?

It's an important question to ask, and the answer is that it is perfectly OK to pull out and say stop. In Japan, you can be unlucky (or lucky?) and have to eat sushi straight off the body of a naked woman, *nyotaimori*, and if there are too many taboos for you in that, then of course you can politely decline (sometimes you can even get a follow-up offer to use the young lady for more private purposes).

Nothing is so important that you should compromise your own core values, but you are of course obliged to consider whether what you can see actually *means* what you think it does. For example, if it's too awkward for you to take a maki roll from the navel of a young lady on behalf of the Japanese, then don't be awkward. Because they are not feeling awkward about the situation, and so neither do you *need* to.

If you personally are expected to do something you find taboo when abroad, then just say no. The people you are with are no doubt fully aware, or at least understanding of the fact, that something is too alien for you.

What you should be more careful about is when other people's behaviour toward each other is something you are opposed to. For example, do you have the right to comment about your male host's polygamy (85 percent of the world's cultures practice polygamy in one form or another, so it is certainly not unthinkable that you will come across it). You simply have no idea whether it is as oppressive for women as people in the West often immediately believe if you do not *know* anything about the women's situation. Unless you are a politician travelling around, there is no reason at all to get involved in such things. Again, you need to look into the meaning for the other people when *they* are the ones concerned, and *they* are the ones doing something. However, if it is a case of limits for what you want to *take part in*, you have quite a different type of veto which you should and may use.

### Can you "sell out"?

"Why should we take our shoes off in their mosque, if they won't take their headscarves off in Denmark?" Cultural encounters unfortunately often develop in such a way here in Denmark (I have in any event heard that type of comment countless times). But that comment expresses a sad, pedantic attitude where people keep precise count of who gives or takes how much. A cultural barter where we talk about "selling our culture out".

In many ways that is an unbelievably unwise way to understand cultural courtesy. Instead of thinking of "doing as the Romans" as a loss, or "adapting to other people's rules", you can choose a pragmatic approach: what is most clever for me, and what do I get the most benefit from? Instead of looking at it as a zero sum game, you can see it as a win for both sides.

The Pakistani man who did not want to shake hands with Anna based his actions on ideas and norms in his own world, not Anna's. He did not want to embarrass her by shaking her hand, but ended up doing *exactly* that. It was unintended, and if he realised that his actions are interpreted in a completely different way in Denmark compared to where he comes from, he ought to seriously consider changing his approach. In Denmark, his action is completely the opposite of what he intends, so it is not just culturally unintelligent, but purely and simply unintelligent if he doesn't *use* his new knowledge, act on it and thus offer Anna his hand.

Sticking to your own cultural norms despite *knowing* that they will be interpreted incorrectly in the situation you are in, means you are acting culturally unintelligently. There can be many possible reasons for that (see box) but if you are on a business trip, the main objective must be to earn money. If you follow the rules of the place you are in, you will be perceived as trustworthy, proper, moral and a decent person. Why on earth would you bet everything on a losing battle for your own norms when you are somewhere in the world where the norms are quite different? Remember, norms are quite random characteristics which could just as easily be quite different. That applies to a lesser extent to morals, and an excellent example can be bribery, which has "become the norm" in the culture you are visiting but which maybe isn't a norm where you come from. In most cultures it is a moral question, so you should not compromise with such issues if you can avoid it.

So if you are afraid of taking your shoes off, or you are a woman who doesn't want to cover up in the Middle East because you think it compromises your identity and that would be "selling out", it actually sounds like you have a personal problem. Remember: you know well enough where you come from, and other people don't think they have "won you over" because you avoid pointing at things with your feet and politely put your hands together to greet people when in Thailand. People who think that they should never "sell out" must perceive the world as a constant cultural battlefield. A very unpleasant attitude, which can almost certainly only be due to having a weak sense of self-identity.

## The art of choosing your battles

Many people who don't have Spanish roots don't like bullfighting. But what do you do if you are not Spanish, but are in Spain, and someone talks enthusiastically about the concept and even invites you to go along to a bullfight? I can't tell you how much you should "give", but what I *can* tell you, is that you have to accept the consequences of the "battles" you enter.

First you need to consider the following, and preferably in this order:

1. Is it my norms, my morals or my ethics which are being challenged?
2. *What* is it they are asking of me, and what *significance* does it have for them?
3. What is my primary task here where I am right now?
4. Why is this principle important to me?
5. What do I think I can achieve by "sticking to my principles"?
6. Is it so important that I want to risk losing a deal / client / colleague / job because of it?

First (1), make sure you understand: is this situation about signals and symbols, or does it have real consequences for people, animals, the environment or for example democratic or economic development in the country concerned?

Once you have determined whether it lies inside the grey area, then comes the difficult decision: take part or not? This is where you have to ask yourself: what do they want? That you like bullfighting, or that you just watch as a spectator? Take part once or several times?

Dip your toes in the water and find out what is expected of you. Remember about the norms. It could be that what you have to do looks worse than it is. Maybe the lovely girl feeding you at an event with the Chinese businessmen has been hired to do just that, and *only* that. Don't assume there is more to it. Remember that they are playing by other rules than you are, and not everything means the same as it would "at home" (that is and remains golden rule number 2).

What of course makes it extra difficult is that taking part in a global world also means that your behaviour abroad can be of interest to people back home. You can thus go against the norms of your home culture by taking part in the local culture's norms, for example when another person is reduced to being used as a serving tray. So it is also important for the international company or organisation to have a clear CSR policy defining the boundaries between norms and morals. Taking part in practices which lead to oppression of women, child labour or are to do with denying fundamental freedoms cannot be disguised as differences in norms.

So if you have a gut feeling that what you are being invited to do won't be suitable for the front page of newspapers back home, then it's a good idea to react to your gut feeling. Decline politely and maybe say that is sounds interesting – which it may do – but that it is illegal back home and that it would therefore give problems for your organisation, and could even cost you your job if you took part.

You can also say you have a migraine…

Anyway, you have to consider why you are there (3). If you are a politician, you are of course there in a completely different way – as a person with opinions. But if you are there as a colleague, business associate, buyer, seller or diplomat, then you have a specific task to complete and that is what you should focus on. So even though you might think you could alter their behaviour, it is best not to. On the other hand, you are obliged to keep considering whether you should take part, or whether you use the excuse with the migraine again. Either for the sake of your own conscience, or because there are limits to what your company likes to be associated with. You don't just have to behave culturally intelligently towards the people you are visiting, but also to the people back home who will maybe hold you to account when you return.

Then you also need to decide what it is about the norm or principle that is so important to you (4) that you don't want to join in. Is it because it requires you to do something you wouldn't want to do if you were at home? If so, then remember that you are not at home, and so things maybe have a different meaning. Then you need to consider what you can achieve by expressing your unreserved opinion about bullfighting, the caste system in India, burkas, the Tiananmen Square Massacre or by keeping your shoes on in a mosque. Again, it is quite a different issue if there is a question of child labour or textile workers unaware of the dangerous fumes they are working with at a sub-contractor's factory, than if you were asked to eat dog meat. So again, we move away from norms to moral and ethical issues which affect you because *you* have direct influence on them. The dilemma becomes ethical, because some people would suffer. And hurting other people is not OK.

The next thing to consider (5) is whether you seriously believe you can change their attitudes and ideas. If not, are you digging your heels in just so you can feel good and for the sake of your own conscience? People don't like being told what to do, and their attitudes and ideas are their own problem. The only exceptions you can react to are their actions. Again, you can of course find things so personally indignant that you cannot live with yourself unless you jump in and criticise what you see and hear. You just have to consider (6) how much a feeling of moral superiority or how much your love of your country's coincidental norms, customs, greetings, table manners and other formalities actually are worth in the specific situation.

It's not about "selling out" but about being pragmatic in a situation where you can't and shouldn't do anything about it.

**Don't say I didn't warn you**
We'll look more closely at specific cultural negotiations later in the book, but here we are dealing first and foremost with the fact that every attempt to force through your own ideas, norms and principles has a price. You can always *hope* that the other people you encounter are culturally intelligent and accept your strange principles and norms, but you cannot *count* on that. So my recommendation will be that you as far as possible try to find your own style and start out from what is expected of you in the situation and location you are in.

The rules are not the same "at home" and "away", and by far the majority of people are very aware of that. So let's look briefly at what to remember and what you can demand. Not forgetting that every situation is unique and depends on what you want to get from the other person. If we only consider doing business at this point, then there is a crucial difference between selling and buying. As Richard Gesteland says in his own book about cultural differences for business people: "In international business, it's the seller who adapts to the client". It's not completely untrue, and most people will come across this pattern. This means that a seller visiting Denmark from abroad will be more willing to follow (or try to follow) Danish customs and usage than a buyer would, as the latter will be more sought after. So with that little difference in the back of your mind, you can list the following abroad / at home differences (as well as all the similarities of course).

- - - - - - - - - - - - - - - - - - - - - - - - - - - - - - - - - - - - - - - - - - -

**Abroad**
- You are the guest, so behave respectfully to other cultures and try to do as they do – that is what is usually expected.
- Ask what to do – as it is your responsibility to find out what that is.

- Be aware of what others do and watch how you "fit in" – let them be the ones to drop titles first and start to use first names.
- Pay particular attention to how they are dressed and make sure you follow their lead ("test the temperature of the water").

------------------------------------------------

------------------------------------------------

**At home**
- You are the host, and as well as being culturally tolerant, as all culturally intelligent people are, you can expect them to do as you do.
- Explain and try to show the guests what to do – you have a responsibility to teach them.
- You can hope that your guests are culturally intelligent, but you cannot expect them to be. So don't be angry or disappointed if they behave very inappropriately – try to show your tolerance and concentrate on the "matter at hand" rather than the individuals.

------------------------------------------------

The examples above are most relevant to business situations and negotiations between companies, but don't let yourself be limited by them. The logic also applies to school parents' meetings, the social services office or in a multicultural neighbourhood. It is just that business situations are the ones which have been investigated and described the most. And in the other multicultural situations you have a responsibility to find out what it is you are there to do together, to talk about the cultural differences when they come up, state each other's points of view and have an open and unprejudiced discussion about the various different ways of looking at the problem.

Everywhere there are people there are rules, but the culturally intelligent job is about investigating which variant of those rules is in play in a given situation. We have to observe the differences and if necessary, explain and mediate between them. We have to explain the rules in our own society and check whether they are being understood or not. Do the others understand the "background" for the rules or not? The latter – understanding – is significant, and we will look at it in the next chapter.

## What is tolerance?

Most people would agree that tolerance is a virtue, yet it is often used to admonish other people. "You're just being intolerant", people tell you, just because you're being slightly critical of something, and with that the discussion is over before it even started. Tolerance is a difficult term, because it is often defined in an unfortunate way as respect for, and acceptance of, anything at all. Tolerance in that way is the same as indifference, because you could just say "I couldn't care less" instead of saying you are tolerant.

So tolerance can in fact mean something else, and a good definition can be found in Thomas Bredsdorff's and Lasse Horne Kjæld-gaard's book *Tolerance – or how to learn to live with people you hate*. To tolerate something means first and foremost:

1. that you in principle reject it;
2. that you do not want to ban it, even if you have the authority to do so;
3. that you try to relate to what you tolerate;
4. that you are sure of your *own* case without being opinionated because you can see how you yourself would appear comical.

The first is the most important point. If you don't reject out of principle something that other people do, that is not tolerance. If you believe eating snakes is gross, or praying five times a day is absurd, or standing up for a national anthem is nonsensical, then that's OK. As long as you don't want to stop other people from doing the same, then you are basically tolerating those who do those things. Something completely different though is stealing a car, paedophilia or child labour. Those are things we would normally reject *and* forbid, so we can quite rightly say that we don't tolerate them.

In other words, it's not necessary to *like* another person's culture in order to tolerate it. *Understanding something is not the same as approving of it.* If you pretend that you should always believe that what other people do is just as good as what you do, then you will lose your own cultural heart, and no one can keep that up for any length of time.

The third point is so important that the whole of the next chapter is dedicated to it. Tolerance becomes a strangely assumed attitude if you don't want to be bothered to understand the other people's point of view. The same applies if you don't try to understand how what other people do has meaning within their system of norms and values. It maybe looks strange, but remember that you seem just as strange to them as they do to you.

When living within your own culture, you often forget how weird you can appear to others. Similarly, you can get so used to different cultural expressions that you fail to see that you are being hypocritically tolerant of certain things because they have been going on for so long, but which if "invented" today would be rejected. This is something often seen in religion. If you are from a predominantly Christian culture, you will have a tendency to accept Christianity's assertions about the virgin birth, the resurrection and miracles – and even though you may not believe in them you probably think of them as less strange than what other religions teach. We tend to be especially sceptical about more neo-religious movements. But these more recent religious movements are not religious in any *new* way at all. They are just *new religions* we have to get used to. Yet we can be scared away from anything strange and weird just because the religion has a strange name or has just been "invented".

## To sum up

To sum up, we can say that the path to increased cultural intelligence looks like this:

The path to cultural intelligence
Prepare
Test the temperature of the water
Learn from / explain to

CRITICAL ACTION
Accept and understand
Choose your battles

Everyone is obliged to prepare themselves (and we can only hope that "the other people" have done the same). It's the first thing you need to do, as it's too late once you're in the middle of things. As soon as things are underway, you hold back with your knowledge, and investigate whether it is even relevant. You test the temperature of the water and avoid reacting as you would to your "own" people. You also *think* before you speak, and *observe* before you conclude.

In addition, you should not be afraid of over-explaining and putting words to the norms and expectations you are used to not talking about. You should make space for people to ask questions and say if you are willing to explain – especially before things go wrong. Feel free to express your bewilderment and make a safe space for others to do the same: there is no such thing as a stupid question.

If things still go wrong, so that critical incidents occur, then accept and understand (more about that in the next chapter) and be pragmatic about considering which cultural battles are important and which are not worth bothering about. Finally, you need to find a compromise based on the rules and norms of where you are at the time. We will deal with the latter in a few chapters' time.

# 3

# Cultural Understanding

Anyone can read about dos and don'ts when travelling abroad. Guidebooks provide lists about etiquette where you can learn not to point the soles of your shoes at an Indian and never to offer four white lilies to a Chinese hostess.

For Indians, and also for people in the Middle East, the soles of your feet are the dirtiest thing possible. During the drama of the "Muhammed Cartoon Crisis" in 2006, Danes gazed in bewilderment at TV pictures of people in Arab countries hitting the Danish flag with their shoes. It was the most insulting thing they could do. Danes just thought it was weird.

Similarly, white flowers (and the number four) symbolise death in China, so such gifts are best avoided. It's rather like giving a wreath of flowers when you go to someone's home for dinner. Which actually happened to a Chinese woman I once taught. She was of course very embarrassed when she realised what she had done, but the Danish hostess was not offended, as she was culturally intelligent enough to understand that her guest from China had bought the flowers with the best possible intentions. She could of course have prepared in advance by asking her local contacts about what to take as a gift. Unfortunately, she forgot before it was too late.

Of course, these are just simple dos and don'ts, and it is reasonable to learn a country's etiquette. Unfortunately, it's not enough just to look them up in the otherwise excellent guides available in print or on the Internet. Checking them is quick and simple, but they do not give you the serious stuff.

The problem with these simple pieces of advice is that they only cover a small number of very specific situations such as restaurants and greetings – in other words the *implicit assumptions* from the onion model in Chapter 1. A general *understanding* of the other culture, however, puts us in a position to understand and analyse much of what a guidebook *doesn't* foresee. It is only through a real understanding of the deeper background, namely the *values* in a society that you can react correctly in completely *new* situations, something which is very useful.

## The difference between *knowing* and *understanding* the rules

Every day, people have to follow rules in traffic. Some streets are one way only, sometimes you have to give way, there are places you mustn't park and there are speed limits. Irritating and inane restrictions on personal freedom, aren't they? No, the rules are there for everyone. They regulate behaviour in traffic, so there is room for all. If you *understand* the rules and the intentions behind them, then you will be happy to follow them, but if the rules are random and irrational hindrances then it is easy to get bitter and aggressive and only follow the rules to avoid other people honking their horns or to stop yourself from getting fined.

That is an attitude which is equivalent to trying to navigate other cultures only by *knowing* their inane and irrational rules without taking the time to *understand* the system and logic they come from. It becomes purely a question of survival, where you are skating around on the surface barely avoiding stepping on anyone else's toes. It's just not a strategy that shows respect for the other culture and any understanding of their world. In the long term, no one wants to hang around people they don't respect or understand. Just as you would probably stop driving a car if the rules you had to follow didn't seem logical, but instead seemed completely random and incoherent.

For people unpracticed in cultural challenges, simple guidelines can appear sufficient, but for anyone who wants a serious relationship with people in other cultures, those sorts of superficial guidelines can quickly prove to be lacking in depth.

In my own work as a consultant, I have sometimes been faced with a brash and aggressive young man who insists that understanding is over-rated. It is all about finding out what other people do and following them. Looking at *why* those other people did what they did was a waste of time, irrelevant and not worth bothering with. Academic rubbish. He was one of those who just wanted to know a few "tricks" or get some "tools" to solve an immediate problem with a Chinese supplier. When you tell them that a China workshop takes all day, they don't understand why. It's not because the consultant wants more money. Well, of course it is, but in truth it's because anything less won't stand the test of time. "A fool with a tool is still a fool". But it can be difficult to convince busy business people that a short presentation about China won't help very much. It's often almost a waste of time. The "tools" they need are not a list of magic tricks they can use in front of the Chinese. It is the *understanding* itself which is the actual tool and that takes time as our brains have our past battling against us.

Let me say it straight: If you are not interested in understanding other people, then you are totally unsuited to cross-cultural collaboration, negotiations or exchanges. You will be awful at handling unexpected situations, and in the long term you will be useless at your job. So it's important to understand *what* happens and *who* the other people are. It is about *understanding* rather than *doing* – about *living* in the other culture rather than *surviving*.

*There is a reason why other people do what they do,* and that is where the understanding lies. It is exactly what John Franklin missed when he saw the Inuits.

As a rule, even norms which are quite random (even if they have clear historical causes) fit into a system, and once you have cracked the code, the "foreign" things start to have meaning. It is a fantastic thing to experience and is quite a relief once you do. The faster you can do so, the better your chances of success in the long term. The more you seek to understand, the more culturally intelligent you become.

## Bachelors and front teeth

When the Koma people in Nigeria celebrate a young girl's approach to adulthood, they knock her front teeth out. This happy event takes place after a long day of feasting which culminates with the local "wise man" knocking her two front teeth out with a club. The girl thus becomes a woman and can return to her people with a broad smile – not to mention blood all over her face.

Well, not everything in life has a meaning, but as I've said, humans both form and use opinions, so maybe you, the reader, want to know why the Koma do this? I'll get to that.

Even in Danish culture, guests can come across incomprehensible native ceremonies and rituals which outsiders find puzzling and exclusive. For example, sometime the natives will weld three or four oil barrels together and fill them with cement, placing them outside the home of a young man on his birthday. This phenomenon is most commonly seen outside the Copenhagen area, although there are reports of it being seen in some of the "less sophisticated" areas of the city. For an outsider it is, to be honest, a complete mystery.

Think of your own culture for a moment. What traditions and annual events do you celebrate? Why do they look like they do? What do you eat and what do you do? And why do you do it in the way you do?

On many of the courses I have given at Living Institute, I have asked Danes to explain their own customs.

When asked, most people can explain that the black tower of barrels is a "Pepper Mill" erected to celebrate 30 years of bachelorhood. "When you get to 30 and aren't married, it's a tradition to tease people in a fun away about it. We do that by giving them pepper." But why pepper? Is there some particular shortage of the substance among young, unmarried men of that age?

This is where most explanations miss their target.

When asked about this ritual, most people answer very specifically about what happens. They refer to historical practice or just say "I've no idea why, it's just something we've always done". It seems we have very little understanding of all our strange ceremonies, rituals and traditions.

"Pepper fellows" was an expression from German trade apprentices in the 1400s. They sold pepper and agreed to stay single so that the trade would not suffer from their being married – with everything that entailed. That is the historical background for the ritual, but how many Danes actually know that? No one knows the historical background, but where it comes from is not actually relevant. Danes are just happy to do things together, because agreeing about *what* to do, not *why* to do it is what is most important.

In all societies, everyone does "strange" things to affirm to each other that they are doing things *together* and that we know how to do them and that it is important to do them right. Most often we agree that things are *meaningful,* but we do not necessarily agree what they *mean.* According to anthropologist Anthony Cohen, we often consciously avoid talking about why we do things in order to maintain the "sense of community". We do things together to affirm that they are important to us, and so we do everything we can to avoid talking about what they really mean. It is only when anthropologists and irritating foreigners come that we get asked all the "stupid questions".

## When there is no real reason why we do what we do

The problem is that little word "why". "Why" is obviously an unavoidable question when we are navigating around in the practical world, where people usually have logical explanations for why they do what they do. *It works for them.* There is a practical reason why the Inuits have chosen to make blubber lamps in precisely the way they do, and as a rule there are practical reasons why almost all jobs are done the way they are. But people also do things which have no immediate *practical purpose* but which have a *symbolic objective,* and here the question of "why" is very hard to answer.

So instead of asking the Indians *why* they throw paint at each other once a year at the "Festival of Colours", or why people celebrate Ramadan, Ashura, Chanukah, Midsummer, Halloween and whatever in all sorts of other places, we can instead ask about *what happens. How* it happens, *what* happens and other specific questions that do not demand *interpretation* by the person being asked.

People often believe, at least they do in Denmark, that other cultures are very well aware of why they do what they do. They imagine that muslims on a pilgrimage to Mecca must have a very clear idea of why they are walking around the Kaaba (the large stone covered in black cloth), or why they should celebrate Ramadan. Or that the Chinese can explain why they burn "ghost money" and the Scots read out poems over a meat dinner (Burns Supper – "addressing the haggis"). Anthropologists generally find that people just can't answer such questions very well.

Interpretation needs ethnologists and other experts. It turns out that we are all really bad at understanding our own culture. Often we have no idea why we do what we do, so we can't expect other people to know much more about their own culture. So don't bother embarrassing them when their explanations aren't good enough. Your own explanations are hardly likely to be any better.

Back to the Koma girls and their front teeth. According to anthropologist Bjarke Paarup-Laursen who has studied the Koma in Nigeria, the strange teeth-ritual has to be seen in a larger context. Boys there are circumcised, and Paarup-Laursen has analysed that for the Koma people, female aspects are soft, whereas what is hard is associated with men. In other words, in order to become an adult a girl has to lose something hard and masculine (her front teeth) and boys have to lose something soft (their foreskins).

When he asked whether the Koma could recognise this explana-
tion, Bjarke Paarup-Laursen got the well-known answers: "no, we just do what we've always done" and "it's our tradition".

Remember that the fourth point in tolerance was the ability to see how comical you appear to outsiders. If you first understand how strange what you do appears to others, then your tolerance for others' peculiarities will increase.

## Why? Because!

Culture is to a great extent an unreflective system of habits and norms people have stopped thinking about. And very often the question "why" will be very difficult to answer. If the "natives" could answer for themselves, there would be no need for books such as this (nor for anthropologists) which systematically try to give readers some insight into how other people think. If they knew precisely how they themselves think, and why, then we could just ask them everything.

But they don't. So if a "why" question needs a decent answer, it requires very culturally aware people, and there are very few of those around. If necessary, we can ask "what would happen if you / I *didn't* do as we usually do" and maybe get more complete answers that way, but in general you have to supplement the questions you ask with additional sources of information. We will look more at what those sources can be in Chapter 17.

A partial understanding of others is hopefully something you will get in the second part of the book. But until we reach that, let's take a look at the Danes. After the next chapter you ought, hopefully, as someone who tries to find meaning in Danes' behaviour every day, to be in a position to answer the "why" question. Maybe even more able to do so than the Danes can themselves. Because Danes wander around inside their own culture wearing cultural blinkers, meaning they have difficulty talking about their own cultural blind spots in what they just regard as normal.

So let's take a look at the values that form the behaviour of the Danes.

# 4

# Why do Danes do what they do?

In this chapter, I will paint a short cultural portrait of Denmark and the Danes. My goal is to start with a culture relevant to you, the reader, and which can form a basis for the second part of the book where we will look at some of the same "differences", but with a focus on other cultures and other expressions.

Understanding Denmark and Scandinavia can in fact be a rather demanding task, as in many ways the Scandinavian people are different and strange, and as I said earlier, it is very difficult to look in from the outside and explain that. Danes have difficulty explaining their behaviour, or even wondering about themselves in the same way as other people wonder about them. They will maybe have a few words about their focus on equality, but it will otherwise quickly end up with a few self-complacent facts about being the happiest nation on Earth. Fine – but what can *you* use that information for? You're not Danish!

This chapter focusses on the values in Danish society and in Chapter 16 we will look more closely at what effect these have on Danish working life and how you can get better at tackling what the Danes do and maybe even challenge them.

- - - - - - - - - - - - - - - - - - - - - - - - - - - - - - - - - - - - - - - -

### The Expat List
The Expat List is a summary of a long list of observations which foreigners living in Denmark have made about Danes and being Danish. The original source of the list is difficult to find, but the list can be found on Facebook and a number of

websites. In reality it has several authors, all expats living in Denmark, who over time have added their own comments.

A whole list of points are presented under the headline "You know you have been in Denmark TOO long if…" – all tongue-in-cheek exaggerations of things non-Danes think are strange but which Danes wouldn't even think about.

Here are a few examples of the funniest ones:

**You know you have been in Denmark TOO long if:**
- You know the meaning of life has something to do with the word "hyggelig".
- You find yourself lighting candles when you have guests – even if it is bright and sunny outside and 30 degrees.
- You can open a beer bottle with almost anything.
- You can't remember what a party without alcohol is like.
- You feel comfortable laughing at jokes about Swedes.
- You say "Skål" at every sip because you can't find anything else to say.
- You buy a hot dog with a credit card.
- You find it normal that shops close earlier at weekends.
- Every time you're in an awkward silence, you have the urge to say "jo-jooooo…".

## Differences that make a difference

In Denmark there are lots of differences which make a big difference, and which mark Danes out from others quite a lot. I've chosen to focus on the following:

- Equality
- Trust
- Independence
- Punctuality
- Formalities
- Openness (private)
- Dealing with conflicts
- Humour
- Religiousness
- Self-image

# Equality

*I never knew any Country where the Minds of the People were more of one calibre and pitch than here; you shall meet with none of extraordinary Parts or Qualifications, or excellent in particular Studies and Trades; you see no Enthusiasts, Mad-men, natural Fools, or fanciful Folks; but a certain equality of Understanding reigns among them: every one keeps the ordinary beaten Road of Sense, which in the Country is neither the fairest nor the foulest, without deviating to the right or left: Yet I will add this one Remark to their Praise. That the Common People do generally write and read.*

Robert Molesworth, British Ambassador to the Royal Court of Denmark (1692)

Whether that is due to the country's modest size or its strong tradition for equality is difficult to say, but the small distance between top and bottom can be very striking to many outsiders. Being able to see government ministers cycling around the city is something completely unheard of for most people from abroad – but why shouldn't they get on their bikes just like the rest of us? Whereas in other countries the chauffeur-driven limousine would be an indication of status, this can have precisely the opposite effect in Denmark. Danes tend to puncture authority with humour – and in some places are surprisingly candid with leadership. In fact, it is in many ways more legitimate to scold management than to do the same to those at the bottom of the hierarchy. People prefer to protect the bottom of the power chain, and challenge the top.

- - - - - - - - - - - - - - - - - - - - - - - - - - - - - - - - - - - - - - - -

When Danes want to have a conversation, they sit down. Danes abroad who feel the need to talk look around desperately for somewhere to sit... This habit is so widespread that it occurs in language as well. When we want to say what Bosnians and Serbs, or Chechnians and Russians should do instead of fighting each other to the death, we don't say that they should negotiate. No, we say that they should *sit down* and have a talk about things. What does that mean? What purpose does all this sitting down serve? Is it just a question of comfort? What actually happens when people sit down?

The first thing that happens is that both sides become more equal. The height differences between people are primarily a function of the length of their legs. There is more difference in leg length than torso length. When you sit down, the differences in height are reduced. We see that as an advantage, because then we avoid looking *up* or being talked *down* to. That matches a widespread assumption in Denmark that communication is best when it takes place between people who are as similar to each other as possible.
Anne Knudsen, Anthropologist

- - - - - - - - - - - - - - - - - - - - - - - - - - - - - - - - - - - - - - - - - - - - - - - - - - - - -

"Similar children play best together" is what we say in Denmark, and that translates best as "birds of a feather flock together" – we don't want people to be too different from each other. This is the tendency Danes often call the "Law of Jante". For outsiders, it can often be a bit difficult to understand what that means. I even met a German living in Denmark who thought it was a real piece of legislation. His Danish colleagues talked about it so much, he assumed it really was a law. But it isn't. It's fiction, but its message gives many Danes an essence of how they treat each other, so it constantly gets used as a (rather poor) method of explanation.

**The Law of Jante (Sandemose, 1933)**
1. You're not to think you are anything special.
2. You're not to think you are as good as us.
3. You're not to think you are smarter than us.
4. You're not to convince yourself that you are better than us.
5. You're not to think you know more than us.
6. You're not to think you are more important than us.
7. You're not to think you are good at anything.
8. You're not to laugh at us.
9. You're not to think anyone cares about you.
10. You're not to think you can teach us anything.

The Law of Jante was devised by the Danish/Norwegian author Aksel Sandemose in his book *A Fugitive Crosses his Tracks* (1933), which deals with his traumatic childhood in the closed and intolerant town of Nykøbing Mors. The law's assertion that you should not think you are anything special is the dominant one, with the other nine simply being variations on the first. But sometimes you can get the impression that the Law of Jante is a convenient excuse from people who are the subject of criticism, because any criticism can be neutralised by suggesting that they are being subject to collective persecution. In any event, many media personalities in Denmark who get criticised argue that the criticism is automatically unjust by referring to Jante.

The Law of Jante is thus often presented in completely the wrong way. The law is not the reason Danes do not boast about their superiority over each other. In reality, the law is just symptomatic of something quite different: Danes' love of equality. As social researchers Gundelach, Iversen, and Warburg wrote in the Danish contribution to a broad investigation into European values (which I will quote from elsewhere in this book), it is "too simple to shout 'Jante' as an explanation: the reluctance to idolise the elite can more likely be seen as having ideals about a close-knit community, which people are afraid of endangering if the elite are given too much emphasis. Instead of eliteness, Danes want equality and community".

It can of course be a bit difficult to get used to as an outsider, especially if you have been given a management position in Denmark and find that the unreserved admiration you are used to at home is noticeably absent here. Danes highly value equality, and that no one thinks they are better than others because of their position, age, gender or whatever. The guy who collects your rubbish has just as important a job as a company director. Imply anything else, and you will quickly encounter big problems.

Basically, it is about Danes putting a high value on homogeneity and unity, because when everyone is the same then it creates trust. Danes really like the idea that the factory CEO sends his children to the same school as the factory floor worker, and shops at the same supermarket. So Danes put high taxes on wealth too, meaning they have obtained a status as one of the world's most equal societies. One which is extremely equal compared to many other countries.

## Trust

As previously mentioned, trust is very high in Denmark because of Danes more or less all being one big family and therefore very similar to each other. Culturally and financially. Visitors from abroad are constantly surprised at the small stalls by the side of the road selling things like strawberries and where there is simply a box to leave your money in. That can only work in a country where people have steadfast trust in each other's honesty.

Danes can thus appear to others to be a little naive, and conversely foreigners in Denmark can often seem to be too suspicious and controlling to the Danes. It's something which is important to remember in cross-cultural encounters, because such big differences in attitude can quickly lead to people treating each other with a lack of cultural intelligence.

I dealt with this particular characteristic in Chapter 1: Denmark is a small country with very small internal cultural differences. And when people are so similar to each other, they trust each other more. This concept is strengthened even further by all the clubs and associations in Denmark, which cross economic, social and cultural boundaries. Around 90% of Danes are members of a club or association, meaning Denmark per capita has one of the highest numbers of such organisations worldwide.

------------------------------------------------------------

Foreigners living in Denmark are often amazed at the enormous amount of trust there is here, and I have heard lots of examples of extremely trusting behaviour which is completely unheard of for them, but which Danes don't think twice about. In Denmark, we just don't think about how unusual this behaviour is. Here are a few things which people from abroad have been amazed by, but which Danes take as given. The nationality of those who mentioned it is in brackets.

- You can withdraw money from your husband's account just by saying you are married and giving his social security number (Polish).
- If the price tag is missing on something, the shop assistant will ask you if you can remember what the label on the shelf said, and then accept your answer without checking it in any way (Scottish).
- We mostly have our children looked after by people completely unknown to us (nursery, daycare) (German).
- In the supermarket, vegetables are weighed not by the checkout assistant but by the customer, who could easily cheat (Spanish).
- When you call in sick to work, you don't need a doctor's note. Not even if you stay at home for the whole week (German).

--------------------------------------------------------

## Independence

When the Øresund Bridge was being built between Denmark and Sweden, there were twice as many accidents on the Danish side as the Swedish. According to Birger Hermansson, who has seen the statistics, the differences can perhaps be explained by the two different cultures. It's all about how people view authority, and what they expect from each other: "Whereas Swedes have more respect for authority, Danes are more anarchistically inclined", says Hermansson, who is Swedish. In other words, when a Swedish worker is told not to enter a particular area he will do as he is told, while a Dane will want to see why for himself. Because "no one is going to tell me what to do"!

Just like if someone says they are not allowed to draw a picture of the prophet Mohammed. "Really? Pass me a pen, I'll show you..."

In the Danes' world, it's not an expression of disobedience or lack of respect for leadership, but showing initiative and thinking for oneself. In that way, Danes have definitely come a long way by thinking outside the box and challenging assumed truths, because their intuition told them that another way was better. This urge to challenge can sometimes also be foolhardy and dangerous, as maybe was the case on the Øresund Bridge, but people seem to be willing to live with that.

Danes are staggeringly "autonomous" in so far as they make independent decisions, don't really believe in chrome-plated truths and never do as they are told. It is a strong Danish value to make one's own decisions and form one's own opinions.

In a large European values survey, 80% of Danes name independence as a core value. That is noticeably more than anywhere else on the continent. By comparison, the figures for the UK, Italy and Romania are 53%, 41% and 28% respectively.

Our ideals are the same when it comes to raising children. The survey shows that 82% of Danes believe that children should be brought up to be independent, with only 13% preferring "obedient". And once again, there is a notable difference when comparing the figures from neighbouring countries.

This, of course, goes well with Danes' mild disdain of authoritarian leadership, and when asked how much influence they have at work on a scale from 1 (no influence) to 10 (high influence), the Danish average is 7.9, which again places them right at the top of the table.

Danes are good at defining their own tasks at work and therefore want management to help them develop their skills and make good decisions, rather than have management make the decisions for them. However, this rather distant form of management can give many foreign staff problems. They cannot really understand that they are often allowed to decide for themselves what they should do, and not always be monitored or given work. In their eyes, Danish independence is often an expression of lack of leadership and structure, even though Danes of course see things differently. Conversely, Danes feel that their foreign staff and colleagues maybe forget to think for themselves. They want rules and procedures, whereas in Denmark people want openness and freedom. When Danes are in management positions where they have to cross cultural boundaries, or when you yourself have to manage Danes, it is very important to always agree expectations. It is something which Danes often forget when they believe that others are fundamentally the same as they are, and the other people can cope with the same high degree of freedom as Danes do. Danes have a tendency to think that everyone else has just not attained the same high "level" of freedom that they have. But that's not always the case.

---

One of our programmers contacted me on MSN from his office in India to ask permission to use the toilet. It was a request I found hilarious, and it order to keep the same good-humoured tone I answered facetiously that he would have to wait until the end of the day, and that actually I would like him to do a couple of hours of overtime that day. Several hours then went by and I had forgotten my joke, when suddenly the phone rang. It was my by now extremely agitated Indian programmer asking desperately for permission to use the toilet.

Palle, head of an outsourcing company with many staff in India

---

## Punctuality

I once heard a man of Middle-East origin complain about a time when a Danish friend he knew bumped into a friend in the street. A close friend he had not seen for quite a while. The old friend suggested they should have a beer later the same day, but unfortunately it wasn't possible. The first man's calendar was fully booked. He had a meeting at his bank. The man from the Middle East was shocked, because his Danish friend was not able to drop a completely impersonal appointment with his bank to see an old friend he hadn't seen for ages. The old friend hadn't even been bothered, as he could perfectly understandably accept that there wasn't time, and they would have to find another day.

Indian Anthropologist Prakash Reddy, who has studied Danes thoroughly on several occasions, has an eye for the same behaviour and describes it as a Danish dislike of spontaneous social events (even though they are very flexible at work). Social gatherings have to be planned, and appointments kept. Reddy writes that Danes are polite and considerate when they meet old friends as described in the example above: "The only things they [Danes] do not have, is time and desire to take part in such interaction". Even though they actually *had* three hours for a cup of coffee (and lots to talk about), a totally spontaneous meeting in the street had to be over within 10 minutes. Because they hadn't *planned* it!

It's because Danes have a *monochronic* perception of time, just like the rest of Northern Europe, where time is a limited resource and everything has to be planned and the plans adhered to. We'll look more closely at this concept in Chapter 14, but it should be mentioned as a special characteristic here anyway.

Danes are a punctual people, who arrive on time. Never more than ten minutes late and NEVER early (they would rather sit in their car and wait till the precise time of the appointment, or take a longer route, when they to their astonishment notice that they are *too early*).

- - - - - - - - - - - - - - - - - - - - - - - - - - - - - - - - - - - - - - - - - - - - - - - - -

**You know you have been in Denmark TOO long when:**
- Your old habit of being "fashionably late" is no longer acceptable.
- You no longer think it's strange that no one ever comes by to visit without being invited and you never show up at anyone's place unannounced either.

- - - - - - - - - - - - - - - - - - - - - - - - - - - - - - - - - - - - - - - - - - - - - - - - -

### Formalities

Titles and deferential expressions of politeness don't have much meaning in Denmark. This is of course linked to the strong focus on equality. People are on first-name terms with their teacher, their boss, their doctor and even, in some families, with their parents. On the other hand, you don't have to travel any further than across the border to Germany before you encounter *Herr Müller* and address your doctor as *Herr Doktor*.

Another thing people often don't bother with in Denmark is civilities such as "excuse me" or "would you mind". In the otherwise very informal USA, it is quite normal to be polite and attentive if you accidentally touch someone with your supermarket trolley – however lightly. There, there will be a plethora of "excuse mes" and "are you alrights?" which many Danes would find over the top. In Denmark it is quite easy to come across situations where people accidentally tread on someone else's toes in a supermarket and just hope the other person didn't notice.

That also means that Danes are often perceived as rude by people from abroad. In Living Institute we have found that one of the most common characteristics of Danes is: "You are just *so* rude". And if you check the expat list, you can also see that many people perceive Danes as a very improper tribe.

------------------------------------------------

**You know you have been in Denmark TOO long when:**
- You can't remember when to say "please" and "excuse me".
- You think someone saying "undskyld" is just a weirdo.
- You call your teacher, doctor and/or in-laws by their first names.
- You think it's OK to walk away from a conversation without excusing yourself.
- You don't look twice at businessmen in dark suits wearing white sports socks.
- You are very surprised when you receive compliments about ANYTHING.

------------------------------------------------

Of course, Danes are not rude by nature. They just have other *norms* and an explanation of their strikingly informal behaviour can again be their great degree of trust. Formal excuses and niceties are good in a society where people don't know each other and so have to spend a lot of time marking out their territory and finding out who everyone is. "Civilised" and "urbane" forms of address such as "excuse me" and "please" (for which there isn't even a word in Danish) are just what the word "urbane" means – to be used in the city. There, where many people live closely together, you have to treat each other a little like rotten eggs, because you don't know each other and so have to deal with each other according to a strict ritual. But such a "meta-language" is not needed in a country where everyone knows each other's basic values and is almost part of the same family. You don't behave in such an over-the-top way to your family, do you?

When you are almost family, and trust each other, then you don't need to over-do your politeness. You can quite easily run your trolley into someone in the supermarket without having to stop and apologise, because the other person is just thinking as you are:

"Please don't make a scene, so I can avoid having to deal with you" – because Danes drop the formalities in order to avoid invading each other's private space (more about that later).

The English sociologist Richard Jenkins has done a thorough study of the mentality of the Danes, and has reached the same conclusion. He believes that the very widespread use of "tak" [thanks] is the key to understanding: Thanks for the meal, thanks for yesterday, thank you and thanks for everything, the latter being what people have written on their gravestones. According to Jenkins, it all fits into the equality ideal. "Would you mind", "may I have" and "excuse me" indicate the status between people. A status where one is asking with a certain amount of humility for a service from the other. "Tak" is about an exchange – of food, attention, friendship or whatever between two equals. "Thanks for the help" – "thank you". No humiliating bowing and scraping, but a perfectly balanced relationship between two equals. People say "tak" *after* these little exchanges rather than make a fuss about the difference between people *before* asking. So people in Denmark don't politely ask for help, they just say it directly: "Will you help me with this?" – not exactly a polite and humble way to address someone. But straightforward and honest.

It is unfortunately very difficult to understand for foreigners and is often mistaken for (passive) aggression and impatient bad manners.

As a negotiator – in business and elsewhere – a Dane will therefore come right to the point. They don't want to do the small talk, because that is about your private life and not about business. Their love of collective decision-making can take time, but they are always focussed on the objective. The process with numerous round-table discussions is not because of an undue love of the process, or because they have to get to know each other through long formal and polite enquiries (or mutual exchanges of respect and recognition) like in Asia. It is rather due to the fact the Danes do not want anyone to feel forgotten or left out. In Denmark, people are measured by their results, and do not get honoured and recognised for dominating a meeting.

Danes can therefore sometimes also appear more sloppy with their attire than in other locations. In Danish companies, *business casual* is the norm, but it is an imprecise term which in Denmark can easily include jeans. No tie, and no jacket. In other words, more *casual* than *business*, one could be tempted to say.

I think that is because people in Denmark see a suit and tie as a presentation of themselves. We sell ourselves with our clothes, something Canadian sociologist Erving Goffman called *impression management*. Goffman also has another term, *face work* which is our honour, renown and reputation, and *face work* is just as much something you give, as something you have.

In stricter, more formal cultures, you *give* face to people by being well-dressed. This means that you show that the other person is worth the extra effort. You dress well for the *other* person's sake, not for your own. It can be difficult to understand in a culture such as Denmark, where dress codes are first and foremost about presenting yourself. In Denmark, people are not used to helping others to save face or to "massaging their egoes". But that is the case for example in Asia, the Middle East and to a certain extent Southern Europe. *In other words, formal behaviour is about showing respect.* Not all Danes find that easy to fathom when they come from a country where you go around treating people as equals and so must not overstate inequalities. In Denmark, everyone shows respect by being at "eye level" with each other (once again, a very Danish expression), whereas in most of the rest of the world you show respect by doing exactly the opposite.

------------------------------------------------

**You know you have been in Denmark TOO long when:**
- You think it's impolite to sit next to someone on a bus if there is a seat where you can sit on your own.
- When a stranger on the street smiles at you, you assume that:
  a. he is drunk
  b. he is insane
  c. he is British
  d. he is all of the above.

------------------------------------------------

## Openness, privacy and individualism

In their long and well-argued book *In the Heart of Denmark*, about the Danish national character, the authors Gundelach, Warburg and Iversen attempt to describe a people who put a high value in individualism, but nevertheless like making decisions collectively and prefer "everyone to be heard". They call it *collectively-oriented individualism*. It is a particular form of individualism where you can do almost whatever you want in private, but have to consider others when there are several people together.

In Denmark, people's sexuality, habits, political views, utterances (and last but not least, drawings of prophets) are their own business. People are to a great extent expected to mind their own business and you will hear things such as: "That's their own business," "that's private," or "they have to sort out their own mess" – which all indicate a deep respect for other people's privacy. It is not necessarily a case of social anxiety, but can just as easily be understood as deep respect for the private lives of others.

Many people have remarked on this way of keeping your distance. When the Indian anthropologist Prakash Reddy arrived in Hvilsager, a small town in Jutland, he was very surprised when people tried to avoid him when he knocked on their doors unannounced. It was because they were not out in the street in a public place when he did so, but had locked themselves behind their closed doors in their little houses as soon as they came home from work.

In another story from Reddy's field work, he tells the story of a woman whose father had far more apples growing in his garden than he could eat himself. Nevertheless, he didn't give any away to neighbours and friends. Instead, he put them in a basket by the roadside with a sign inviting people to help themselves. He did it while no one was looking in order to maintain the anonymity of both the giver and the receiver. Most days the apples were all gone by the evening. Prakash Reddy asked the woman whose father put the apples out why he didn't just give them to people who didn't have apple trees. Her answer was that people would have been too embarrassed to accept them from her father, as they would have been suspicious of his motives.

It is not easy to be generous in a country where people keep each other at arm's length, as Reddy wrote. It is easier and more polite to help each other anonymously.

- - - - - - - - - - - - - - - - - - - - - - - - - - - - - - - - - - - - - - - - -

I wondered why so many small lanes in summer house areas were marked "private" – even beach areas were marked too. As well as the many "private" signs, the owners had put thick fencing up so that they couldn't even see into each other's gardens.

I've found this "privacy" to be a Danish characteristic. It expresses itself as a form of reservation or modesty about showing feelings. It can be perceived as a lack of interest in others (...). Maybe the fact that Danes shy away from conflict, coupled with modesty, is a serious source of loneliness?

Tone Saugstad Gabrielsen, Norwegian author, in the book *How Danish are Danes?*

-------------------------------------------------------

As we will see later (in Chapter 8), there is a big difference between what is "private" and what is "public" in different cultures, but in any event the Danish home can be classified as very private.

As Reddy wrote: "Someone's house and the land it stands on are a castle, a secret place which no one, not even a neighbour, has the right to violate. Other people even feel that they are not allowed to park their car on the public street outside your house for a couple of minutes". And he continues: "In Denmark, a good neighbour is one who never calls".

So in Denmark, being invited in is something very big. People can work with Danes for many years without ever being invited to a colleague's home. Danes keep their private and work lives separate and only 56% of Danes say they have close friends at work. The average in other countries surveyed is 71%. In Denmark, almost everyone leaves work at 4 pm, and offices are left empty. They have gone back home to their families. They stay there until they leave it again for a planned activity, or to go to work again the next morning. So working in Denmark and building a network outside the workplace is often very demanding.

The arm's length relationships mean that Danes "don't want to impose" and in fact take it to such an extreme that foreigners perceive it as coldness.

Similarly to what we just talked about in the previous chapter, it is extremely important for foreigners to *understand* why Danes do what they do, and that things probably look worse than they really are. It is a very fine line between tolerance and indifference, of that there is no doubt, but Danes definitely prefer the arm's length option over a return to the old traditional forms of living where everyone knew everything about everyone, and "normality" was defined very narrowly. In Denmark, people leave others alone and so there is a very high tolerance threshold for sexuality and other private matters. Denmark was the first country to allow same-sex civil unions. Again, it is because your private life is your own affair, and no one else's. Keeping one's distance thus also has clear democratic consequences, depending on the political climate.

In the same way, the arm's length society also helps keep corruption at a very low level. When you need something done, you don't ask a civil servant for a personal favour – and pay. Just because you know his cousin, neighbour or closest relatives. There are very few people who come close enough that Danes dare to ask for personal favours. The rest are held at arm's length.

------------------------------------------------

A deep feeling of solitude doesn't just pervade Danish literature, but also nature and day-to-day life for Danes. As a foreigner coming to Denmark from more southern latitudes, you can feel Danes' deeply-ingrained solitude even more than your own as an outsider. This feeling can fill you with fear, but also with fascination and bewilderment for people who in their own unobtrusive fashion know how to handle one of life's biggest challenges: being alone and daring to be alone.
Maria Pilar Lorenzo, Spanish lecturer, in the book *How Danish are the Danes?*

------------------------------------------------

For the same reason, it can also be particularly difficult to build a close relationship to Danes if you have moved here and are not a member of the "family". It is most definitely one of the biggest problems for guests and people who move here, if I am to judge from the comments of the many people I have come into contact with from abroad through my work. Danes appear to be reserved, cold, aloof and distant.

Traits which are confirmed by a survey undertaken in 2010 by Oxford Research, where more than 1,500 knowledge workers from abroad were asked to say if Danes were "open and inviting". Only a third felt that to be true. Not very impressive, and when they were asked how easy it is to make friends with Danes, only 14% said they thought it was easy. 69% said it was difficult – an overwhelming majority. Unfortunately.

This is partly due to the high rate of working women, which is one of the highest in the world. This means that small children are not looked after at home, but sent to day care. So there is a natural limit to how late both sexes can work if the children have to be collected by 5 pm. In addition, Danish parents spend a remarkably large amount of time with their children, and this has only increased over the past twenty years. So Danes with children are very difficult to get hold of outside working hours. Children have a very high priority.

But it can't just be that. Because the same pattern is seen among Danish students, who don't have to rush home to children after school. In other words, it must be something cultural.

### Handling conflicts

Danes avoid conflicts. Maybe that is because they have such a big need for things to be "cosy" and "nice", but Danes will go to great lengths to avoid conflict rather than have open confrontation. Another related observation which is often associated with Danes is *consensus culture*.

- - - - - - - - - - - - - - - - - - - - - - - - - - - - - - - - - - - - - - - - - - - - - - - - - - -

An unwritten rule in Danish culture is that we are not very explicit. We are much too implicit and take it as a given that people understand a lot regardless of their cultural background. When we have people from a different ethnic background coming in, we find that there are some things which we take as given and which become apparent. One of the limits of being so implicit is that sanctions are left unsaid. If you do something wrong, no one tells you directly. Instead, you get frozen out and ignored.

Agi Csonka, HR Manager at TDC

- - - - - - - - - - - - - - - - - - - - - - - - - - - - - - - - - - - - - - - - - - - - - - - - - - -

When Danish anthropologist Karen Lisa Salamon undertook a study of Danish club and association culture at the beginning of the 1990s, she discovered that one of the reasons for the large number of associations was that many had been formed as a result of splits from other associations. The splits had mostly come about because of a small and insignificant disagreement. Instead of confronting the conflict, raising their voices and arguing about it, those involved decided to leave and start a new association which was more or less identical to the one they left. The Danish club landscape is thus teeming with almost identical organisations with almost identical objectives and charateristics, with the exception of whatever it was that led to the disagreement. Maybe that is also reflected in the Danish political landscape. It's quite normal for four or five MPs to leave their parties and become independents during the lifetime of each parliament. Danes are apparently bad at dealing with internal differences of opinion. And when a majority of politicians demand a "broad agreement", but try to use the power they have won, it gets called "block politics" and is condemned. Because everyone should agree "regardless of party lines".

In Denmark, people avoid discussions where things get too heated. The Indian anthropologist Prakash Reddy, who has studied Denmark very thoroughly for decades, sees this as an expression of Danes' need for privacy and desire to keep their distance. They can discuss politics well enough, but usually stop when things get too heated. Maybe that is also the reason why people only usually guess how others vote, but almost never actually ask. To avoid an open conflict no one wants to have. As long as they can just guess instead of ask, they can guess that they are "fundamentally in agreement". And that is so wonderfully uncomplicated. So everything is nice and "cosy" again…

The English sociologist Richard Jenkins believes that it already starts in school, where young Danish children learn that challenging the group is the worst thing they can do. They thus learn to take on the group norms and attitudes very early on, because anything else would be extremely anti-social. Danes may be individualists, but they are also afraid of sticking their heads above the parapet. It all points back to the equality ideal, and Jenkins concludes that *"individual diversity is safeguarded by accepting that one should in important respects be similar to everyone else (…) That the result in Denmark has been a valorisation of negotiation, compromise and conflict avoidance is not surprising"*

The Indian sinologist Triloki Nath Sharma describes in his portrait book *Danes* a well-known situation from a train compartment designated as a "quiet zone", where someone dains to speak. Everyone is well aware that this is wrong, but no one dares to start a conflict. After a long time, a woman breaks the silence and admonishes the culprit.

*Her action broke a new norm: one does not admonish others. The other passengers in the compartment were instinctively aware of her situation and in order to help her deal with her embarrassment, they consciously chose to pretend that they hadn't noticed anything. They didn't look at her, but pretended to be even more deeply engrossed in what they were reading, not revealing that they had in fact seen it all happen.*

Many Danes, and possibly you yourself, have been in such a situation.

When conflicts nevertheless occur at work, they take a strange form, according to integration consultant Mehmet Yüksekkaya. As an immigrant woman once said to him: "It's easy to talk to a Danish colleague about a particular conflict on a one-to-one basis, and they always show understanding for your point of view. But as soon as the conflict gets taken up in a larger group, no one wants to talk about it, and no one says anything specific".

The above also expresses a special culture of moaning in Denmark. It's also called "sluice room gossip" in Danish. It often consists of moaning and aggressive comments which seldom make it to larger gatherings, but which exist as a particular social behavioural norm in some (but not all) Danish companies. And even though there is no research which directly backs up the assertion that we moan more than other nations do, a study from 2005 shows that 70% of 1,500 surveyed members of the 3F trade union said that there was often or very often moaning at their workplace. So there is definitely something there.

When conflicts are pushed out to the "sluice room" and not dealt with openly, it may be the strength of the value about being nice to each other, having a good time and most of all being "cosy" together. So things often end up with people going their separate ways, saying that they are in fact in agreement, and insisting that there never was a conflict at all. A final possibility is of course to express the criticism in a more understated fashion. Danes are experts at that. Try this sentence:

*We'll finish a bit earlier today so you can also help to clear up the coffee cups.*

When I say that sentence in a Danish context, the people on my courses usually smile and say that they know that type of communication very well. It is our ability to say things between the lines or "sideways". It's due to a very sophisticated form of communication which can only take place in a relatively small population such as there is in Denmark. It is tone of voice, and the common history the staff have together, which is crucial, and which here means: you haven't been very good at helping to clear up before. Danish members of the tribe will understand the tone of voice perfectly and (perhaps) make amends. Colleagues from abroad, however, will not always be communicating on the same wavelength.

The clever thing about this form of understated communication is that it puts the conflicts into words, but that the criticism can always be withdrawn again if an unpleasant personal conflict arises. "No, that wasn't meant as criticism" is how you can defend yourself later. Conversely, if the other person does not understand the real meaning, you can say that "it was made reasonably clear that we weren't happy with your contribution". But "clear" is exactly what the statement wasn't.

Overall, Danes tend to keep criticism to themselves, skirt around it, use irony or just round off a heated discussion with "basically, we agree, don't we?" Even though everyone knows that's not the case. Nevertheless, they nod and smile, and woe betide anyone who later says he is in complete disagreement. We can't have that – because we've just "put a lid on things".

## Humour

In Denmark there are two types of humour. Danish humour and bad humour – at least if you ask Danes. In a study from 2009, 59% of Danes questioned answered that Danes had a better sense of humour than other nations (only 7% felt it was worse). So they're not exactly unaware of this, and Danes regard humour as a significant part of their national character and a significant aspect of good relations with work colleagues.

But humour is neither "good" nor "bad", humour simply differs from culture to culture.

What is interesting is *what* people laugh about in Denmark, and even though there have not been many studies done about it, many people would agree that sarcasm and irony play an important role in Danish humour.

------------------------------------------------

I don't think you can say that irony is something particularly Danish. Irony can be found all over the world. But there are big differences between cultures about what to be ironic about. And what you can say about Danish humour is that we use irony with everything. There are not many things left which are taboo, and that was what I had difficulty grasping when I was trying to understand Danish humour as a child.
Naser Khader, Syrian-born Danish politician, speaking in 2005

------------------------------------------------

In Danish, irony plays an extremely important role. Once again, this is due to irony requiring a lot of understanding between people, which can only easily be achieved in a small, homogeneous nation. Danes use irony to affirm the secret codes on which trust is based. When someone says "excellent parallel parking!", then every Dane *knows* that it most likely was exactly the opposite. Members of the tribe know that it is simply a more palatable way (again) of expressing criticism.

Danes' uniqueness in this is apparently so special, that sociologist and vice-chairman of the Association for Ethnic Equality, Halima El Abassi, suggested introducing irony-free workplaces in 2005. Apparently inspired by a study by Catinét which showed that irony led to serious problems with understanding. To my ears, forbidding irony seems to be an over-reaction, but in any event, it indicates that it is something that creates difficulties for good collaboration.

The example of Palle and the Indian employee needing the toilet (in the section about independence above) is a shining example of the lack of cultural care which is found when Danes believe that everyone understands their "good Danish humour".

Danes themselves think that a "fresh" and sarcastic tone is liberating, and that is due to them being the most impudent people in the world who can therefore easily cope with being made fun of. We have science's word for that. Danes come bottom of the world table in *gelotophobia* which means "fear of being laughed at". The lower the percentage of the population who are gelotophobic (1.62% in the case of Denmark), the more people can cope with being laughed at. The result comes from a large study made of 72 countries by the University of Zurich. Among those scoring highest were for example Middle East countries, where as many as 25% of people are gelotophobic. People there are much touchier about friendly jibes, they lose face faster and feel that they personally have lost their honour. Once again, the Mohammed cartoon crisis is a shining example. Danes did not understand that other people were so sensitive, because everyone has to be able to take a joke, don't they?

Of course, but some people are better at it than others, and in Denmark we don't take things so seriously. We are not so worried about what other people think, and there are two reasons for that: firstly, an individual's own self-image is formed to a greater extent by what they think of themselves, rather than what others think. Secondly, it is not so dangerous to be laughed at by people you know and trust. This Lilliput-society gives a safe haven where people are not afraid of being laughed at, because those around us know that we are "good at heart". Neither do we have to build a good reputation up *from scratch* among lots of outsiders if we have been made fun of.

Some would say that Danes are dishonourable, while they themselves would say that they are just a bit more thick-skinned and self-assured. That they have grown to be independent of collective judgment and now only judge themselves.

### Religion

*Danish bishop Jan Lindhardt once said that Danes' attitude to religion is like a lottery scratchcard. Scratch the surface, and Christianity will eventually appear. I scratched and scratched, and found nothing.*
Religion sociologist Phil Zuckerman (quoted from memory)

- - - - - - - - - - - - - - - - - - - - - - - - - - - - - - - - - - - - - - - - - - - - -

Believe in life after death:
Danes: 30% – Americans: 81%

Believe in Heaven:
Danes: 18% – Americans: 88%
Believe that the Bible is the word of God:
Danes: 5% – Americans: 33%

Phil Zuckerman, Religion sociologist, 2008

----------------------------------------------------

If you come from the very Christian USA to a country where very few people believe in life after death, even fewer believe in Heaven and hardly anyone thinks the Bible is the word of God, then you're going to be in for a bit of a surprise. The American religion sociologist Phil Zuckerman was also surprised when he undertook a study of Scandinavian and in particular Danish religiousness in 2005 and 2006. Or maybe we should call it a study of the lack of religiousness. Only about half of Danes believe in a god, which means we are one of the least religious nations on Earth. Nevertheless, just under 80% are members of the Church of Denmark, and being a member seems to mean a lot to them. Danes don't believe in God very much, but they do believe in the Church. In other words, Danes are predominantly "cultural Christians". This means that they take part in the rituals, call themselves Christians and feel that they have a mutual bond with other Christians. We could say that there is plenty of religion (as an institution) in Denmark, but not much *religiousness*.

This means that for Danes, God doesn't play anything like the role he plays in day-to-day life for many other people around the world. When asked, only 9% of Danes say that God plays a large or very large role in their lives. In other parts of the world, people come across religion several times a day – when they eat, think and go about their daily chores – and that they have to pray, think and execute rituals at certain times. Religion comes nowhere close to that for Danes. It only gets a look-in at special events.

Maybe this is one of the reasons why Danes are so obsessed with other religions. Discussions about religion, and particularly the religions of immigrants to Denmark, have been flourishing in recent years, just as opposition to these "strange religions" has too. Part of the opposition is that Danes tend to be "middle of the road" as regards religion, and don't like any type of extremism. They are not impressed by people with strong beliefs, and are in fact perhaps scared of them, which of course can lead to cultural misunderstandings when they come across people with much stronger beliefs. Remember what Molesworth said about the Danes: *"no enthusiasts, fools or fantasists. Everyone is pretty much the same as each other"*. That also applies to pseudo-religious ideologies such as nazism and communism. Neither has played any serious political role in a country where people have always been sceptical about "great truths". Danes are pragmatists, not idealists.

----------------------------------------------------------

**You know you have been in Denmark TOO long when…**
- You know that "religious holiday" means "let's get drunk!".

----------------------------------------------------------

Added to that is one thing I have noticed myself, namely Danes' tendency to believe that religion determines almost everything in other cultures. When you are used to religion having so little meaning, then you have a tendency to over-do it when it comes to others. I remember an Indian vegetarian who took part in one of my courses, and who was completely fed up with Danes thinking that he didn't eat meat for religious reasons. No matter how much he explained, they still thought "it's something he's not allowed to do because of his religion". Because in these situations, Danes think that "other people", who are not Danish, are the sort of people who are controlled by all sorts of restrictions… Finally, he gave up and just said they were "right". "Yes, it's my religion that says I mustn't eat meat". Then his Danish colleagues insisted cheerfully that in their religion, everything was allowed.

A study by Danish ethnologist Ina Rosen confirms this very well. Danes in the study distinguished between religion as a personal belief and as cultural heritage, and as institutionalised religion with rules and regulations about how to behave. The first was about going to church for weddings, funerals and the like, and Danes thought that was OK. But dogmatic religion was something they weren't happy with. People in Denmark don't like religious restrictions on personal freedom. They think it is weird that someone is not allowed to eat, drink or draw whatever they want, or for that matter even sleep with whoever they want to. When Danes regard religion as something bad and dangerous, it is often because it restricts freedom. That is the negative consequence Danes see that religion has in the rest of the world.

As regards religion, Danes are well aware of how different they are from the rest of the world. But that doesn't make it any easier for them to understand other people's religion.

The deeper cause of Danes' modest belief in God is rather that Denmark has a national church, which as Gundelach, Warburg and Iversen describe it, is the "world's weakest church monopoly". It doesn't encourage Danes to have anything more than a rather indefinable belief and being a member is something almost automatic, which means that people don't really have to decide what they believe in. It is a "lazy church" as Phil Zuckerman wrote. If a Dane had to actively and constantly decide what he or she believed in, then many would get much more in touch with their spiritual side. If a Dane actively chooses a different religion to that offered by the National Church, then he or she will quickly be regarded as strange (and *suspiciously* religious) – so most Danes just choose the state's "standard" product.

------------------------------------------------------------

In Denmark, "God" is one of the most embarrassing words you can utter. People would rather walk naked through the streets than talk about God.
"Jokum", a priest, 36 and one of Phil Zuckerman's interviewees.

------------------------------------------------------------

Religion is also a taboo in Denmark. If someone at a dinner party starts talking about a good film they saw last Wednesday, then everyone listens intently. But try saying "I heard a fantastic sermon last Sunday" in the same company then everyone is embarrassed, stares down at their plates and tries to change the subject – in any event, that will be the case for most people in the country. As I once heard religious historian Tim Jensen say: "The only right way to show your Christian beliefs is *not* to show them".

Several sociologists have noted how difficult it is to get people to talk about belief, and again this is due to it being a private matter. It is people's "own affair" and so not something which concerns others. Maybe it is because religion is linked to "morals" and "judgment" and so smells a little of inappropriate poking into other people's business. It is simply too intimate a question to ask about beliefs. We mustn't get involved in that.

This means that when people from other cultures with a much more open attitude to religion (USA, for example) ask what you believe and what religion you belong to, they will likely be met with an embarrassed silence in Denmark. Direct religious utterances and behaviour can make us feel insecure, which is one of the most significant reasons for the deep debate in the country about Muslim immigrants, their prayer rooms, eating habits, headscarves and unwillingness to be naked in swimming pool changing rooms, among other things. As well as signalling other *norms* than those of the majority, it also shows that there are some people who do not keep their beliefs private, but who instead parade them in public. That is something difficult to swallow for a nation so modest as the Danish.

### Self-image

*If we look more closely at some Danish peculiarities, we can see that many have to do with our small size as a nation. Over several hundred years, we have got smaller and smaller, a fact that doesn't match Danes' self-image. We believe we should be big.*
Jens Smærup Sørensen, author

Most people are happy with their nationality. Brazilians, Poles, Italians and Japanese – they will scarcely want to be something else. But Danes can sometimes give a very strong message that everyone else in the world would really want to be Danish given the chance.

Danes' strong feeling of pride in themselves and their significance in the world, despite the country's small size, can sometimes get out of hand. It can be an annoyance for non-Danes, so it has to be mentioned here.

There is nothing at all wrong with being proud of your country, but smugness and excessive self-satisfaction are not very nice characteristics. Many people sometimes get the feeling that Danes see themselves at the centre of the world, and that we may be small but from a moral point of view ought to be much bigger – and in fact already are!

"It is difficult to imagine that a country of 5 ½ million people can make any significant difference to terror, poverty and civil clashes.

Maybe that is the reason why happiness with security and welfare in Denmark can so easily be covered in self-satisfaction – and delight. It is peaceful here and not dangerous, so we must be something special because it's so good here, Danes are taught to think." Gundelach et al, 2008.

91% of Danes said they were either "very proud" or "rather proud" to be Danish in 2008. Of course, that is not at all alarming, but by comparing it with other surveys, we can consider whether this self-satisfaction might not lead to some blind spots.

In a study by Peter Gundelach published in *Danish Sociology*, Danes were asked whether they agreed with the statement "My country is better than other countries". 42% answered yes. As a comparison, enthusiasm was more tempered in Sweden and the Netherlands, with 12% and 7% respectively saying yes.

21% of Danes also agreed that "It would be better if all other countries were more like mine". Something which only 6% of Swedes, 5% of Norwegians and 3% of the Dutch agreed with.

"People should support their own country regardless" had 26% of Danes agreeing. Again, noticeably higher than other countries.

What is interesting is the difference to other countries which are otherwise very similar to Denmark. That perhaps explains why Danes are sometimes seen as very self-satisfied.

Of course, Danes are not the only patriots, but some things could point to them particularly liking to tell other people how good things are here, and how everyone else should "come up to our level". According to Bertel Haarder, a former government minister and Member of the European Parliament, Danes suffer from something in between an inferiority complex and delusions of grandeur. That leads to them having difficulty with European collaboration, which doesn't always involve other nations learning to do how the Danes do things. When the Danes are afraid to "come down to the level of the others", then they back out, implying that everything that was Danish was a question of progress. Danes perceive themselves as a "spiritual superpower" and that maybe gets a bit tiring for everyone else to listen to.

- - - - - - - - - - - - - - - - - - - - - - - - - - - - - - - - - - - - - - - - - - - - - - -

In the European Parliament, I have had the opportunity to observe Danish players on the international stage at very close quarters. I have to conclude... we are not very well liked. We have a reputation for being self-centred and conceited – in strong contrast to the Finns, for example. We see our greatest goal as getting others to be more like us.

I remember one day in Parliament, when a Danish member started – as usual – to talk about how we do things in Denmark. A Dutch member interrupted: "We don't want to hear about Denmark, we're talking about what to do in Europe".

I have even had someone warn another colleague in Dutch not to listen to my arguments. "You can't count on the Danes", he said, "they have a completely different agenda".
Bertel Haarder in *Soft Cynicism*

- - - - - - - - - - - - - - - - - - - - - - - - - - - - - - - - - - - - - - - - - - - - - - - - - -

The word "Un-Danish" is thus an expression that something is bad. In that way, "Danish" is used as something especially moral and as an expression of something just being "good". Just take a look at how many companies call themselves something beginning with "Dan": Danferie, Danisco, Danfoss, Danæg, Dan-spil, Dan dryer, Dan-Bo, Dan Jord, Danglas, DK benzin and DanKort. The list is endless, and more examples can be seen on the Facebook page called "Dan this, dan that" setup by various expats here: http://www.facebook.com/group.php?gid=105485402833836&ref=ts.

Many of the same companies also use the Danish flag in their logo, which is the latest thing that confuses many foreigners and supports the argument that Danes are chauvinistic and egocentric. But in this case they are wrong, as the Danish flag is not nationalistic in such cases. Sociologist Richard Jenkins, who has investigated Danes' attitude to their flag more thoroughly than anyone else, believes it is more a question of unreflective use of the flag than anything else. It's just something that comes out when there's something to celebrate. For people from abroad it can be very "in your face" when a supermarket has an anniversary and puts flags up all over the place, but it mustn't be confused with any sort of nationalistic symbol. The English researcher into society, Michael Billig, called it "banal nationalism".

In particular, Germans and Swedes have difficulty with the Danes' extensive use of flags, and I can also remember an English colleague at the University of Aarhus needing to wait a long time to steel himself to ask why we had a flag on a two-metre pole in the canteen. We explained that it was to put outside someone's office when it was their birthday. He shook his head and said that in the UK such a flag would be seen as being in especially poor taste and a very hefty political statement. In the USA too, the flag is much more political than in Denmark, and is afforded a much greater honour. It would not be stuck on top of a cake, even though it appears in many other places and on many other occasions.

In Denmark, most people were therefore relatively relaxed about their flag being burned in the Middle East during the Mohammed cartoon crisis. For them it was nothing particularly political, but just a mutual symbol of celebration and community. It rather seemed a little out of place.

## How Danish is that?

The Danish characteristics I have painted in this chapter can be applied as a whole to the Danes, but some aspects can also apply to other nationalities. It is the *combination* which gives culture its special signature. Thus, Americans are very self-assured. A Dutchman apparently has the same crusty and sarcastic humour and irony as the Danes, something which is also very widespread in southern China. In Sweden, they believe in God just as little as Danes do, and the other Scandinavians are similarly very focussed on equality.

Remember too, that it is not that interesting or particularly easy to describe how people *are*. It is much more interesting to look at how they are perceived by others and differ from each other. In other words, it is the *differences* which are interesting, because when you compare cultures, you can do interesting analyses of who the other people are. Danes of course see themselves as polite, and if the world only consisted of Danes, it would be meaningless to say that they can appear rather impolite. After all, they are polite enough for each other. But *in others' eyes* they are unfortunately the opposite, because they have other codes and standards they adhere to. To say that Danes are rather "impolite" requires a comparison.

Because cultures only become cultures when there are *other cultures* around. So Danish characteristics depend to a certain extent on *who* is talking. For the same reason, you could very well disagree that Danes are not very polite. That is the challenge of writing a book about Danes for everyone who isn't Danish. Your culture may very well have a lot in common with Danish culture so that many of the things I have mentioned don't seem particularly different or strange to you. Of course, I hope you as the reader will bear with me about this, as it is almost unavoidable when the target group for this book is readers who are not Danish (in other words the whole population of the world minus 5 ½ million). What you see, quite naturally depends on who you are.

For example, compare these two very different statements about Denmark and the Danes:

(A) So for me it's about speed. Speed of decision making and negotiations. We have talked a lot about Danish productivity (sigh!) but I don't think I can see it. It's mostly about going to meetings and generally wasting time and investment in time. I'm not so sure that Danes are particularly productive.

(B) Danes are so focussed. They have no time to waste. So when your working day is from 8 till 3 or 8 till 4, then you are there to work, and keep to your schedule. If you have a meeting, then when you go to it you know exactly what it's about, what is the expected output and you leave the meeting having understood. Someone from my country would go to a meeting, discuss things for ages and not reach a conclusion.

Don't be fooled. Both A and B have been in Denmark for a long time, and both of them have worked with Danes. But their impressions are as different as night and day. Try to work out where you think A and B come from.

B's picture corresponds to the general picture I gave about Danes being punctual, where A doesn't. That is because A belongs to one of the few cultures where punctuality plays an even more important role than it does in Denmark. Germany.

B however is from Brazil.

This doesn't mean that all national characteristics are useless, because it all depends on who you are comparing with. In many ways Denmark is SO special, that Danes really are very different to all other cultures in the most general terms. Conversely, it is clear that we only have half the explanation for culture conflicts between Danes and foreigners if we *only* know about Danes. So we have to know a little about other ways of being different. We therefore have to compare lots of different countries in lots of different ways.

# Part 2

## Mapping – where are we different?

After a short chapter about methods we will look at the areas where we humans differ from each other. At the differences that make a difference. We will compare various countries and give some tips about how to handle those differences.

# 5

# Can countries be compared?

Imagine you are sitting in front of a door, and you have just heard
that in one minute, a man and a woman will come through it. You
have some money to bet. You can double your money if you guess
the following correctly: (1) The man will be taller than the woman
or (2) the woman will be taller than the man.

My guess is that you will go for the first option.

But isn't it just completely sexist and stereotypical to assume that
the man will be taller? It could be the other way around.

Generalising is always negative. We always do it, because otherwise we just can't keep control of our surroundings, and – even
worse – we can't *plan* according to our surroundings if we don't
have any usable ideas about the statistical probabilities. We are used
to generalising about everything, but we often feel bad about generalising about people because all individuals are unique. But even
unique people fit into some boxes: women, doctors, the middle-
aged, mothers, people from Jutland or whatever. These give certain
statistical certainties for one thing or another, and if you forbid
people from generalising, because it is not "nice" or not "politically
correct", then you take away one of the most used, reliable and
necessary tools there is.

As anthropologists we generalise constantly. We simply have to,
because we study social life. Which means we have to make divisions
somewhere or other. Not being able to tolerate that means finding
something else to do. Despite all the logic in generalisations, it is
nevertheless astounding how much difficulty people have with
understanding statistics in general. I can still come across a situation where I am teaching about how the majority of single women
in their 40s do something particular according to statistics, and yet

suddenly hear a "smart" student at the back mention his aunt who matches the demographic, but doesn't do that. The young genius then expects my statistics to be wrong for ever more. Of course they are not. If masses of those "exceptions" pop up, then obviously the theory has to be rejected, but until then, all the small exceptions you have found are not worth a thing. In social science, they are known as "anecdotes".

Here is something very important: the internal difference in a group of men, for example, will always be greater than the general differences between men and women. You can see that if you look at height: there is a greater difference in height between the tallest man and the shortest man than the difference between the average height of men and the average height of women. In the same way, the political differences between journalists on a left-wing and a right-wing newspaper respectively are without a doubt greater than the general difference between the two newspapers. That doesn't alter the fact that there are lots of areas where men and women differ, just as in general there is a difference between the two newspapers' political attitudes. When you take all men and make an average and compare it to the average for women, there is a measurable difference. The same applies to newspapers and countries.

When you compare Denmark and Sweden, the internal cultural differences between the almost 9 million Swedes are similarly greater than the general cultural differences between Sweden and Denmark. But there is nevertheless a difference between two "amounts of cultural differences", which we call Sweden and Denmark respectively, and it is *this* general picture we can measure.

I'm sorry if it bores you to have this explained in this way, but in my experience it is statistically really difficult for many people to understand, and the material I am about to present consists partly of statistics. Material which has been checked again and again, and which has shown, in the big picture, to be significant and stable. Nevertheless, there are some reservations it is good to know about, and which I will write a little about in the following. If you are not interested so much in statistics, source criticism and evidence, then you can just skip straight to Chapter 6.

## The difference that makes a difference

As I have described previously, we humans are fundamentally identical, but have different values – our cultural differences. According to Dutch sociologist Geert Hofstede, values are about all cultures having a "general tendency to prefer certain situations to others". Values are about what people consider to be good/bad, clean/unclean, just/unjust, decent/indecent, ugly/beautiful, natural/unnatural and forbidden/permitted. It was the third layer of the cultural onion in Chapter 1.

Most people agree that what is beautiful, good, clean, natural, just, etc. are things to strive for. Where we *differ* from each other is *what* we regard as beautiful, natural, good or clean. This is where the cultural differences enter into the picture.

The areas where our values differ are what we will look at next. It is the differences that make a difference. For Danes it is fair and just not to emphasise the differences between people, whereas in Japan the opposite is true. For most Danes it is "natural" for someone to be homosexual, but not everyone in the world thinks the same. Being four hours late is "indecent" in Denmark, but definitely not in Africa or South America.

Remember that no one wants to be unjust, indecent, rude, bad or dirty, but because our criteria are so different, that is exactly what we are in the eyes of others – which is why it is so important to understand and be aware of these differences. To realise how other people see what you see – but just in a different way.

However, it's neither possible nor desirable to list all the specific examples one by one. On the other hand, we can outline some general patterns for the fundamental characteristics which form the basis for culture. This is where statistics come in. Anthropological and sociological research can tell us something about how people in certain cultures relate in general to some values which form the basic pattern of their culture. We'll look at seven of these types of pattern:

- Chapter 6: How people deal with hierarchies.
- Chapter 7: How dependent some people are on building relationships in order to establish trust.
- Chapter 8: Whether people are more group and society-oriented or whether they are more independently minded.

- Chapter 9: How secure people feel about change, and how afraid they are of uncertainty.
- Chapter 10: How competitive and self-promoting each person is, and how great the differences are between men and women.
- Chapter 11: How expressive people are about their feelings.
- Chapter 12: How people deal with time.

## The countries chosen

Of course, it's impossible to examine every country in the world, but in order for a book such as this to have a practical use, there needs to be a broad, stable basis for comparisons. So I have chosen 18 countries to compare so you can get an idea of the spread of geo-cultural differences. They have been chosen on the basis of which countries Living Institute and I myself have experience with, and of course because there is sufficient data available.

| Denmark | Japan | Romania |
|---------|--------|---------|
| Sweden | Vietnam | USA |
| Morocco | UK | India |
| Poland | China | Germany |
| Turkey | Russia | Italy |
| Australia | Brazil | Pakistan |

At the end of the Notes there is a list of the main sources used in the comparisons.

# 6

## Some are more equal than others...

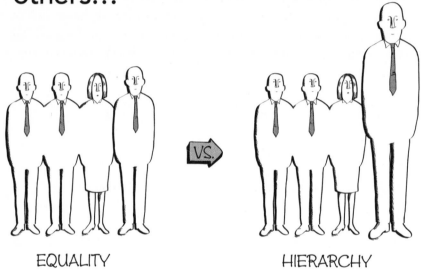

EQUALITY        VS.        HIERARCHY

---

**Come back another time...**
A Danish company sends a delegation of middle-ranking managers to negotiate with a large company in China. They send a list of who is going beforehand. The Danes arrive expectantly at the first meeting.

They talk and talk, and their Chinese hosts smile and look happy and ask them to continue the meeting the following day. The Danes are used to decisions taking time in China, so they are not expecting to seal the deal on the first day.

But concrete solutions don't even appear on the second day. On the third day, something happens. The Chinese have very little left to say, and the meetings become quiet and unfruitful.

Finally, the Danes ask if they have a deal. The Chinese reply that they are not in a position to make such a decision, and will have to talk to their management. The Danes are rather surprised, as they thought that they were negotiating with decision makers.

The Danes have to return home without a deal. All the way home, they discuss what went wrong, and how they can be better prepared in future.

What do you think went wrong? How did the Chinese perceive the Danish delegation, and how did the Danes regard the Chinese? What did each side expect from the meetings, and how could they have avoided disppointing each other?

It's not difficult to work out that the Danes believed they were negotiating with people with more authority than those people actually had. In China, they are very careful to match people. When the Danes announce they are sending middle managers, then they will be met with middle managers in China in return. But middle managers in China are not the same as middle managers in Denmark – and in this situation the Danish delegation had more decision-making authority than their Chinese counterparts at the table. In China, there is always someone higher up the chain who has to be consulted.

In the fourth chapter we will look at how Danes regard inequality as slightly unjust, whereas cultures with stronger power hierarchies don't have any problems with some people being more important than others. That is the system they are most comfortable with.

## What values do they have?

Sociologist Geert Hofstede divides the societies he studies into two extremes: societies with high power distance and societies with low power distance. In this book, I will call them hierarchical and egalitarian societies respectively. If we focus on the way companies function and are managed, we can see the following characteristics:

----------------------------------------------------------------

### Hierarchical societies

- Everyone expects that power is unevenly shared
- Status and rights depend on one's place in the hierarchy
- People expect some to have more privileges than others
- People wait for orders and execute them without question
- People are very dependent on their leaders
- Centralisation
- Many middle-managers and levels (steep pyramid)

----------------------------------------------------------------

----------------------------------------------------------------

### Egalitarian societies

- All use of power must be justified and shown to be legitimate
- Inequalities between individuals should be minimised
- The ideal manager is one who unifies and not one who uses power
- No one has fundamentally more privileges than anyone else
- Tasks received may be questioned
- Decentralisation
- Fewer middle managers (flat structure)

----------------------------------------------------------------

So it is important to understand that the values of those with power are to a great extent the same as the values of those without power, and that having an unequal system is accepted and valued. That doesn't mean that people will accept absolutely anything, but that inequality is seen as something quite normal and necessary. (Just as a Danish manager, as a rule, is not totally opposed to the Danish equality culture, just because he himself has made it to the top).

Geert Hofstede measures a culture's *power distance* by looking at how much respect people have for their managers and what sort of leadership they prefer.

Power distance is also a question of obedience. Do people do as they are told, or question their orders? Do they even dare to ask their manager anything, or would that be impolite and disobedient? In general, we can say that power distance measures *people's willingness to submit to authority*. The greater the power distance there is in a country, the more inclined people are to do as they are told, and to believe that management's ideas and suggestions are always the best.

## Who's who?

The cultural researchers I use in this part of the book all focus on hierarchies, and it is striking how much they all agree with each other. If we use Hofstede's model as a basis, then our 18 countries look like this as regards power distance:

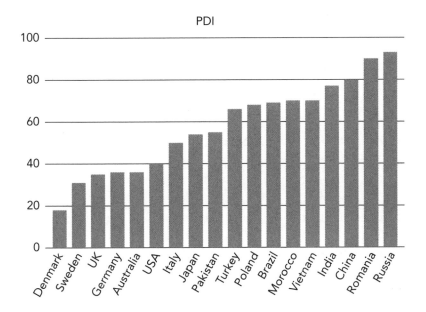

Not very surprisingly we find the obedient, egalitarian country with the high tax rate for the rich and a widespread tradition of scepticism for authority right at the bottom. Denmark. Conversely, a number of the former communist states are at the opposite end of the scale. Countries which were known for surveilance of their citizens, giving orders and top-level control of all aspects of life. Sweden is slightly higher up than Denmark, which also fits with many Danes' perception of Swedes as having slightly more belief in authority and being a little more elitist than Denmark. Remember how well-behaved and sensibly obedient they were when building the Øresund Bridge.

**How do you acquire status?**

In a hierarchical society, everyone is also on the alert for people with more official status than others. It is a society marked by status, and when the community allocates you a particular position, there is no longer any need to justify this. In egalitarian societies, people have to a greater extent to keep "performing" in order to maintain their status. Fons Trompenaars and Charles Hampden-Turner call it the difference between societies with *attributed* and *attained* status, with attributed dominating in hierarchical societies.

**Attributed status:** means that you are something because of your age, position, gender, family background or connections.
**Attained status:** means that you are something first and foremost because of your results, your education, ability, financial success or knowledge.

Having attributed status seems rather strange for Europeans in particular, and most especially for Americans, who are very sceptical of anything that smells of nepotism and inherited prestige. The latter is of course due to the fact that it was immigrants to the USA who rejected the idea of having respect for people purely because of the family they were born into. There were of course lots of European kings and queens who lost their thrones – and heads – in a rejection of blue blood having special priviliges, but that was a long time after Americans had lost patience and rejected European family snobbery.

If you believe in attained status, then you believe that *everyone is reponsible for their own destiny* and that no one should be born into wealth and status just because you happen to have the right gender, the right race, or because you have grown old. In cultures with attained status, such as Denmark, people can't really understand that old people enjoy so much unreserved respect as they do in Asia or the Middle East – because anyone can get old! Getting old is scarcely an achievement. In more traditional societies, people regard it as quite natural to gain status with age.

If we believe the studies by Trompenaars and Hampden-Turner and other researchers such as Richard Gesteland, these cultures of old, powerful men can especially be found in Asia, the Middle East and Latin America, to a lesser extent in Southern Europe and to a very limited extent in Scandinavia and North America.

## Obedience

As mentioned, a classic indication of a hierarchical society is that obedience is expected. Don't ask stupid questions. If the boss says "jump", the correct response is "how high?".

That can be difficult to understand for people from countries where asking questions is an expression of independent thinking, and which is therefore valued highly. People from such countries have difficulty accepting that asking questions in hierarchical societies is perceived as an expression of disobedience and bad manners.

For example, if you are giving instructions to a group of Chinese, and ask if they have any questions, then you shouldn't expect many hands to go up. Their respect for you means that it is not natural for them to ask questions. You might lose face, because that would mean that you had not given good enough instructions. Similar circumstances with Danish workers, who would constantly ask questions, would be considered as unbelievably rude.

A cultural value such as accepting inequality gets ingrained in people at a very early age. Both because people quickly find out how much inequality their parents accept with regard to other adults, and because accepting authority is solidly anchored in children's relationship to their parents. In the World Values Survey (1995-2001), a question was asked about how much value people placed on obedience when bringing up children. Countries such as Denmark, Sweden and Germany all had the lowest figures (all under 2%). A much higher percentage of Indians, Russians and Pakistanis placed obedience as very key, with Turks being at the top of the list with 15%.

## Meetings of opposites

People from **egalitarian cultures** can perceive **hierarchical cultures** as oppressive to a greater or lesser extent, maybe a little feigned and superficial, because all the reverence appears theatrical. They will perceive a hierarchical organisation as very rigid, but possibly also easier to understand as regards lines of decision making and division of responsibility.

On the other hand, people from **hierarchical cultures** can perceive **egalitarian cultures** as lacking consistency and as impenetrable. Reponsibility can be difficult to localise and appear to be rather spread across the whole organisation (which is often the case). The lines of decision making are difficult to determine, and it seems like things get made up as they go along. In addition, egalitarian cultures can often be perceived as lacking in respect and honour, because authority is not automatically respected. "How do I actually punish my Danish staff?" a Jordanian manager asked me on a cultural training course. We needed a rather long talk…

## Problems for egalitarian-oriented people in hierarchical cultures

**People from egalitarian cultures believe that workers from hierarchical cultures have to have everything explained**
They feel that they lack initiative and independence, if they are used to being lower down in the hierarchy.

*Solution:* If you are a manager from an egalitarian culture, you have to decide whether to give direct orders or to teach your staff to make their own decisions. If you choose the latter, then be prepared for it leading to a lot of uncertainty. Keep a close eye on what happens – more so than you are used to. Giving more direct orders is probably easiest, and as you have to make more decisions yourself, you can also be sure that things are being done as you want them.

**In negotiations it takes a long time before you get to speak to a decision maker**
If that happens to you, then the reason is probably that you have not sent people high enough up in the hierarchy. Maybe you have sent younger staff, who are seldom respected as much as older staff. Maybe you even sent a woman, which can be a problem in societies that afford men more attributed status.

The same problem can occur for a young member of staff who suddenly finds that an older client asks to speak to the person in charge.

*Solution:* Always take care to tell people who they are meeting. Whether it is in the social welfare office, at a parent-teacher meeting or in a negotiation, you have to show and explain who you are much more, and who the people you have with you are, and what their decision-making level is. Otherwise, the others will just use their stone-age brains to determine how they perceive and deal with you, and what your decision-making powers are.

Alternatively, a company must always send its most senior manager to negotiate – or perhaps even better – to close the deal in its final stages. Danes and others from egalitarian cultures who negotiate with people in Asia, for example, have to learn that the negotiators they send out first may be decision-makers back in Denmark, but that equivalent ranked people in Asia are considered to just be negotiators. It is only once the negotiators have removed the hurdles that the big boss is sent into the room. That type of difference in decision-making power was likely the reason why things went wrong in the example I started with.

This lack of understanding was one of the reasons why the COP15 Climate Conference in Copenhagen in 2009 went as badly as it did. The fact that India's and China's leaders expect to turn up right at the end, sign the deal, make a speech and take all the glory was overlooked. As the Indian environment minister explained to Danish Prime Minister Lars Løkke Rasmussen during a visit to India shortly before the conference: "Leaders give guidance, leaders don't negotiate". During the final days of the summit, when government leaders had to negotiate directly because the original plan had failed, it was a very embarrassing situation, particularly for those from Asia. The lack of cultural intelligence among the Danish Presidency of the conference therefore bore a significant part of the blame for the poor result, according to many observers. Just like many other Danes, the Danish politicians were convinced that the Danish method was best, and that Scandinavian wisdom would triumph over all the other foolish cultural ways.

It didn't.[1]

- - - - - - - - - - - - - - - - - - - - - - - - - - - - - - - - - - - - - - - - - - -

**REMEMBER: You are the person you are encountering**
In hierarchical societies, you measure your own status according to who you are equally ranked with. So the higher the

---

1 The Danish Prime Minister's very Danish rebuke of the delegates' boring obsession with "procedure, procedure, procedure" remains as a mark of shame for Danish arrogance about formalities and lack of cultural empathy.

status of your representative, the more respect and recognition you give to a Japanese or Chinese business partner. In one of his books, Richard Gesteland tells the story of an Egyptian business associate who was left alone at the end of the evening with a young, female member of staff, while the Danish manager gave his excuses and left. He had an early flight the next day. The Egyptian also went home the next day – angry to have been subjected to such shameful treatment.

You *are* the person you are brought together with, and that was simply too insulting.

- - - - - - - - - - - - - - - - - - - - - - - - - - - - - - - - - - - - - - - - - - - - - - - - - -

So remember to tell people in advance *who* it is you are sending to negotiate for you, and to close the deal. Alternatively, you can give your representatives a "few extra stars on their shoulders". You can do that by giving them a fancier title than they would normally have at home. Many Danish companies have started to have two business cards: one to use at home in Denmark, and one to use abroad in hierarchical societies. The latter has been "inflated" a bit, so that "Sales Manager" becomes "Head of Sales".

Several Danes I have spoken to are staggered at such an approach, but maybe that's just Danish modesty at play? If so, then it needs to be dropped. Neither is inflating job titles a question of *cheating* others, but in many cases it is rather a question of correct *translation* of your title (controller, sales consultant) to what it actually *means* in the other side's context (*manager of...* or *expert, team leader, head of...* etc.) My God, those titles have already been inflated! So just keep on going. It can mean the difference between coming home with the contract or coming home empty-handed.

You also need to agree what you want to get out of the negotiations. If you want decisions to be made in the meeting, then you need to signal that by sending people who are *credible* decision makers in the more hierarchical world. You can quickly be seen as frivolous or lacking in respect if you clearly send middle managers to meet with senior, top-level bosses. It is a very embarrassing state of affairs for a high-ranking person in a hierarchical society to have to make decisions with people lower down the ladder than he is (see box below).

**My work isn't being recognised!**

If you are used to being judged on your immediate and most recent results, it can feel unfair to be judged by seniority and titles. In a hierarchical leadership system you can find that the short-lived additional influence and recognition that results from a successful job can be completely non-existent. People still bow and scrape for the "old man" who has not done anything for years (he doesn't need to). And for women things can be especially hard.

There is nothing else to do except explain how things are for you. At the end of the day, we have to give far more explanations than we are used to. Cultural intelligence is about understanding the limitations in one's own and in the others' perspectives, and showing willingness to understand and to help others to understand. That doesn't mean that we should criticise what in our eyes is an "old-fashioned" attitude about how to reward people, but that we should make it very clear what we expect and what we are used to. Otherwise, how will they know?

## Problems for hierarchical-oriented people in an egalitarian culture

### Hierarchical-oriented people do not understand decision processes

In "tribal" societies such as Denmark in particular, organisational structures are very difficult to see, and it can be very difficult to work out who is in charge.

There are of course decision processes (it is not complete anarchy) but they do not follow the same chains of command as people are used to in steep-sided pyramid societies. It's not just a question of going up the chain of command, but of moving up and down and from side to side. In Danish companies there can easily be a "gatekeeper" in the form of a capable and respected receptionist somewhere in the organisation, who officially is low down in the pyramid, but who has an enormous amount of informal power and significance. Or it could be an experienced nurse who gives young doctors the runaround…

You can't avoid power, and especially in flat structures like in Denmark, some very capable exercisers of hidden power can be hibernating here and there. People who have a lot to say, but no official responsibility. So they are never held to account for their power, because "we are all equal here". There is only one thing to do: get things out in the open and ask the official Danish management to deal with it.

*Solution*: Do a favour for people visiting or working in our egalitarian culture. Tell them about the structure, the way things are handled and how decisions are made (depending an how long they will be there). Maybe hold some meetings to explain. Danes themselves often need to find out who actually decides what, because flat structures create confusion about roles for everyone. There is decision-making competence in many parts of the organisation, so take the trouble to describe and show that competence with regard to *who* and *what*.

### Hierarchical-oriented managers lose their privileges

If you are used to having a reserved parking space, your own bathroom and an executive dining room, then you can find things difficult in many egalitarian cultures, including in most Danish companies. It is up to each company to decide to what extent "class differences" should be maintained, or whether they will teach a new foreign or hierarchical-oriented manager about how things work in Denmark. In general, if you come from a radically greater hierarchical culture, you need to consider dropping your most "exclusive" habits, as these will backfire in the long term in a Danish company if management gets too much obvious special treatment. Trust and respect for management would slowly evaporate, and a manager is nothing without those.

Vulgar over-consumption of high-end luxury goods can also have the same effect, and it is a good idea to keep the "bling" at home in private. It doesn't necessarily command respect for the boss to park his Porsche in the best parking space when the culture is more egalitarian. It can almost be perceived as a provocation (but a large, sensible Volvo would probably be OK).

### Fewer special privileges – and definitely not for the family

Giving special pay rises or privileges to family members, or turning a blind eye to problems with staff related to you are all quite normal in hierarchical societies. But in egalitarian societies, where status is to a greater extent attained instead of just given, you are treated equally regardless of family ties. Helping family into jobs is quite widespread in Denmark, but from that point on people are treated equally.

In brackets it can be said that nepotism in Denmark is like cheating on your taxes: most people do it, but nobody will admit it. The difference to hierarchical countries is that there, people are completely open about helping family members: it is of course quite normal. No one is ashamed of it, because anything else would be deeply illoyal.

*Solution*: hierarchical-oriented managers in an egalitarian country have to understand that nepotism is (officially) undesirable, and that it takes a lot less before anyone starts to use the words "abuse of power". What in Denmark would be called an *abuse* of power, would in hierarchical societies simply be considered *use* of power.

------------------------------------------------

**The golden rule – start high and see what the others do.**
"Dressing down" is always easier than "dressing up". In other words, it is easier to take a tie off than to have to make a tie out of whatever you can find on your desk. It is easier and less obvious to undo buttons than to do them up. And taking your jacket off is easier than putting it on, if to your surprise you find that other people are keeping theirs on.

So start with a tie, jacket and smart trousers, or a skirt and makeup and take things from there.

------------------------------------------------

### The path to cultural intelligence
In the case we started with, the Danish staff had sent the wrong people, or else they had not agreed expectations. We had a critical situation. So let's take another look at the Path to Cultural Intelligence I first introduced in Chapter 2.

### In encounters with hierarchical cultures:

### Prepare:
- Consider what titles to use, and whether you can inflate them a bit.

- Find a spokesman who is older and "higher-ranking", and decide whether in fact to send a man. If you have to choose the latter, then make sure it is a decision any female staff can support – for example by giving them other challenges in different situations.
- Find out who to talk to, and remember to match them in status (find out in advance by contacting local sources and people who have been there before).

**Test the temperature of the water:**
- Look at how people treat and greet each other according to their status. If you don't know what status you have, you can look at how they treat you (how they greet you, where you are placed in relation to their manager, etc.)
- Be aware of who sits where, and what placement means – and remember it.

**Learn from / explain to:**
- Tell staff from hierarchical cultures what we perceive as good management and a good member of staff. Show responsibility and explain what is expected, and be ready to *talk* about what everyone is *thinking*.

**Accept and understand:**
- Hierarchical cultures are effective, have clear divisions of responsibility and chains of command.
- Remember that even egalitarian cultures most often have had periods in history with steep hierarchies. They don't have to go back more than fifty years to remember when bosses, doctors, teachers, civil servants and not least parents were sacrosanct figures of authority.

**In encounters with egalitarian cultures – such as Denmark:**

**Prepare:**
- What counts is experience and concrete results, not what title you have, so to sell yourself it is there you need to focus.
- Prepare for cultures where status symbols mean less and where managers can be well-served by "toning their appearance down" a little. People will likely be positively surprised at that.

**Test the temperature of the water:**
- Notice how status is marked much more subtly than you are used to.
- Don't believe that the way the official hierarchy works is necessarily the same as the unofficial hierarchy, so remember to look around and be aware of invisible power structures.

**Learn from / explain to:**
- Tell staff from egalitarian cultures what we perceive as good management and a good member of staff. Get them to understand that it is not about being "power crazy" but about taking responsibility and that it is that which is rewarded and respected where you come from.

**Accept and understand:**
- Egalitarian cultures may not always be as effective, but on the other hand they often have high buy-in from staff and can move quickly once decisions have been made.
- Egalitarian cultures are very flexible and ready for change, and individual staff members have greater incentives in the form of recognition at all levels.

# 7

## Those we know, and those we don't know so well

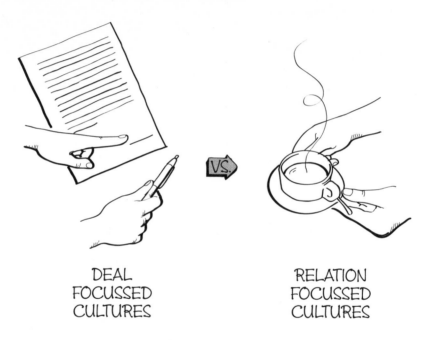

DEAL
FOCUSSED
CULTURES

RELATION
FOCUSSED
CULTURES

---

**Negotiations in Japan**

During the past week, Ole from Denmark has been in Japan to negotiate with a partner firm about extending production and hiring more people. The Japanese factory manager smiles and listens, but still constantly asks questions and indicates very clearly that he thinks Ole's suggestions are poor. "It could be nice with something completely new" he says several times, and Ole can do nothing but interpret this as him simply needing to propose something else. But maybe the interpreter is not very good at getting the message across?

Tired after several days of negotiations, Ole and the Japanese manager go out to eat together. Ole invites him to a place used by some of the other Danes in the company. That evening, the place is filled with several of Ole's colleagues, including one of the company's local Japanese staff, Yamashita. He quickly spots Ole's difficult Japanese partner (they are the only two Japanese in the company). They have a quick chat. Yamashita knows about the problems in the negotiations and after a few minutes talking to his Japanese colleague he turns and says to Ole in English:

"The manager says," explains Yamashita, "that he prefers hiring new people for the jobs in the new team rather than retraining old staff".

Ole raises his eyebrows and looks at his Danish colleagues in surprise. That's not a problem at all.

"So is that what we should do?" Ole asks Yamashita, relieved that it wasn't more difficult.

"Yes", he says, and adds "But you don't need to do it right now, he's happy to follow your original plan".

"Why?" asks Ole.

"I said that I thought your original idea was the best", answers Yamashita.

"And he's listening to you just like that?" says Ole, thinking about the many hours of negotiations he has had without making progress.

"Yes, he knows some of the same people I know" he says and smiles knowingly. He leaves it at that.

Why can't these people say things directly? – thinks Ole.

- - - - - - - - - - - - - - - - - - - - - - - - - - - - - - - - - - - - - - - - -

## How knowingly do we communicate? – High or low context?

Think about how you talk to your spouse or other people from your closest family. How you can finish each other's sentences, and how a simple look or word can say everything. Twins in particular are very good at that. They don't need to explain very much because *it's not in the actual words that the information is to be found*, it is in everything else around. In the *context.* It is all the common knowledge which precedes and which we only need to refer to, not repeat.

According to American anthropologist Edward T. Hall, some cultures have more context than others, in other words *esoteric* cultures where people don't need to go into the details. Cultures can thus be divided into two types: those with a high context and those with a low context.

### High context cultures

In high context cultures, agreements depend on *who* enters into them rather than *what* they are about. When *someone* says something is OK, then it is OK almost regardless of *what* it is. It is the person and the person's context/connections which mean something. That is what was happening in the example I started with. When Ole made his suggestion, it was not as good as when Yamashita subsequently made exactly the same suggestion.

In such a culture, it is more about being part of a network with a high degree of trust. Certainty is achieved not through abstract legal agreements, but through personal contacts, and with dignity and honour.

There is not much to obtain outside the network, and the lack of knowledge of people cannot be compensated by precise descriptions of what they can expect of each other – no, they would rather consult inside the network before such "outsiders" get their act together and want to *join* the network.

### Low context cultures

Low context cultures are cultures where people communicate with lots of different types of people who they don't necessarily know particularly well, and where they therefore do not put so much emphasis on the context. In such situations, they are dependent on a very precise use of language, where things are not taken as a given. There is not much room for interpretation, so people make sure they are very precise and detailed in their descriptions and messages. Formal and clear legal agreements are given a high value, and overall, it is important to get things written down. Agreements are things on paper. A verbal agreement is not enough, because verbal agreements can be misunderstood. How could we otherwise know that we agree?

In low context cultures, people have relatively limited networks, and instead prefer to have a small core of close acquaintances.

However, as deal-focussed culture versus relationship-focussed culture are more manageable terms than low context and high context, I have chosen to use these expressions in the next section instead. But high and low contexts are a significant element in the two types of society, and in research it is the terms high versus low context which have traditionally been used the longest.

- - - - - - - - - - - - - - - - - - - - - - - - - - - - - - - - - - - - - - - - - - -

### Guanxi – Chinese for networks

One of the most appropriate examples of how relationship-focussed societies function is the Chinese expression *guanxi,* which means connections in Chinese. It covers a person's network, contacts and the services they are due from various people.

You undoubtedly know about networks in most other countries, but in China it is so widespread that it needs its own word – which the Chinese use a lot themselves. Where we pretend that we cannot remember who owes us a favour, the Chinese are quite explicit with their expectations to their network and like to phone each other in the middle of the night if they need a favour, information or something else from their connections.

You can have good or bad *guanxi,* and everyone is expected to use a lot of time looking after these connections, simply because they are often necessary to get what you want. Just like when Sidsel, one of the China consultants associated with Living Institute, was asked, right out of the blue, by her Chinese partner's family whether she could start work as an estate agent. A job she had absolutely no qualifications or experience for. But that didn't matter. Everything could be arranged, it was all just a phone call away.

Nevertheless, she politely declined.

- - - - - - - - - - - - - - - - - - - - - - - - - - - - - - - - - - - - - - - - - - -

## Why do we have to sing so much karaoke?

I'll get to which part of the world we're talking about, but I'm sure that the well-travelled reader will already know which particular

Asian country can be characterised as especially relationship-focussed. There, any negotiator will have to drink far too much sake with his new Japanese friends, be pressed into visiting one restaurant after another and be introduced to one person after another whose names you can't ever remember anyway. And anyway, what do my abilities as a karaoke singer mean for the deal we're about to close? Surely it's the business that is most important?

But it's not that simple. Because you only know business through the people who bring it to you, and if you don't know those people well enough then there is no point in spending any time on the business.

In deal-focussed cultures on the other hand, people concentrate on the specific deal and the information which deals with the specific issue – not how your wife is, whether you are happy with the new house you just bought, where you want to go on holiday and whether you had a nice stay at the hotel. In the USA, people couldn't care less about that sort of thing, but on the other hand they are very focussed on the legal and formal details (no one wants to be sued for something): "Come on guys – let's get on with it! Do we have a deal or not?". They don't necessarily trust each other, but they are so sufficiently covered by the legal niceties that the personal relationship takes second place. If we can't trust them, then we'll just sue them anyway.

In a deal-focussed culture, like both the Danish and the American cultures, people take it as a given that you *can* trust each other (or rather that no one dare do anything other than follow the rules of the game), otherwise it's a waste of time signing the deal. But in relationship-focussed cultures, that trust can only be established if you *know* enough about the other side, and you actually like them. So there is no way of avoiding the sake, the small talk and the karaoke.

For the same reason, telemarketing doesn't work in Asia. How on earth could you want to buy something from someone you have never met? In the USA, however, there is no peace from irritating cold callers.

## Trust – again
This doesn't mean that relationship-focussed cultures are cultures where everyone knows each other as if they were closest family. In

fact, the general level of trust in relationship-focussed countries is very low, that is why they have such a great need for a close and understanding network.

In Denmark, people are so relatively similar, that they don't need special networks. The general level of trust is high, but because it is a case of dealing with "strangers" you don't know, then in Denmark people compensate to a great degree for the superficial relationships with legal documents and written agreements. You have to be quite sure that you understand each other, but there is no need to get to know the others very well before entering into any agreements. Danes, and other deal-focussed cultures, just let the agreement be wordy and precise enough, and then everything will work.

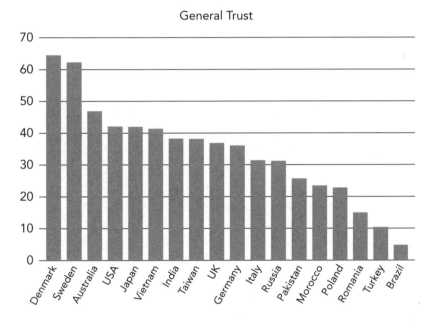

General Trust

Denmark is very much the highest scorer for trust. In this survey, trust is at 64.5%, while other surveys give an even higher result. If you ask Danes directly whether they generally trust people, 78% will answer that they do. In other European countries outside Scandinavia (but with the Netherlands as an exception) only 20-30% say yes to the same question. How you answer such a question of course depends on what you understand as "generally". The survey in the table above is therefore a little more thorough and a more precise measurement of "general trust".

It is also very noticeable that former communist countries have surprisingly low levels of trust. That could be seen as a reaction to having lived in a decidedly "snitch culture" under communism. But maybe it is also the result of a societal model which forbade liberal professions and free trade, where people learn to build independent and trustful relations to each other rather than only looking to the state and their closest family.

## People are everything, paper is nothing

In relationship-focussed cultures, it is thus very necessary to have good relationships to people, so you can sometimes need a "broker" or maybe what we would call an "ambassador", "wingman" or "informant". A local person you trust who can open doors for you. He or she will also be in a position to understand the hidden meanings and indirect communications better than we are. If Yamashita had been at the first meeting in the example I started with, he would most certainly have understood what the Japanese manager meant by "it could be nice with something completely new". The puzzling comment which none of the Danes understood.

During a culture course with a large Danish company, I experienced how frustrating it can be to deal with relationship-focussed cultures, when one of the Danish participants constantly had to answer his telephone and leave the room, and come back shortly afterwards. Each time more annoyed than before. "I don't understand why we suddenly have to pay double. We had an agreement!" said the purchaser. Apparently the Chinese supplier had found out that they could sell their goods to someone else, so now they thought there was no reason to keep the contract with the Danish company. "But we had a contract" exclaimed the purchaser, frustratedly.

Well. The contract is just a piece of paper, and many Western companies (not least American) have over the years found out that their "bullet-proof" agreements have just been cancelled on the spot by their Asian business partners. And it is rarely worth making a big legal issue out of it.

*The agreement is worth nothing without good relations,* so the Danish purchaser will have to put the phone down and just buy a ticket on the first plane to Beijing. Had the Chinese partners considered him as part of their network, they would also have felt a personal obligation to keep to the agreement. But the Danish purchaser had only met the Chinese salesman a few times, and if you don't allow more time for such meetings, you might as well not bother. It's better to go for a long time and have the opportunity to build up relationships than save money by going for a short trip, holding a couple of meetings and coming home with an agreement which just isn't going to last.

## Don't get too close!

*Danes in China always seem to be on the way home again. As if things just have to be concluded quickly so that they can get back to Denmark.*

Chinese course participant

In the chapter on Danish culture, we saw how Danes are perceived as a particularly private and closed nation. They keep people at arm's length and are nervous of getting personally involved with people they don't know. It sounds as if Danes' private zones are very large, but in fact it's the other way round. In any event that is the case if you use two terms developed by Fons Trompenaars and Charles Hampden-Turner. They distinguish between specific and diffuse societies[2].

The specific naturally dominates in deal-focussed cultures, when people prefer firm contracts and legal details, which are not susceptible to "soft" values such as personal relationships, or whether people in fact even like each other. There, everyone knows what their role is and sticks to it. They are either professional or private. So the Danes' private zone is in fact very limited, because it is only covering close friends and family. As for everyone else, they are more or less professional and keep people at arm's length. So Danes often have difficulty explaining to their partner or spouse that they have to go out for a beer with their new staff from Iran or their Japanese business partners. Because that's just enjoyment – in other words private!

---

2  Again, these terms can also be compared with Hall's theories. It can seem a little strange that theorists can just reinvent each other's terms with new names, but I would rather say that they are elaborating on them and finding even better ways to describe them. The main reason is that it is the same societies which are low context, deal-focussed and specific.

It isn't, however, for the relationship-focussed Iranians or Japanese. For them, the dividing line between "professional" and "private" is much more diffuse.

Danes are quite open in other ways. For example, they are used to being half naked on a beach, and isn't that something quite private? At the same time, they express themselves in much rawer and more direct ways than others do. Danes let the state get involved in the most intimate details of their lives, and let other people look after their children and elders. They also have a high degree of trust in the public system, and are happy to delegate to the state what Asians would call family issues. Nevertheless, Danes' core of close relationships is very narrow and limited.

Trompenaars and Hampden-Turner call this type of society, which is primarily deal-focussed, "specific" societies, because there are specific roles in the public / professional space. Danes have many different specific roles. When they are at work, in the bowling centre, at a meeting of the school board, out drinking with their friends or shopping in the supermarket. There are many roles to play. When they are at home, they are "themselves", and that is something quite different and private and very exclusive. Not everyone gets access.

Graphically, it can be drawn as below, where the small space in the middle is the private space, where people are themselves, and all the fields outside are the very specific professional / public roles they have.

## SPECIFIC CULTURES

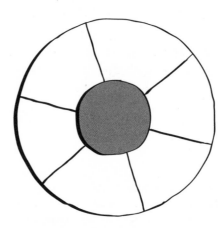

In deal-focussed cultures, the roles are clearly defined. On the other hand, in relationship-focussed cultures, people have more "diffuse" relationships to each other.

This means that in relationship-focussed cultures, the public space where people meet each other *anonymously* and at *arm's length* is very small. In order to have anything to do *at all* with other people, you have to strive to get away from the very limited professional space and into the space which is partly or completely private. You can't do very much with people without knowing them. In order to get access to play all the roles which other people may consider to be very public and professional (be a good colleague, be on a committee together, close important deals as equal negotiators), you therefore have to enter into lots of private contexts (eating together, enjoying each other's company, fishing, playing golf and talking about the family and other private niceties). Because these sorts of things are well and truly mixed – the line between what is private and what is business is flexible and diffuse.

## DIFFUSE CULTURES

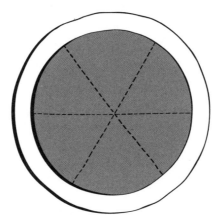

So what is private space (the covered area in the model) in relationship-focussed cultures is very large and divided up as above into fields with dotted lines because the "role change" inside is nowhere near as significant and marked as it is in specific societies. In specific societies, such as Denmark, there can however be a marked difference between how people behave to their colleagues, when they are out shopping, and when they pick up their children from day care. In the relationship-focussed cultures, there is a greater tendency to be more open to personal relationships to all sorts of people, where we would rather consider a professional and more adapted relationship.

- - - - - - - - - - - - - - - - - - - - - - - - - - - - - - - - - - - - - - - - - - - - - - -

### Spanish "amigos" and the Danish "ketchup effect"

Spaniards are relatively more relationship-focussed than Danes. Spaniards have a small public space and therefore a broad private space, which you are expected to be part of if you want to do business or get decent contacts.

Anette Villemoes, a lecturer at Copenhagen Business School, has looked at encounters between Spaniards and Scandinavians with a special focus on the latter's problem understanding the Spanish term "amigo".

Spaniards like to hold business meetings in bars and in general are very happy with passionate socialising which culminates in calling each other "amigo". Then you can do business together.

The problem is just that the Scandinavians misunderstand the term amigo and then believe that they have become really good friends, in other words that the Spaniard is now part of their private space in the same way as they would be in Denmark. That's not the case at all, and as a frustrated Spanish businessman said to Anette:

"Foreign businessmen who come to Spain are overwhelmed by our hospitality – assumed or genuine. We do somersaults for them and show them everything in the few days they are here. We just can't stop ourselves.

Then they go home and start writing letters, calling or whatever, want us to keep in touch and come to their daughter's wedding.

They think we're friends. But it's over now. We gave them the big tour, and now we're giving it to some other people. So they're quite wrong: they haven't got any friends in Spain!"

I've heard southern Europeans talk about the Scandinavian "ketchup effect" when they describe how difficult it is to get close to a Dane, for example, who wants to keep an arm's length relationship for as long as possible. "It's like a bottle of ketchup, where you keep hitting it and hitting it and nothing happens – and then suddenly it all comes out at once". Then the Danes suddenly let all their feelings flow and tell you all their intimate and private details, and get much too close.

If, like Danes, you come from a culture where the boundary between private and public space is very closely guarded, then the more diffuse way people have of being private in southern Europe can be very confusing. Suddenly you find that you've let far too much out of the bag and got far too close – and intrusive. Danes' cultural map can simply not show us the right way to turn in southern Europe, because it is tuned into the Scandinavian cultural "landscape" and the Scandinavian private space.

------------------------------------------------

I have already described how Danes, just like the rest of the people in Scandinavia, are from typically distanced, specific and deal-focussed cultures, which also makes them very lonely souls in the eyes of others. In Scandinavia, you don't need to know people very well before you can do business with them. So perhaps you don't bother getting to know people at all. They stay level-headed and professional with other people. When I am teaching Danish students at university, I limit myself specifically to that role. I couldn't dream of asking anyone about their private life, and they mustn't hear about mine. We almost exclusively only talk "business", and that is what we feel most confident doing.

For people from elsewhere, Danes appear cold and formal when we decline an invitation to a cup of coffee after work, or look completely frightened when our Middle East colleague suddenly invites us to his daughter's wedding in two weeks' time. It sounds really nice, but the Dane will scarcely "impose" on you and so often decline so as not to get involved and send the wrong signals. But what the Danes are forgetting is that what is private for them can be a more or less public event in Syria. And when you are working with each other every day, then you have partly come in to his private space, which in his culture extends far further than Danes are used to. So declining would be impolite and very bad for your work together.

As Gilles Maria, CFO at Rockwool, said in an interview in Berlingske Tidende: "I have invited Danes back to my home, and it was nice to have them visit. But the strange thing is that they never called and invited me back to their place. In France, I would have received an invitation". And he continues: "It's very delicate to ask your colleagues why you didn't get an invitation from them".

Gilles Maria also tells about a situation where, at his 50th birthday reception, he wanted to give his staff champagne and was surprised how difficult it was, as the company had very clear guidelines about the size and scope of such a reception. Again, this is a typical characteristic of a specific culture such as Denmark's, where social activities are planned in very strict frameworks. In France, which has a more moderate relationship-focussed and more socially relaxed culture, social activities are much more of an opportunity for spontaneity.

## When social relationships mustn't pay

In Denmark, everyone is equal, as already known, and if someone comes and establishes too close personal connections, then that equality disappears. Everyone is guaranteed the same treatment, so it doesn't do to wallow in special treatment and exclusive agreements with other people. That is second nature to every Dane. I even once had a note sent home from my daughter's day care centre which said that parents should not become Facebook friends with their staff. Such social relationships can have rules made for them in a specific, deal-focussed society such as Denmark. You are not allowed to benefit from your connections. Entering into personal relationships with the staff mustn't be something worth doing. Everyone gets the same treatment. Everyone is equal, and there are clear boundaries between roles in the public space. They do not have the same diffuse boundaries which are open for negotiation as in more relationship-focussed societies.

In Denmark, people do not need to have any special relationship with each other in order to get decent childcare or care for the elderly. That type of work is run by the state in Scandinavia, but it quite naturally makes close personal relationships to a great extent unnecessary, and is maybe one of the reasons why it is not only the climate but also the people in Scandinavia who are considered to be cold.

The positive aspect of deal-focussed societies is of course the low level of corruption. When you don't go around keeping an account of the favours you are owed, and when you don't have that good private connection to the people who work at City Hall, then it follows that corruption is not very widespread. Your neighbour may be a policeman, but when he's off duty, he is first and foremost your neighbour (so he can't do anything about your speeding ticket if you mow his lawn for him). The boundaries between roles for Danes are very specific and are respected by most people. In Asia's relationship-focussed societies, Danes can on the other hand have difficulty finding out which diffuse role they have been allocated, and how immodest they are allowed to be at using their contacts. Even those in government…

Danes can quickly come to perceive southern cultures such as France, and even more so Asia, as very exotic in just this area, but in fact you just have to go to the USA to see the difference between public and private. An American home, for example, is a relatively open space, and if you have ever been to an American barbecue, you will know that this does not mean it is an invitation to anything private or to intimate friendship. You mustn't believe that you've suddenly become close friends!

The heartiness with which Americans welcome people with open arms and open doors, is therefore easily misunderstood by Danes, who can quickly come to perceive American hospitality as another expression of how "superficial" Americans are. A sad and stupid misunderstanding which I myself have experienced all too often, and which uncovers a banal cultural misinterpretation which could have been avoided with a little preparation and knowledge about how far private space extends from culture to culture. Having enough cultural intelligence can thus save us from many unreasonable and mistaken impressions about our fellow human beings. Everyone, in all cultures, should quite simply get a better handle on what is public, what is private and in that way understand how our cultural worlds differ. And again, the best way to do that is to operate with more openness with regard to mutual expectations.

## Who is what?

Allow me to summarise here. We have two cultural types.

High context cultures with diffuse roles, with a focus on personal relationships, and which for simplicity's sake we will call **relationship-focussed cultures,** and low context cultures with specific social roles and a focus on legal aspects, rules and concrete agreements, and which we will call **deal-focussed cultures**. Here are some of the most noticeable differences:

- - - - - - - - - - - - - - - - - - - - - - - - - - - - - - - - - - - - - - - - - - - - - -

**Relationship-focussed**
- Focus on connections
- Trust is created through relationships
- Esoteric and unspecific communication
- The public and anonymous space very limited, as is the interaction people can have with each other in such a space
- Meetings do not appear to be particularly planned
- Conclusions and summing up are not particularly important (because of course we agree, don't we?)
- What is right and wrong depends to a great extent on the person (and the situation)
- Written agreements are nothing compared to personal relationships
- It takes a long time to reach a good agreement (so that you can get to know each other)

- - - - - - - - - - - - - - - - - - - - - - - - - - - - - - - - - - - - - - - - - - - - - -


- - - - - - - - - - - - - - - - - - - - - - - - - - - - - - - - - - - - - - - - - - - - - -

**Deal-focussed**
- Focus on agreements (written)
- Trust can be regulated and legislated about (so we'll just assume that)
- Specific and precise communication
- Public space is large enough for most roles to be played out without getting too close to other people
- Meetings are planned in detail
- Conclusions and summing up are important so that we know we agree
- There are rules about what is right and what is wrong, and exceptions will not be made for anyone
- Personal relationships take second place to written agreements, the latter always being what counts
- A good negotiation is effective, short and unambiguous

- - - - - - - - - - - - - - - - - - - - - - - - - - - - - - - - - - - - - - - - - - - - - -

In practice, there is seldom an *either or* – rather a *greater or lesser degree*, so we can't get closer than dividing into three boxes with: a pronounced relationship focus, a group where the countries are more moderate, and a final box where the countries are decidedly deal-focussed.

Relationship-focussed ← → Deal-focussed

| China, Japan, Vietnam, Italy, Brazil, Pakistan, Turkey, Morocco, India | Russia, Romania, Poland | Germany, Sweden, Denmark, UK, USA, Australia |

As a rule of thumb, we can say that the old Germanic and Anglo-Saxon territories as well as their former colonies (Australia, USA) belong to the deal-focussed area, large parts of central Europe and Russia are more moderate, whereas the rest of the world goes for closer relationships and limited public space. Asia and the Middle East are very definitely relationship-focussed areas. Just think how insulted the Indians were by Richard Gere's total transgression of their modesty norms in Chapter 2. Private space starts closer to home in India, and such harmless flirting which the American "didn't mean anything with" is not allowed there. It was just a "role" he was playing in public. Such behaviour doesn't belong in such a limited public space as that in India. Intimacy is not public.

**In the details**
The Chinese and the Japanese are the most noticeable examples of relationship-focused cultures, but Southern Europeans and Latin American countries are also in there too.

As regards the middle box, the cultures in there also prefer to build close relationships, but as opposed to the radically relationship-focussed countries, they have a different, direct style and are less indirect and esoteric (highly contextual) in their speech.

If you look at the group Denmark, Germany and the UK, a good and reliable study shows that the Germans have an even lower context than both Denmark and the UK. The UK uses more indirect language and allows business connections to become personal to a greater extent. This positions the UK as the least appropriate example of a deal-focussed culture among the three. The Germans get quickly to the point, are precise and do not allow much small talk, something which several theorists have noted. Again, they are slightly more low context than the "cosy Danes", who despite everything also like a bit of gossip. But again, compared with the extremes at the other end of the scale, the small differences disappear into the big picture. That's how it is when you compare cultures. The broader you make the spectrum, the fewer differences it is possible to see. But that doesn't mean that they're not there. It all depends on *who* you are comparing to.

### Meetings of opposites

**Relationship-focussed cultures can perceive** deal-focussed cultures as cold, difficult to access and far too obsessed with words and rules. Relationship-focussed cultures believe it is a shame that the deal-focussed cultures regulate their social lives as much as they do. They think there is far too little time for spontaneity and unexpected social events. They hardly dare invite someone from a deal-focussed culture such as Denmark to anything at all social, because that would simply embarrass him! In addition, people from deal-focussed cultures can appear ill-mannered and untrustworthy because they (especially Americans) believe they can make very important agreements without even showing a minimum of interest for the people they are negotiating with. They just come barging in and think money can buy anything. Very inappropriate and disrespectful!

**Deal-focussed cultures can, on the other hand, perceive** relationship-focussed cultures to be unusually slow. It seems like they don't trust you (which they don't). It seems as if you're not worth anything before you have taken part in every possible ritual which, when it comes down to it, are not "real" personal connections, but just a strange *diffuse* something in between. They get confused about being a "friend" but not a "real friend" as they know from their own culture. Couldn't they just keep the roles completely separate like we are used to at home? Why do they have to be so pushy, couldn't they be more "professional"?

If we were to put the conflict into a diagram, it would look like this:

# SPECIFIC AND DIFFUSE CULTURES IN A "CLASH"

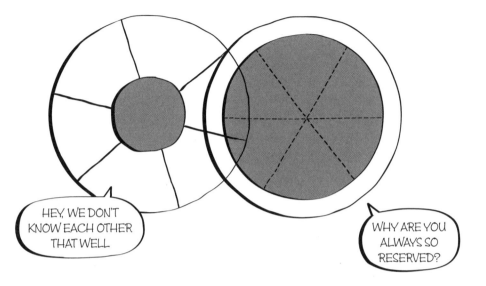

The relationship-focussed culture (on the right) has offered something which the people from the deal-focussed cultures regard as very private. Something which the relationship-focussed culture has placed in public space, where the deal-focussed culture doesn't believe it belongs. But the model can also be understood the other way round, as when someone from the deal-focussed culture (for example Denmark) does things in the relationship-focussed culture which the relationship-focussed people consider to be especially private, but which in Denmark happens in the greater public space. For example it could be the straightforward Danish attitude to nudity. In public life in general in Denmark, child nudity is nothing special, but it would be so private in relationship-focussed cultures, that in most of the relationship-focussed countries it would be regarded as very inappropriate. In fact we don't have to go further away than the USA before child nudity is completely undesirable in public. So Americans are slightly lower down the axis towards a relationship-focussed culture than the Danes are. (In any event as I have defined it here, but not necessarily in Trompenaar's and Hampden-Turner's version of the term.)

### Problems for relationship-focussed people in encounters with a deal-focussed culture

Relationship-focussed people perceive deal-focussed people as sloppy and frivolous, whereas deal-focussed people perceive relationship-focussed people as unfocussed

How can you make a deal with someone you have only spoken to on the phone and exchanged a couple of e-mails with? And expect everything to be OK? That's what relationship-focussed people think. Whereas the deal-focussed people, the Danes for example, are burning with impatience in the middle of all the mishmash of gossip, breaks for refreshments, "now you have to see the factory" and "now let's go out to dinner" chat.

*Solution*: There is not much which can be done about these feelings. You have to play on their terms. They don't trust you without first having established a personal relationship, and even the best assurances can't do anything about that. If you want deals which stick, you have to meet people personally (of course only after a cost-benefit analysis which takes the size of the deal and its importance into consideration). That means long stays (with open tickets) – so clear your calendar, be flexible and try to get as much out of your trip as possible. Limit communication by e-mail and telephone to questions and planning of meetings, *never* use them to negotiate or agree prices or to start a relationship. I'm sorry, but there is no real compromise to be made here, it's on their terms or not at all.

As a schoolteacher, doctor, lawyer or other professional, where you may be invited to events which do not fit into the way professional relationships work here, you can politely decline. It can be a very good idea for an organisation to draw up a common policy for this, so that everyone knows what guidelines apply.

### Problems for diffuse cultures (relationship-focussed) in encounters with specific cultures (deal-based)

People from more diffuse private spheres think that people from specific cultures regulate their social life in a very impersonal and cold way. Danes, who are extremely specific, appear particularly lonely, cold and distant in their whole way of being. Conversely, specific cultures believe that the diffuse are too insistent, and so they are often, modest as they are, afraid of imposing by accepting invitations.

*Solution*: People from diffuse and relationship-focussed cultures need to be better at explaining what it is they expect and why they do what they do. Then things will be easier for both sides. So it is your responsibility to ask more. Conversely, the more specific, such as the Danes, also need to lighten up a bit and understand that the others do not think the same as they themselves would do if they just showed the same strong desire for socialisation long into the evening (like in Asia), the friendly arm on the shoulder (like in the Middle East) or their close and intense contact (like in Southern Europe and Latin America). Similarly, people need to understand that the invitation to dinner at home is not an invitation to see the whole house[3].

Just because you go to the daughter's wedding doesn't mean that you'll go on holiday with them the following year. Keep calm!

Remember the golden rule of cultural intelligence: Don't judge others in the same way as you would judge your "own people", things don't mean the same to them as they do to you.

### Keep control of your social connections and let others do the same for theirs

- Draw social diagrams (social maps of people you know and what connects them to each other) in order to keep control of your networks in these countries. If you have staff from relationship-focussed cultures, let them put their own team together (and even hire friends and family). They will be very happy to be able to help the network, and you can be sure of getting a workforce where people trust each other. People from the West are inclined to look down at that type of behaviour, but often forget how much they help each other at home – the only difference is, as I mentioned, that people *pretend* that they did not get the job through family or friends, whereas in a relationship-focussed culture, people are open about it and happy to have used their connections. Just what we could do with.

---

3 It is quite the opposite to what is intended in Denmark, where people happily show new visitors just about everything including the toilet and the bedroom. A private dinner in France is just that: the dinner, so it will be very inappropriate to enter other rooms. Those are the REAL private areas rather than the semi-private event you have been given access to (Trompenaars and Hampden-Turner: 1998:86)

### Be careful about replacing staff who have built up trust

- It goes without saying that when you are negotiating with relationship-focussed cultures and planning to maintain contact with them for many years ahead, then it is not appropriate to replace people so that the guy they knew so well is suddenly replaced by someone they have never heard of. Of course, people can change jobs and even companies, and that is why it is important not to send "lone wolves" to negotiations, but instead send larger teams so that in the future there is a greater chance of them meeting people they already know. Otherwise, you have to start again from scratch. Remember, in relationship-focussed cultures you deal with people, not companies.

### The path to cultural intelligence

The unspoken comments in the Japanese case could not be understood by everyone, but you can be prepared for them and take the necessary action. That is the culturally intelligent way to deal with relationship-focussed, diffuse cultures with high context.

### In encounters with relationship-focussed cultures:

### Prepare:

- Get a handle on who you are going to meet, your network, your contacts, your informants, your staff and everyone who can be considered to have relationships to the people you are going to negotiate with, hire or in any other way have contact with – let them be sparring partners in all aspects, and let them be ambassadors for you.
- Find out what is private and what is public in the culture you are dealing with. Look at literature, ask locals or people who have been there before. How private is an invitation to dinner or a fishing trip? What shouldn't you ask about, or ask others to take part in?
- Have plenty of time and plenty of space in your calendar. Things can very well drag on.

### Test the temperature of the water:

- Listen to what is being said. In relationship-focussed cultures, there is more to what is said than just the words. Note and analyse

BEFORE you react. Give yourself time to understand the contextual significance.

- Notice signals that you may be going too fast. If they insist on breaks or whatever to *avoid* concluding, it may be because they think they are being pushed. They may confirm that you "have an agreement" just to please you. In reality, they may not agree about anything at all.

### Learn from / explain to:

- It is absolutely essential that you ask and keep on asking. What do they really mean by what they are saying, what can you do and what can't you do? What do they expect from you? What is your role? How private are private aspects in reality?
- Explain to to the relationship-focussed people you will be dealing with that your deal-focussed countrymen are neither lonely, arrogant, dull, angry nor cold-blooded, but just a little nervous about overstepping the boundaries. Remember to tell them that we behave like that to each other in much the same way. It's got nothing to do with them being foreigners.

### Accept and understand:

- Relationship-focussed cultures often occur in societies where the level of trust in the general population is very low. So you have to be very certain that you can depend on those you are with. The Danes are used to relying on each other in a different way, so we don't need all that "feeling around". So maybe the Danes that you might be travelling there with sometimes behave very naively – and think a deal is closed prematurely – or they simply ignore the relationship building.
- Remember that when your business connections or maybe subcontractors in relationship-focussed cultures do not really open up with long rounds of introductions, company visits, long speeches and beating about the bush, it doesn't necessarily mean that there is something they're trying to hide or avoid saying. If they're going to meet you, maybe for the first time, that's just what they're going to do. Don't push things, just wait. To be pushy is very insulting and hurtful.

**In encounters with deal-focussed cultures – such as Denmark:**

**Prepare:**
- Be prepared for people wanting to get down to business immediately. If they have said exactly how much time things should take, then you can count on that being exactly what happens.
- If you're going to meet with people from deal-focussed cultures, then avoid tiring them too much with lots of social events; give them a chance to have a few evenings to themselves.
- Find out what is private and what is public in the culture you are dealing with. Look at literature, ask locals or others who have been there before.

**Test the temperature of the water:**
- Look out for obvious signs of impatience. Looking at the clock does not mean that you are not worth spending time on, but just that they want to keep to the schedule you agreed.
- If you invite them to various events and they start talking about there being no need for you to spend so much time on them, and that they are happy to entertain themselves, then it's probably because they don't really enjoy your company and would rather be on their own.

**Learn from / explain to:**
- In this type of culture, people will typically be reasonably clear and easy to understand, so if you agree expectations about how much time you should spend together, and how quickly you expect to get things finished, then as a rule that will be very well received.
- Explain to the deal-focussed people you will be dealing with that your relationship-focussed countrymen are slow, unsure, maybe like drinking a lot and don't take their working time very seriously. They just see it as part of business to use a lot of time on social aspects.

**Accept and understand:**
- Deal-focussed cultures like to be effective, and they have done away with all those "provincial" ways of thinking in communities, where everybody knew everything about everyone in the

village, and which people thought were limiting and controlling. Instead, they think it is more stimulating to keep a distance, and conversely to be very precise about what we expect from each other's behaviour. That way, as mentioned, they avoid everything that resembles corruption.

# 8

## For my sake, or the group's?

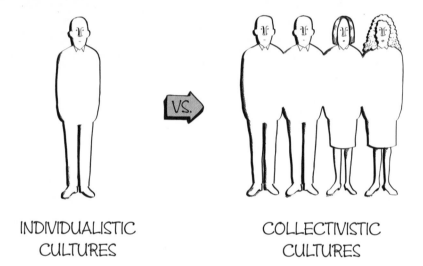

INDIVIDUALISTIC
CULTURES

COLLECTIVISTIC
CULTURES

- - - - - - - - - - - - - - - - - - - - - - - - - - - - - - - - - - - - - - - - - -

**The vote**

A Danish organisation has received a delegation of members from an Indian sister organisation, and everybody is looking forward to an interesting time working together during the week. A number of decisions are to be made with relevance for their future collaboration, much of it of a purely technical nature.

For example, during the first meeting there is a suggestion about a new type of software for member registration. Until now, two different systems have been used in the two departments, and the Danes in particular feel that now is the time to converge the systems a little more.

There are pros and cons with both systems, and many opinions about the issue, and after about a quarter of an hour's debate, the meeting leader thinks that they can conclude by quickly moving to a vote.

The Danes are very quick to raise their hands, but the Indians look around the room in dismay. A spokesman protests and says that they cannot just vote like this on this type of thing. The Danes say that this is the most democratic way. After much discussion back and forth, the Indian shakes his head, and has a short conversation with his countrymen.

The Danes ask if they are ready, and the Indian nods. At the first vote, all the Indians raise their hands at the same time. Not a single one votes differently from the rest of the group.

It is thus decided which programme to use. But the Danes cannot help thinking that the vote had not been quite as democratic as they had imagined.

---------------------------------------------------------

Do you work best in a group or on your own? Do you think it is necessary for everyone to be heard, and that consensus is much better than votes – like in the example?

Whether you think that things work best if you give individuals personal responsibility, or prefer to consult the group, is not just a question of who you are as an individual – it is to a great extent also a question of which culture you come from.

For example, the Indians did not like having to vote, because it gave potential for lots of individuals to fight each other. Instead of agreeing on things, you let each individual be responsible for his own opinion. The majority wins, and the Indians thought that was extremely unsatisfactory. They prefer the group to act as one. So they voted together – almost certainly according to the orders of their spokesman – because they felt better knowing that everyone in the group agreed, even if they actually didn't.

The Danish attitude is a typical sign of an *individualistic culture*, and the Indian attitude is typical for the *collectivist*.

## More than the sum of its parts?
Is a group just the sum of its parts, in other words, of the individuals who make it up? Individualists would say so. To talk about societies,

communities or groups as something which have needs, wishes or will is something purely abstract. That has nothing to do with reality. Groups cannot "can" or "want". It follows that particularly in the West, people first and foremost take their own needs into account and are true to who they are. People are encouraged to express their opinion and develop a strong personality.

If you are applying for a job in a country with an individualistic culture, those are the sort of words to use in your application. Of course, you could also write that you work well in a *team*, and like teamwork, but if you are not independent as well, that is seldom sufficient.

Conversely, too strong a focus on a strong personality and personal will can be seen in a collectivist culture as potentially damaging, disobedient, egoistic and as an expression of an immature lack of willingness to collaborate. In such a culture, a strong independent personality will more easily be rejected.

In general, the differences can be drawn in the following way:

-----------------------------------------------

**Collectivist cultures**
- Think "we" before "I"
- They share with their group to a great extent
- Who you are, depends on your relationships to others
- They work best in groups
- Teaching: Primarily, there is a need to teach people to act
- One's own actions infect the whole group
- What the others believe is very important for what you yourself believe
- Rules can be avoided if it is to the group's advantage
- Conformity is highly valued
- Dependence is a strength

-----------------------------------------------

**Individualistic cultures**

- Think "I" before "we"
- They only share with the group what has been agreed, otherwise everyone expects everyone to look after themselves first
- Who you are, depends on your own personal history and development
- People work best on their own
- Teaching: It is about teaching people to learn
- One's mistakes are one's mistakes and no one else's
- Other people's opinions are not as important as what you yourself believe
- Rules can be avoided if it is to your own advantage
- Conformity is a weakness
- Independence is a strength

Collectivist cultures can be characterised as having the family play a very large role, and families can also be very large. This is known as an "extended family" and means that the feeling of family extends much further than immediate "core family".

Extended families are very normal in developing countries and traditional societies, where the allocation of land and resources is often decided by inheritance rules within the family. In these cases, it is important to maintain contact with great cousins, who in some societies are also potential marriage partners. Because it is best to keep things in the family.

But the group can also be much more than just the family. Examples of other groups which people typically take into account before looking after oneself are: friends, the company, the working group or team, the school class, the party, the country and those with the same religious faith.

## The whole or the part?

In an individualistic culture, the community is simply an instrument and not an objective in itself. Individuals are part of the group because they have better chances there than on their own. There is something pragmatic about community.

Things are completely different in collectivist societies. Personal success is nothing like as important as group success. How good an individual has been can first and foremost be measured by the group's results.

In collectivist societies, people are very close to their networks. Networks will also be looked at in the final chapter. Relationship-focussed societies with diffuse personal relations also have a tendency to be very strongly collectivist. Such networks are in fact almost an inseparable part of the individual. You are nothing except what you are because of your relationships. All others outside the close network are very far away. That is why they have to take so much time to find out who other people are.

Psychologist Richard E. Nisbett, who has studied the very collectivist societies in Asia, has drawn up the following model which shows how we perceive the relationship to ourselves and others in individualist societies (such as the Western world) and collectivist societies respectively. He had a particular focus on Asia and the Far East.

## THE RELATIONSHIP TO GROUPS

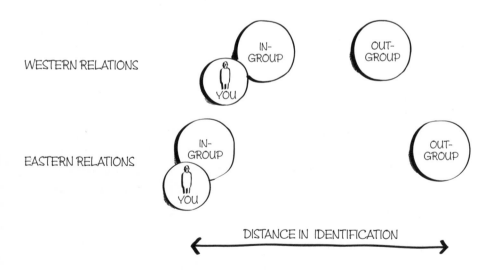

The Western and modern individual can in fact understand him or herself independently of the group, of the family and of close friends and work colleagues. He or she also finds it easier to identify with and understand other groups which are immediately outside. There could be another company he or she is to negotiate with, friends of friends or the other parents at day care.

Societies with a larger collective identity, and here I mean primarily Far East societies, are different. There, the individual is very closely connected to the group. For example, people do not make very many decisions without asking the rest of the family: "May I get married to him or her?" "Should I accept that job?" etc. Because the individual is part of the group, and the group is also part of the individual. Decisions for one person therefore affect them all. Everyone else outside the group is very far away.

In individual societies, people like to introduce themselves with the name and what they do for a living. In Denmark, you can be sure to get the question from the head of the dinner table about what you do for a living within the first 15 minutes. In a collectivist society, people prefer to introduce themselves as someone's son, wife or friend, as that is what people will ask before anything else. Westerners, such as Danes, will often think that this goes a bit too far, because it is not the relationship which determines who you are. Whereas Danes first ask much later in the conversation about whether you have any children, and only enquire about your marital status when they have acquired some courage from a couple of drinks, such private questions can well be the very first ones a Chinese, Indian, Egyptian or Japanese will ask. So you need to remember to be culturally intelligent: it is not impolite or pushy if they expect the same behaviour from you.

The staggering thing about this focus on groups and individuals (and the reason why it is worth spending a whole chapter on) is that this way of thinking permeates many different areas and can be used to understand many of the fundamental differences in the world. For example, people from individualist societies like to differentiate themselves in many different ways. In order to test how deep this desire lies, social psychologists Hee-jung Kim and Hazel Markus did an experiment a few years ago. They asked Koreans and Americans to choose from a selection of ballpoint pens. The result was that the Americans had a tendency to choose the pen which was most special. The Koreans, however, chose the most ordinary one they could find. They had no desire to differ from the norm.

## The special way of thinking in Asia

In his book *The Geography of Thought*, Richard E. Nisbett shows lots of interesting examples of how people in Asian societies think. In Asia, people are often influenced by Taoism and Confucianism, strong philosophies which emphasise harmony and knowing your place. The search for peace and order are better than the search for abstract truths. We cannot know what is right for all eternity, but we can try to establish harmony and context where we are.

Western culture looks differently at things and according to Nisbett, these two different views of the world are so old that they are the reason why East and West have developed so differently from each other.

The ancient Greeks wanted to understand how the world was made up, and they tried to think towards the "spirit" which had to be found behind the visible world; the order, system or strength which ran the world. But because they focussed so much on individual things, they made some mistakes. For example, when Aristotle imagined that stones fell to Earth because it was a characteristic of stones that they fell fast. Conversely, a characteristic of feathers was that they fell slowly.

The Chinese, however, had worked it out. Gravity works on everything in the same way, but air resistance is different, meaning that the stone falls faster. The Chinese found it easier to reach the correct interpretation, simply because they were concerned with relationships. They understood how stones and feathers interacted with the element they were in, namely the air. Whereas it was the "individual stone" which was interesting for the Greeks.

When you talk to people from the East, you can still see that that's the way they think. They see the whole picture before they see the individual parts. Nisbett tested this very specifically by showing both Americans and Japanese pictures of fish swimming around some plants in water. When he asked the Americans what they saw in the pictures, it was most likely that they pointed to the individual elements. They said they saw a fish, a stone or a plant. The Japanese, however, said that they saw a dam, a lake or an aquarium.

Asians see the whole picture first and then the individual elements.

That is also how people work in Asia. Asians can appear unfocussed on an individual task, because they suddenly switch to doing something completely different. Where in Denmark people normally finish A before they go on to B or C, in Asia they don't see things as quite so separate. In Asia, they would rather come back to things later so that the work is spread a little more over the whole picture.

If you have to tell an Asian about a small but important detail, you need to tell them about how this detail is part of the big picture. In the machine, in the organisation, in the group, in the business strategy, in the school class, etc. It is crucial that they understand the *context*. If they get stuck in the detail, which the Chinese in particular do, then it is precisely because they maybe lack context in the big picture. There, people never say yes to a contract, a plan or process before they are sure about how it all fits into the big picture. Once they can see the big picture, then they get going, and then they move very fast. That is another reason negotiations in the East take such a long time.

Which pair do you think belongs together? Is it the cow and the hen, the hen and the grass, or the cow and the grass? If you grew up in a Western society, you will probably answer "the cow and the hen." If you are from China or Taiwan, it is more likely that you will answer "the cow and the grass." why? Well, because the cow eats the grass.

In the Western world, we look at which category the objects fall under. The cow and the hen are both "animals" and therefore belong together. But in the Eastern world one looks at relations, rather than abstract categories. Here it is more natural that the cow and the grass belong together.

Nisbett's observations apply particularly to Taoist and Confucian cultures such as Asian (primarily Japan, China, Vietnam, Taiwan and Korea) and not for all collectivist cultures per se. In Asia, collectivism is particularly linked to their philosophical teaching but also expresses another way of seeing the big picture rather than the individual elements, the context rather than the *individual* issue, or the *individual* object, or the *individual* person.

## Dirty Harry

Right at the other end of the scale is where we find individualism, which is strongest among Americans, who scored the absolutely highest scores on the individualism index in Hofstede's studies.

The American dream, as we know it, is about finding happiness on your own, and there are at least two reasons for that: the first is that the USA, as previously mentioned, came about from a resistance to the European nobility and the power of the monarchy, where family status determined your success or lack thereof. The other is that the country was built by pioneers who had to look after themselves on the prairies. So Americans like individualists who stick to their principles, and who are not afraid of meeting resistance from their surroundings.

In the large study of the American "spirit", *Habits of the Heart* (1996), a number of researchers studied Americans' great love of the mythological lone avengers we often see in films. People such as the private detective, the cowboy and of course the hard-hitting policeman who constantly has problems with his superiors because he does things his own way. Clint Eastwood's character Dirty Harry is almost the personification of these lonely figures who prefer to work alone and never do what they are told.

It is important to emphasise that this ideal is not about egoism. On the contrary, there can be an overriding well-developed sense of social justice involved, but instead of talking to the group about how to attain the social justice, people act on their own – and on their own initiative. That is what Dirty Harry does when he breaks the collective laws to catch the criminal. His own moral compass is pointing in that direction and so there is not time to ask what other people think. There is a lot of respect for that type of individual action in American society and in many other Western cultures. This way of acting is simply not understood in collectivist societies, and people there don't like it in the same way that individualists do. The Danes can also experience conflict with Americans in this area when the more collective-oriented Danes think that things should be discussed in the group before taking things into their own hands.

In individualistic societies, such as the USA, people think that societies' values are in fact being maintained because of individuals who take responsibility and who are willing to defend them. They do not see individualism as an opponent of the community. Quite the opposite: strong individuals are a prerequisite for the community being able to function. Who would otherwise defend law and order, morals, decency and justice if there were not strong individuals, who should therefore not be held back?

Individualists should have some elbow room. They must have a lot of freedom and be allowed to fight for their issue in the group. It is individualists who don't have anything against voting instead of taking a long time to reach consensus. According to studies, it is the individualists who obtain better results when they are on their own than if they work in groups. Conversely, collectivists perform much better when they work together with others.

## Universal rules versus special rules
Individualists prefer deal-focussed cultures because we are better at arm's length with others than if we are in a suffocating, limiting social community. In deal-focussed cultures, people prefer fixed laws and rules because they cannot take special account of each other. There, everyone is an equal, free individual. "I know my rights", as Americans say.

That is why Americans like to turn up to the first meeting with an army of lawyers, which seems extremely hostile to many collectivist, Eastern societies. Americans' tendency to sue each other to find out who is right, is connected with their strong belief that it is individual rights which guarantee their freedom. As opposed to my friends, my network and my family. I am not bound by them. If I don't fight the battle, then no one else will do it for me. So I therefore need very *specific* laws which regulate my relationship with other people. As opposed to the *diffuse* rules which apply in many collectivist societies.

It goes without saying that this gives lots of difficulties when working across the cultural gap.

**Honour killings, the collectivist extreme**

An unconditionally tragic and awful crime is so-called honour killing. It can seem completely incomprehensible to Westerners that members of the same family can kill each other because of a matter of honour, but if you look more into how collectivist societies work, it can be easier to understand what happens. Understand but not *accept*, of course.

In collectivist societies, you do not bear the guilt and shame alone if you do something which is not compatible with cultural norms. Because you are your family, and the family is also the individual, the shame infects everyone. Everyone in the family thus becomes "worth less" from a moral point of view, if an individual does something he or she should not. The responsibility for what happened is also collective. The family is also liable when someone does something stupid.

In order to save the family's honour (for example, the market value of an unmarried daughter when it comes to marriage), it can be necessary to take the consequences and kill that member of the family who brought shame on the rest.

In individualistic cultures, people believe that impudent actions are an individual's own problem and own responsibility. But that doesn't work in cultures where responsibility and honour are collective.

It should be said, however, that people in collectivist cultures generally believe that honour killing is too extreme an action, even though they understand the principles behind it more than individualists do.

In a large study, cultural researchers Fons Trompenaars and Charles Hampden-Turner asked who would report a friend to the police in a theoretical case of a dramatic accident where the friend had been speeding. In collectivist societies such as South Korea, China, Egypt, Venezuela and India, there was a much greater willingness to protect the friend despite the breach of the law, as well as an expectation from the friend that the others would cover for him to a certain extent. In more collectivist societies, rules are about *who* should follow them, not the actual conformance to the rule in itself.

That is not an understanding that people in individualist societies have. Dutchmen, Englishmen, Swedes, Australians and, of course at the top of the list, Americans, all believe that the law is the law and that it applies to everyone regardless. Relationships are not a mitigating factor.

## Why do people in the East lie?

- - - - - - - - - - - - - - - - - - - - - - - - - - - - - - - - - - - - - - - - - - - - - - - - - - -

A Danish company is in the process of buying a large shipment of electronics from a Chinese company, but the Danes are nervous about whether the components meet certain European safety standards. They pick up the phone and ask the Chinese. The Chinese say that they do indeed meet the standards. A few weeks later, the Danish firm receives the components, but despite the assurances they do not meet the requirements. There are also some problems with the format.

The Danes have previously received good, low-cost and not least well-functioning components from the Chinese company, so they decide to give them another chance.

The Chinese call again, give lots of apologies and say that they will sort things out. Then they go through the specifications with one of the Danish engineers on the telephone, and it sounds like they have understood everything correctly.

The Danes ask if the parts can be ready in two months, which is precisely enough time to get things installed so that the company's own orders will be ready on time. The Chinese give a clear yes.

A week before the deadline, the company receives an email from the Chinese which says that the components will be ready for delivery in six weeks. Now the Danes will have their own production delayed by another month. How could things go so wrong?

- - - - - - - - - - - - - - - - - - - - - - - - - - - - - - - - - - - - - - - - - - - - - - - - - - -

Lots of Danes who do business in one way or another with Chinese, Japanese, Koreans, Indians and many other Eastern nationalities know this problem well. They've been promised everything but suddenly it can't be done.

We have previously seen how lack of trust means that verbal and even written contracts can suddenly be cancelled, but in this example there is something else in play. In China and a large number of other Asian countries, "yes" does not necessarily mean "yes".

In fact, there are different ways of saying no in Asia. Danish China consultant Hannah Leanderdal has compiled a number of examples of how "no" can sound during negotiations with the Chinese.

----------------------------------------------------

**Ways of saying "no" in China:**
- "This question will require further study"
- "It might be difficult"
- "I'll see what I can do"
- "I'll think about it"
- "It's not a big problem"
- "I need to report to the boss"
- "We will see"
- "Maybe"
- "Yes, yes"

----------------------------------------------------

All the sentences can actually mean a definite no. But why don't they just say that, we Westerners ask.

Does it mean they're lying? Yes and no. Some are clearly lying, and some more than others. In China, a little white lie is not a big problem. They are much quicker at lying there than people in Denmark are, and studies show that the Chinese are in fact so used to lying that their bodies don't give things away with the same signals that ours do.

So it is important to understand that the Chinese seldom regard it as conscious deceit and therefore as an actual lie.

What happens all over Asia is once again the focus on harmony and nice-looking "big pictures". The Confucianist belief in order and wholeness is also employed here (and in countries such as India, which is not Confucianist, but where there is a similar demand for harmony and completeness, for example in Hinduism). So people don't say "no" when they are asked. A "no" would break the harmony, and upset an expectant buyer, so people avoid saying the truth.

But can a country function if people don't trust each other? Yes, it can, if everyone takes into account that people are striving for harmony, and the last thing they want is to lose face to an outsider. The latter is also important, because the lie is to cover up the fact that the Chinese company is not as good as it wants to be. As long as you are prepared, you have the opportunity to interpret things correctly.

In the East, people know very well that a question that can only be answered with "yes" or "no" is a bad question because you will always get a yes regardless of the actual answer. So they don't even bother asking each other questions like that, because they know what the answer will be. Instead, it pays to ask a question where the person being asked has to give information in order to answer, rather than the questioner coming with a long, informative question such as "can you have a delivery ready in 14 days?". That type of question is called *closed questioning*, because it can only be answered in the affirmative or the negative.

The converse is of course *open questions* where instead it is possible to give a more detailed answer. Open questions are also what we call "wh-" questions: when, what, which and who. So instead of asking *can* you deliver in 14 days (closed), the Dane should have asked *when* can you deliver (open).

Remember too, that for Asians who live in a very esoteric, relationship-focussed culture, it is very easy to understand that "I'll just have to talk to the boss first" means "no". In such cases, people automatically take account of the big picture, the process, the situation and the need to maintain good relationships, all of which are more important than the truth. They have no problem understanding what is being said between the lines, and take it into account.

So Asians are therefore very often dismayed about how rude and direct people in the West are (and especially in Denmark and the USA). In the West, you just say "no" if you think things can't be done. The truth is placed higher than politeness, and so Danes, for example, are perceived as impolite and unsophisticated, particularly by the Chinese. You can avoid that by learning to say no in a polite way. Consider using the same excuses as in the box above. The

Asians will immediately understand that you have said no, yet you will have done it in a polite and respectful fashion.

------------------------------------------------------------

**An Indian no**

This dialogue comes from Craig Storti's useful book about how to communicate in India. Try to see for yourself how many times there is a no, and how much Sumitra tries to avoid the question in order to avoid being as direct as Brigitte clearly wants her to be.

**Brigitte:** I was wondering Sumitra, if your team can come in on Saturday?
**Sumitra:** Saturday?
**Brigitte:** Yes. Just for a couple of hours.
**Sumitra:** I see
**Brigitte:** Just to finish up that application test.
**Sumitra:** Right.
**Brigitte:** I think Ram's team is coming in also, so it should go pretty fast.
**Sumitra:** Yes. They work quite fast.
**Brigitte:** So what do you think, Sumitra?
**Sumitra:** That's probably OK.
**Brigitte:** That's great
**Sumitra:** Let me ask my team and get back to you
**Brigitte:** No problem

------------------------------------------------------------

## Generosity

It goes without saying that in collectivist societies, people make sure they give as much back to the group as possible. So those types of societies are often extremely generous. People buy each other drinks and stand up to give other people the best seat. They put themselves in the background. A good example is from Japan: Sony's possibly greatest invention, the Walkman. Whereas in the West, the portable cassette player was marketed as allowing people to listen to music without being disturbed by others, the motivation was completely different for Sony's founder Akio Morita, who desperately wanted a player which would not disturb his fellow passengers when he wanted to listen to music on his many flights around the world. It was not about his *own* experience of the music, but about not disturbing anyone else.

Of course, part of this generous practice of giving gifts and favours also has another objective: self-promotion, or showing that one is willing to suffer for others' sake and for the sake of the group. A good example of this is the Greek term *filótimo* (Φιλότιμο), which is a measurement of how much a person is willing to suffer for his group. A man who generously helps others before he helps himself has a lot of *filótimo* and thus enjoys great respect.

Small signals that you honour your fellow citizens and take a back seat are a sure way to gaining points at little cost (depending on what you're willing to sacrifice, of course), when you are dealing with collectivist-oriented people. So remember that generosity and (overdone) attention from your side pays in a collectivist society, where people are always aware of other's needs. Danes come from a more modest culture, where people often don't dare to buy someone else a beer or give them gifts because they do not want to create any sense of obligation for later… But the whole *idea* in many collectivist societies is just that: that people *should* feel an obligation and encourage others to feel mutual obligations.

In China, you can often find that people almost come to blows with each other to pay the bill. You should also offer to pay. You can always choose to "give up" and let the others pay after a while. They will be very grateful to you for that. You can call it a win-win situation.

Deep down, we are all interested in being liked by other people. We cannot avoid other people. But some people use more energy on it than others. For them, the community is much more important for their understanding of who they are. That is why we see these great differences.

## Who is what?
The special focus on the big picture and harmony is, as I said, a very specific Asian phenomenon, and the Taoist and Confucianist values put a stronger focus on family and relationships than on the individual. The special way of thinking I have described above, is not found in quite the same way in other collectivist regions such as the Middle East, Africa or Latin America, but nevertheless they have

many things in common. In studies, the focus on the big picture and harmony often fit very well together with the degree of general collectivism.

So who are collectivists, and who are individualists?

Geert Hofstede has undertaken a very thorough study of how individualist or collectivist various countries are, and presented the following breakdown between the 18 countries I have chosen to examine in this book. The higher the IDV figure, the more individualism measured in the country concerned.

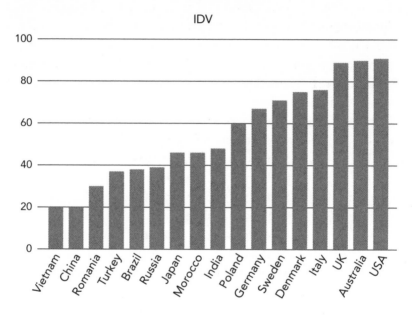

### In the details – Focus on Scandinavia

As shown in Hofstede's study, Danes are slightly more individualistic than Swedes, and even though the difference is not very large (Sweden IDV 71 and Denmark IDV 74), then there is nevertheless something many people have noticed.

The Danish journalist Kirsten Weiss has studied differences in Scandinavian business culture, and her interviews with Scandinavian bosses, analysts and staff do indeed confirm that those differences exist. The Swedes are slightly more collectivist than Danes. In Sweden, everyone is just as good as each other, and one of the things that means is that everyone has to be heard before a decision is made.

Many Danes have no doubt insulted a Swedish delegation because
in Denmark it is much more normal to take decisions about
something if there are no immediate objections. Danes are slightly
more impatient than Swedes and even though in Denmark the
whole group should really be heard first (just ask the Americans),
Danes reach a limit for how much discussion they can tolerate
sooner than Swedes do. Danes try to conclude earlier than Swedes,
or suddenly put things to a vote.

In her book, Kirsten Weiss explains that such behaviour is
regarded as very rude. The Swedes prefer everyone to be heard and
thus included in the process.

The more individualistic Danes can thus quickly come to seem
like thugs who are just trampling all over the community and don't
care about anyone else than themselves.

Danish children leave home sooner than any others in Europe.
The average age is 20. By comparison, it is 23 in France, 27 in
Spain and 28 in Italy. One of the reasons is that parents in
Denmark insist that their children should show independence.
Source: Cécile Van de Velde (2008): *Devenir adulte. Sociologie
comparée de la jeunesse en Europe.*

## Meetings of opposites

**Collectivist cultures perceive individualist cultures as** egoistic and self-centred. In particular, the relationship which individualists have to the family can appear especially cold to collectivists. That their children are expected to fly the nest and look after themselves is completely unheard of in other places, and is one of the reasons why the integration of immigrants from collectivist cultures has often been difficult in Denmark. They feel that they should take more responsibility for their family. Danes, however, perceive this as unnecessary control, depriving young people of their freedom.

**Individualist cultures perceive collectivist cultures** as interminably slow and difficult to negotiate with. When everyone always has to be included and heard – even though it's still usually the boss who makes the final decision – everything just sometimes appears to be one big piece of theatre of generous friendship and undue attention. In addition, collectivist people appear very lacking in independence, and sometimes it seems as if they don't even have a personality. They change their mind according to the circumstances... The excessive politeness is something individualists see as dishonest and lacking in independence, and the lack of attention to detail which the "harmonious" Eastern peoples have seems to them to be a little flimsy and unfocussed.

- - - - - - - - - - - - - - - - - - - - - - - - - - - - - - - - - - - - - - - - - - - - - -

### With Bo Bendixen in Japan

The Danish artist and graphicist Bo Bendixen tries to get into the Japanese market, but very quickly gets the feeling that the place is both hierarchically organised but also extremely collectivist. However, there is no doubt where the decision-making power lies, even though everyone has to be involved. As the secretary Yuki Araki explains:

"There is a whole organisation behind the decision-making process in a Japanese company. For example, as the secretary I know all the details of the business, but I have no title so I have to ask my section leader and the section leader has to ask the department manager, and then the department manager has to ask the divisional manager. Sometimes the question has to go all the way up to the director or the Chief Executive. At Bo Bendixen's introductory meeting, they were all there together".

---------------------------------------------------

## More good advice for dealing with collectivist cultures

### Come in groups when you are negotiating
- People who negotiate on their own, without having the group with them, are not to be trusted. Coming alone either means you have no status or you have no decision-making power. In order to impress in a collectivist culture, the rule is: the more people you send the better.

### Family is a good topic of conversation
- Ask about what really means something: the family. Remember the information you get. It is not insignificant to be able to remember how many children people have.

### Be careful about mixing groups
- If you are managing people with very collectivist ways, then give them a lot of self determination as regards forming the group. It is not irrelevant who people work with, and they know their "in group" better than you do; they know who they can trust and work with. An individualist might think that it is a good idea to "shuffle the pack", so that everyone gets to know everyone else, but that can be almost frightening for a collectivist, who prefers to remain with his "in group".

### And...
- Remember that things take a long time
- Be prepared for nepotism, favours for friends and lots of people who are invited to everything you can think of, but you nevertheless never find out who they are.
- Be generous and self-sacrificing – show attentiveness
- Prepare social activities

### Peculiar Danish collectivism
It might seem strange that in some areas, Danes come across as both collectivists and score very highly on the individualism

spectrum in Hofstede's study. New research also shows that individualism in fact therefore ought to be measured as two separate parameters. The large international GLOBE project distinguishes between in-group collectivism and institutional collectivism. Danes and other Nordic peoples score very low on the first parameter and very high on the second. This means that Scandinavians in general do not get their identity and self-understanding from the group (for example the family) but that they still regard society's institutions as very important and that wealth, influence, power and responsibility should be very equally spread in the collective. Danes are therefore very much more willing to give up part of their independence to the state, for example, but very unwilling to give it to individuals or the family. We can say that Danes behave as little collectivists at work and in their welfare state, but as little individualists in all other areas.

### The path to cultural intelligence

As the case in the introduction illustrated, it is not a good idea to decide things by a show of hands when in a collectivist society. Instead, you need to take plenty of time to listen to everyone and find a compromise. Avoid playing people off against each other, but respect that there is going to be one person who concludes for the group.

**In encounters with a general collectivist culture (in some regards, a Danish workplace):**

**Prepare:**
- Make sure you have plenty of time available for yourself and your relatively large group, and make sure you get all the information you can about the people you are going to meet.

**Test the temperature of the water:**
- Be aware of signals that you are moving too fast. If you are asked whether you all agree in your group, then it is important to underline how much you have talked about it and that everyone agrees. Remember to emphasise how both sides have gained something from the situation. People love win-win situations in countries which are based on harmony and balance.

**Learn from / explain to:**

- If you have staff from in-group collectivist societies (not Denmark), they will try to get family and friends placed in advantageous positions. In such situations, you have to make it clear to the collectivists that the results mean more than the relationships before you start to trample all over them by talking about nepotism and favours for friends. If the person they recommend appears qualified, there is of course no reason to reject him or her just because of your own culturally-dependent principles. You need to choose your battles carefully.

- Teach them to make decisions independently. That is easier said than done, but remember to emphasise to them as well, that they will be held individually responsible if something goes wrong – it will not affect the group, because we are not working with collective responsibility.

**Accept and understand:**

- You can go a long way with loyalty in collectivist societies, and group work works for them. Another positive element in these societies is that there is nowhere near the same tendency for families to split up into various different fractions who do not speak to each other. Someone dying alone without any family happens very rarely here. Individual freedom is limited, but the upside is often a very much greater mutual level of care for each other.

# 9

## How much change is allowed?

UNCERTAINTY AVOIDING
CULTURES

UNCERTAINTY TOLERANT
CULTURES

---

### The company's rules

When Thomas starts work at a Romanian factory, he immediately notices the large noticeboard in the workshop. "Rules" it says in large letters on it. Most of the staff speak very poor English, but they have understood that this notice sets out some rules for the company.

Thomas has been asked to make the company more efficient, and it occurs to him that many of the rules are rather strange. "Do not wear safety helmets outside the factory", "no trucks inside the factory building" – examples of unnecessary rules, as, for example, the doorway is not even high enough to let a

Danmarks Tekniske Universitet

Dear participant from the Danish Living Crash Course

We have finally received the book written by Dennis Nørmark; *"Cultural Intelligence for stone- age Brains – how to work with Danes and beyond"*, which was a part of the course material, but at the time for your attendance wasn't finished.

The book has been paid for as it was included in the price of the course.

We hope you will enjoy the book and that it will entertain you.

Best regards

**Kamille Ivalo Lehn Strouhal**

International HR Specialist, International Faculty Service

Coporate HR

Danmarks Tekniske Universitet
**Ledelse og Administration**

Anker Engelunds Vej 1
Bygning 101 A
2800 Kgs. Lyngby

Tlf.   45 25 25 25
Dir.   45 25 10 84
Fax   45 88 17 99

www.dtu.dk

truck drive in. Or the unreasonable: "Food is to be eaten in the canteen".

In addition, many of the rules are consistently not followed at all. So in order to show goodwill, he takes the notice down and replaces it with three fundamental rules which take account of most of the issues.

After a few days, however, someone has found the original notice and hung it back up again, and the foreman explains to Thomas, that he had made the men rather nervous. They had doubts about what to do. Thomas explains that they appeared not to understand what the rules really meant, and anyway they were not respected, so it doesn't appear to make any difference. "They could just use their common sense" says Thomas and smiles. The Romanian foreman looks at him as if he doesn't understand what he means.

"You could have discussed it with me", he says, and shrugs his shoulders before he goes off to eat his lunch. In his own office.

------------------------------------------------

## When "usually" will not die out

Some people are more unsure about the future than others, something the sociologist Geert Hofstede calls *uncertainty avoidance*. Uncertainty avoidance is a measurement of how far we are willing to go to avoid change, uncertainty and new situations. In evasive cultures, people feel threatened in situations which are not unambiguous, or which include too many unknown elements.

Many things can be used to avoid uncertainty, with some of the most common being:

- Strong and authoritative leadership
- Clear guidelines and lots of rules
- Religion – which sets out what is true and false in advance
- Lots of fixed traditions, procedures, taboos and rituals

In cultures where people are generally more uncertain, nervous and afraid of change, there is also often a very large power distance, but not always. When Geert Hofstede undertook his studies, he found out that uncertainty avoidance had to be seen as an independent parameter. Just because there is a large power distance (PDI), there is not also automatically high uncertainty avoidance (UAI). China has a much lower uncertainty avoidance than Germany (30 and 65 respectively), but a much greater power distance. The Chinese are much less bothered about unexpected situations than the Germans are. But neither are the Chinese as focussed on "right" and "wrong" as the Germans are, instead they perceive right and wrong to a much greater extent as determined by the context. That shows a high degree of flexibility. The Germans, however, like guidelines, and as a British sociologist once said about the Germans: if a train is late you can hear that the man announcing the fact is actually feeling really bad about it, because it comes across in his voice so clearly. It's not just unfortunate that the train is late, in Germany it's decidedly tragic.

In China and India, people are more used to things not necessarily going to plan (or the timetable), so people are very good at finding alternative solutions. So that also means that safety is not always quite as good as it should be, because some solutions are simply rather *too* creative.

-------------------------------------------------

**High uncertainty avoidance (UAI)**
- A generally high level of fear and stress
- A love of standards and known solutions
- Many taboos
- Change should be avoided
- Great truths sought
- High level of loyalty to employers
- People expect staff to be stable
- Laws and rules do not have to be *explained* (it is less important whether they are or are actually respected)

-------------------------------------------------


-------------------------------------------------

**Low uncertainty avoidance (UAI)**
- Generally low level of fear and limited stress
- High willingness for new thinking and different solutions
- Few taboos
- Change is exciting
- Sceptical of great truths

- Low level of loyalty to employers
- People expect staff to be flexible
- Laws and rules must be understandable, rational and changed if they do not work

---------------------------------------------------

## Who is what?

Let's look at how our countries are distributed by uncertainty avoidance according to Geert Hofstede. The higher the number, the higher the uncertainty avoidance by people in the country:

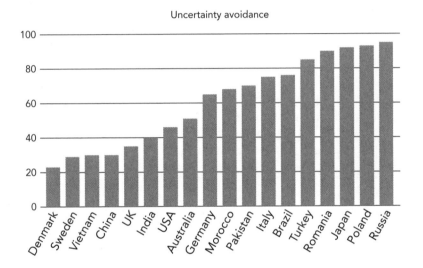

Uncertainty avoidance

Once again, the Scandinavians are bottom of the league, and I wonder if the Danes and Swedes can recognise a difference between their two countries by the difference between a more rule-based Swedish reality with many more taboos and the more easy and relaxed Danish attitude? Those are Scandinavians' own prejudices about each other, so maybe they may actually be right? Incidentally, Norway is even higher up than Sweden, with a score of 50. A figure which matches well with Norway's reputation for being a very careful country with a very great reluctance for a lot of change. In Norway, there is a lot of focus on old-fashioned things and what is "Norwegian" and the country's own strong traditions, which according to Norwegian anthropologist Thomas Hylland Eriksen mean that the country often appears very smug and isolated.

As I have already mentioned, many Asian countries are relatively well prepared for change, which may also be one of the reasons why their economies have been so successful in recent years. Japan is, however, still solidly placed as absolutely the most conservative and change resistant country in the Far East. For example, it is still normal to tell someone who is going to be surprised by a "surprise party" about it beforehand. Otherwise it would simply be too unpleasant.

In addition, people in the former Eastern European communist countries who have experienced their fair share of turbulent change are also most inclined to avoid change. For example, the surrounding world regularly looks on in amazement as Russians time after time re-elect Vladimir Putin with an enormous majority. Asked why, Russians repeatedly reply: Putin means stability and certainty. The Russians don't want anything new, they would rather carry on as before. A typical prioritisation of a country with an extremely high uncertainty avoidance. Law and order and as little change as possible please![4]

### Fear of change

Another area where uncertainty avoidance can be seen is people's willingness to take chances and try something new. In Japan, where uncertainty avoidance is high, people happily stay working for the same company all their lives, whereas Chinese staff are known for being pretty unfaithful to their employers.

In Scandinavia, where the safety net is large, there is also no lack of scruples about changing jobs. People are not so nervous about it, and so their loyalty is not that great. There, people are loyal to themselves and their own interests. Overall, flexibility is the order

---

4 Conversely, Russians are very inventive at finding new ways of avoiding laws. They behave surprisingly flexibly when it comes to this. It is very likely a relic of the old USSR days, when the law was what it was but respecting it meant it was very difficult to survive in the long term. So even though they were used to unnecessary rules, they also found a way around them.

of the day when it comes to Scandinavian workers. They are known for being able to take initiatives and being prepared to change. That is one of the cornerstones of their business culture. If you come from cultures that are much more avoiding of uncertainty, you will want to know what is right and what is wrong to a greater extent. Preferably for eternity.

The differences are often due to history. If you grow up in countries where there is high stability, then you are naturally less guarded about change. Neither is there any great danger linked to the changes which actually take place. Maybe there are also better resources for handling the changes that occur. If you live in countries with high unrest and uncertainty, the risks are greater, and so people will naturally tend to move towards what is more stable and *avoid* situations where uncertainty occurs. The people there can be very good at *handling* the chaotic situations when they are in the middle of them – but they will do their best to *avoid* getting into them in the first place. They say no to change, no to flexibility and they are afraid of the unknown. Uncertainty avoidance is not so much about the ability to handle uncertainty, but more about the need for *avoiding* and *fleeing* from it.

### "Relativism" versus "great truths"

As we saw in the chapter about Danes, they are among the most sceptical. They do not believe in great chrome-plated truths and would rather have their doubts about things. Generally, Danes are not particularly fearful people. In studies about general happiness they repeatedly score very highly, something which is typical for people with low uncertainty avoidance. The reason for that is that the fear which people with high uncertainty avoidance feel is not necessarily directed at anything in particular. Which is why in societies with high uncertainty avoidance, people are more willing to believe in great truths which explain and protect them in their daily lives. According to Hofstede, uncertainty avoidance also correlates with indications of neurotic behaviour.

In Scandinavia, however, people are more inclined to believe that truth varies and doesn't have any particular fixed size. This is one of the reasons why people in the Nordic countries are so "unreligious". Countries with high uncertainty avoidance are generally more religious than other countries, because religion helps to remove some of their general fear (but also generates new fear, such as the flames of hell et cetera). People feel good knowing that there is someone "in charge", and if they just do as they are told then nothing bad will happen. That is incidentally another reason why Norway scores so high on this parameter compared to Denmark and Sweden. Christianity is stronger in old pious Norway than in the rest of Scandinavia. Where there is religion there is fear, and where there is fear there is religion.

Countries with low uncertainty avoidance will also typically have fewer *taboos*. Taboos are the way that fearful people keep pleasant and unexpected things at a distance. When there is something you mustn't eat, mustn't do or mustn't say then you can create a calming illusion that danger is something you can identify very specifically, and which can therefore very specifically be kept at a distance. If we just follow what is prescribed, everything will be OK. So there will typically be food that mustn't be eaten, or words that mustn't be said in cultures with high uncertainty avoidance. The Muhammed cartoon crisis in Denmark was a very good example of how much difficulty a country with low uncertainty avoidance has with understanding that there might be rules about what you are allowed to do with a pen and paper.

---

*For example, in Muslim countries there is a lot of irony and implied humour. But we just don't make fun of the same things that Danes do. In Muslim culture there is a large number of taboos which people do not touch and definitely don't make jokes about. For example God, the King, authorities, heroes of olden times, women and sex. Danes are not always aware of these taboos, and in such situations Danish humour can give rise to some serious cultural conflicts.*
Naser Khader

---

## Meetings of opposites
## Good advice for living among people with high uncertainty avoidance

### Indicate the "correct" solution – instead of offering a "free choice"
"What is the right thing to do" is something that people from cultures with high uncertainty avoidance will ask again and again. The more a Scandinavian answers "what do *you* think?", the more uncertain and fearful they will become. In other words, management of people from the more fearful parts of the world means perhaps focusing more on certainty and clear rules, and sometimes the Danes will just have to forget the "everything is relative" attitude and just say: "that's what's right".

They will relax, and you will get peace.

### Your new slogan: Change to maintain
In encounters with uncertainty avoiding cultures, you will quickly discover that there are many things which just can't be done when you are with people who prefer to avoid new thinking and want to stay with what they already know. So you have to make sure you tone down the risk, and focus on the good old conservative slogan "change to maintain". In other words, argue that in order to maintain what we have as we have always had it, we also need to implement some new insignificant changes. We have to break with tradition in order to maintain traditions. Focus on certainty and stability. Changes are necessary so that we can keep things as they are in the long-term.

That is how the status quo is maintained. At least superficially.

### Be careful about asking "why"?
If you are dealing with countries with high uncertainty avoidance, you will find that many rules exist just for their own sake. There are things you mustn't do because... because you mustn't do them! Don't bother asking too many questions about that. Regulations and rules feel good in a world where people like to have clear guidelines. This means that asking questions about the rules of practice which sometimes get in the way of other and maybe better suggestions, is unwelcome. It may be that their rules do not appear to be particularly rational, but they are rules and should be respected,

and if you try to argue for the rule not being good, you can quite rightfully be perceived as talking down to them.

In Russia, they naturally have a smart way of avoiding rules, yet you still don't question them – out of principle.

- - - - - - - - - - - - - - - - - - - - - - - - - - - - - - - - - - - - - - - - - - - - - - - - - - - - - - - - - -

The correspondent for Danish newspaper Weekendavisen in Moscow, Anna Libak, has been allocated a chauffeur. She wants her chauffeur to wash her car too:

"That met with resistance from the security guards at the car park. "It's not allowed for car owners in cities to wash their cars themselves," they said. "The law says that it has to be done in proper car washes, so your chauffeur can't wash your car here. Of course we do advise you to have your car washed, as you can be fined for driving around in a dirty car in Moscow".

I asked them how they manage to wash their own cars at the car park, seeing as it was illegal.

"Oh, we just do it at night when the police can't see us," they explained".

- - - - - - - - - - - - - - - - - - - - - - - - - - - - - - - - - - - - - - - - - - - - - - - - - - - - - - - - - -

## The path to cultural intelligence

Thomas, whose story I started with, was not prepared for Romanian culture, where rules help to create stability – even though they never get followed anyway. On the contrary, Thomas' three simplified rules, which very explicitly encouraged staff to just use their common sense and own judgement, were perceived as disturbing and revolutionary. "You make the men nervous", he was told. In cultures with high uncertainty avoidance, fear is a much larger part of daily life than people with other cultural backgrounds are used to, and when working with those sorts of cultures there are a number of things to take into account. Generally, Danes put it like Thomas did: "find out for yourself", but that is difficult to under-stand when you are used to looking for the right solution. Even if you always try to find creative solutions which end up having to be made up anyway because the rules are impossible to follow exactly.

Danes are also very creative, but conversely they are quite open about that kind of "independent thinking" being what they expect from people. Creativity is not just a solution for them, but the actual *number one* solution.

This can especially be seen in the way Danes treat new staff. They barely give them more than a desk and a computer, and just let them get on with it themselves. People who come to Denmark to work are often puzzled by the lack of instructions. Something as simple as a job description is barely used here any more, and I have met many people from abroad who desperately want a piece of paper where it says what is expected of them. If you come from a culture where people like to know precisely what they should do, then there is actually nothing more anxiety-inducing than all the freedom in Denmark – so consider asking the Danes if they couldn't just be a little more specific…

**Prepare:**
- Get yourself an overview of the rules and taboos in the society. Is there something you mustn't say, or are there things that you mustn't ask questions about? You can be sure that a culture with high insecurity avoidance has many illogical rules from the point of view of someone from a culture with a very low uncertainty avoidance. The best thing you can do in advance is to learn them.
- Take everything into account. Get your arguments supported by all the data you can find – people have to be convinced before they are willing to make changes.
- If you yourself come from a country with high uncertainty avoidance, and are working in a country with low uncertainty avoidance such as Denmark, then remember that mistakes and sometimes also risk-taking is much more accepted than it may be back home. This means that it is OK to try something without being totally sure, as long as you are completely open to your colleagues about what you are doing and never try to cover up minor mistakes you make. You do not need to know everything before you act, you just feel your way along.

**Test the temperature of the water:**
- Yes, it can well be that there are many rules in an uncertainty avoidance culture, but it is by no means certain that people follow them. Keep an eye on that. Rather than trying to work out why, maybe you just have to accept that things regulate themselves

despite appearing to be overregulated. Can the people say that something is impossible, yet find a way of making it happen later anyway. They just don't want to admit to being disobedient.
- Make changes slowly and make them together with your staff.

## Learn from / explain to:
- Make it clear to your staff from uncertainty avoiding cultures what is expected of them and make sure you always tell them what the risks are (and of course, that there are always risks that can be coped with) – remember that these people are often looking for a way out – both literally and figuratively – and one of the first thoughts they have is: "how can I get out of this in time?"
- Explain the advantages of the changes to them. For Danes, it is true that "change is a pleasure", so people are always used to explaining what is good about a change. For Danes, change in itself is nice, but people in uncertainty avoiding cultures do not necessarily feel the same way. There, you have to take the time and explain the reason for the change – or just avoid introducing changes if they *were* just for change's sake.

## Understand
- Many of the uncertainty avoiding cultures have very bad experiences with change. Their existence has been marked by uncertainty and fear, maybe political unrest, maybe because of poverty, of unpredictable climate or because there is a certain tradition of apathy in the countries where changes have never really helped. Their experience is that stability is the best thing of all. Better to have lots of laws and regulations than the lawlessness they might have had before.
- The uncertainty-willing Danish culture is conversely a culture where there is very high trust and certainty in day-to-day life. So people can take a few more risks here because the really big catastrophes are few and far between. There is a safety net in Scandinavian countries which in some ways is a very radical attempt to handle uncertainty, but precisely because it IS handled by rules, then Danes can relax.

# 10

## Gorilla or mother hen?

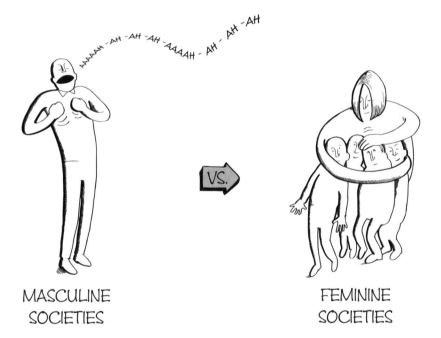

MASCULINE
SOCIETIES

FEMININE
SOCIETIES

**So you're the expert on this machine**

Benny is a supervisor in a Danish firm of engineers which has recently started production in the USA. Benny has gone over to teach the American workers something about maintenance. Benny is to train Bill, who after the initial small talk asks a very direct question: "So, I guess you're the expert on this?". Benny smiles and says modestly that he is "OK", and that they will get things working fine together. Bill does not seem completely satisfied with the answer, but Benny ignores that.

Benny wants to be very thorough, but there comes a point when he can see that Bill is not happy. He thinks Benny is too long-winded, can't they just get going with the work so that they can be finished before the others? "I want to get my bonus" he says. Benny says "it's not a competition," and Bill replies with a grin: "Maybe not for you". "I'm just trying to be thorough," answers Benny, and finally Bill says resignedly "You know, what I really want is for someone to come and teach me this properly rather than have a second-rate worker come and show me". Benny is rather startled, because he is definitely not second-rate, he assures Bill. Bill shakes his head: "So why didn't you say that?" Benny can tell that Bill has absolutely no trust in him.

- - - - - - - - - - - - - - - - - - - - - - - - - - - - - - - - - - - - - - - - - - - - - - - - - - - - -

When Geert Hofstede undertook his large study of cultural differences around the world, he found out that not everyone is equally interested in promoting themselves, competing with others or generally putting themselves and their own abilities at the forefront. Some are much more reserved and are uncomfortable with being the centre of attention. They don't talk so much about what they want to achieve, their successes, their abilities or their results.

When people like Benny come into contact with people who are used to hard competition or elbowing others out of the way, they can quickly appear incompetent and "second-rate". Bill wants to know whether Benny is an expert. He doesn't want to waste time with someone who cannot bring him success. But Benny is from Denmark, where Jante's Law applies, and where, as we know, being reserved is a virtue, and so in all modesty he doesn't believe he should be called an expert. Bill, however, is from a country where people prefer to oversell rather than undersell themselves. If Benny does not want to call himself an expert, he must be really bad at his job.

They have both totally misunderstood each other because they are used to two different ways of presenting themselves. Benny is from Scandinavia, which is *extreme* in just this regard. In the USA, however, it is all about selling yourself and showing what a success you are. Just take a look at all the TV programmes from the USA which are about being the best in an elimination race. "I want to be succesful, I have always wanted to be nothing but the best, and I think that I *am* the best and I'm gonna prove it!". It sounds normal coming from an American, but Danes seldom say it with the same conviction. That would be too much – yes, it would even be considered as a conscious provocation. People don't want to be too self-centred and egocentric, maybe even too "American". In the USA, self-obsession is the most natural thing in the world. In Hofstede's terminology, the USA is a typically *masculine* society, and Scandinavia a typically *feminine* society.

## Why "feminine" and "masculine"?

You can also say "gorilla" and "mother hen". The gorilla jostles his way forward, bangs his chest and always makes sure he finds the highest tree where he can sit and shout about his superiority. On the other hand, the mother hen is interested in there being room for others than herself, and that the weaker ones should not be pushed out of the henhouse. Instead, she takes care of them. The gorilla, however, will go for the clear winners so that they get *even better*. The gorilla would say it is about a winning mentality. While the mother hen would talk about caring for the weaker ones. It's not surprising that Hofstede has measured the mother hen attitude as being strongest in the caring and supporting welfare states of Scandinavia.

That one type of behaviour should be more masculine and the other more feminine may not be to everyone's liking, but it is in fact an argument which is very well supported by evidence. In nature, the males generally dominate. They fight each other for the females and only produce offspring if they themselves get to the top. This pattern is also found among humans, where men also compete with each other (and with women, but first and foremost with each other), whereas women to a greater extent seek consensus and balance. It is often men who are the most visible in culture and the media. They have always been the ones who write more symphonies, books, poems, songs, philosophical tomes and constitutions than women have. They have been speakers, painters, dictators and preachers. Men are good at putting themselves in the spotlight, whereas women are good at looking after others. Culture can of course strengthen or weaken this tendency, but whether it is our culture or our nature which causes this difference is really not that relevant for the argument here. The difference, however, is a fact.

The American cognitive linguist George Lakoff has written quite a lot about how feminine and masculine morals look and their connection to politics. Masculine morals are often conservative and right-wing, focussed on giving people moral support to look after themselves. They believe in abilities people are born with, in talent and self-assertion. They don't wait for other people to come along and help, they get on with things themselves. Conversely, feminine morals are more left-wing, and build on the assumption that an individual is shaped by his or her environment. An individual does not have an inner core, everything is created by external loving care, help and support. These are morals which are a natural extension of the very different tasks the two sexes traditionally have: the woman as caring and the man as outgoing and focussed on dominating his many competitors. The woman has no competitors at home and can thus focus on caring.

I can remember my mother, who worked as a manager in a large Danish company, telling me that when she was interviewing women for a vacancy, and she asked them about whether they knew a specific computer programme, they often tended to answer that they knew a little bit about it even though they had actually been on a training course for it previously. Men, however, who had only tried the programme two or three times, had absolutely no qualms about saying that they were "experts" or "super users". In other words, men found it harder to be reserved than women. That is the same difference which Hofstede and others have noticed. In a study by Gallup in 2010, for example, 54% of men stated that they were more intelligent than others. The result for women was only 35%.

The difference is thus found at the individual level (i.e. between individuals and especially between men and women), and that caused Hofstede to suggest that it can also be found at group level (between societies/countries).

## Masculine and feminine values

- - - - - - - - - - - - - - - - - - - - - - - - - - - - - - - - - - - - - - - - - - - - - - - - - -

**Masculine societies are characterised by:**
- Ambition is a virtue
- Competition helps create winners
- Sell yourself!

- It's good to have differences between men and women
- You are in it to win
- The strong should be supported so that they become even stronger
- Second best is not good enough

- - - - - - - - - - - - - - - - - - - - - - - - - - - - - - - - - - - - - - - - - - - - - - - - - -


- - - - - - - - - - - - - - - - - - - - - - - - - - - - - - - - - - - - - - - - - - - - - - - - - -

**Feminine societies are characterised by:**
- A good person is a caring person
- Competition helps create divisions
- Be modest
- Equality of the sexes is best
- The weak should be supported and protected from the strong
- It is not about winning, but about joining in

- - - - - - - - - - - - - - - - - - - - - - - - - - - - - - - - - - - - - - - - - - - - - - - - - -

## Who is what?

Societies with more feminine values are not necessarily collectivist societies – the two factors are quite independent of each other. That is due to it being quite possible to focus on care, helping the weak and place importance on modesty without at the same time believing that community means more than the individual. People should care not necessarily for the collective good, but just as much for their own sake and their own values. In Denmark, feminine values such as care and support dominate, but Danes also believe in the individual's right to think independently of what others think and to find their own identity independently of the group. However, Danes score highly on institutional collectivism (the desire for protection and equality guaranteed by various institutions), which we looked at earlier, and this can very well be the tendency which in Hofstede scores Danes extremely low on masculinity parameters.

Hofstede does not measure feminine values, only the masculine ones. The higher an MAS score a country has, the more the masculine values push the feminine into the background. It is due to more people in these countries concurring with masculine values rather than with feminine values[5].

---

5  Shalom Schwartz also has a value here which correlates with Hofstede and supports his results. Schwartz calls the masculine characteristic "Achievement".

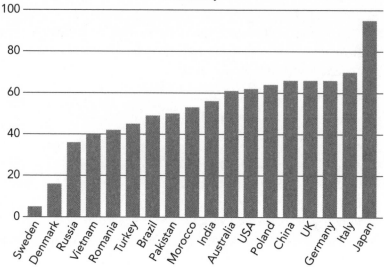

As clearly shown, Scandinavia is an extreme here too. The variations on a global basis are however not so great for this parameter. Japan is at one extreme and Sweden at the other. Once again the internal differences within Scandinavia can be clearly seen. Whereas Danes are perceived by many Swedes as being noisy and lacking in seriousness, Swedes have conversely a much greater preference for listening and letting others speak. Even though Danes are mother hens outside Scandinavia, they quickly take on the role of gorillas within the region. "The Italians of the North", as they are called in Sweden, or: "Southern Europe? – that starts on the Danish side of the Øresund Bridge", as some of my Swedish friends said when I lived in Stockholm.

- - - - - - - - - - - - - - - - - - - - - - - - - - - - - - - - - - - - - - - - - - - - -

**When Thor Pedersen declared war on Sweden**
Back in 1993, when Sweden declared that Barsebäck, the nuclear power station across the Øresund strait from Copenhagen (which was temporarily shut down), would be switched back on again that summer, the then Danish Interior Minister Thor Pedersen, said that he realised it was against the law, but that he was inclined to stop Barsebäck opening using military means. "Unfortunately, the law does not give me the opportunity to ask

the Defence Minister to send the Navy, the Army or the Air Force across to Sweden, even though I would like to", he said.

This enraged Swedish Prime Minister Carl Bildt so much that he said that Thor Pedersen's words had started a serious crisis between the two countries. "Pedersen's statement shows a gross lack of knowledge and also has a tone which I find incompatible with the atmosphere which we ought to have in Nordic cooperation," said Bildt, who was going to protest formally to Danish Prime Minister Poul Schlüter about the Interior Minister.

I am sure many people in Denmark still remember Thor Pedersen as a typically masculine personality who sometimes appeared rather brash. In any event, that is what people perceived him as in Sweden. It may be that Sweden also has people like Thor Pedersen, there just aren't as many of them as there are in Denmark.

The issue disappeared of its own accord, but it definitely confirmed the prejudices the two Scandinavian peoples have about each other. The Swedes got confirmation that Danes are loud and self-promoting and can't take anything seriously. The Danes got confirmation that the world's shortest book is still *Five Hundred Years of Swedish Humour*.

- - - - - - - - - - - - - - - - - - - - - - - - - - - - - - - - - - - - - - - - - - - - - -

## Gender differences are good and natural – versus gender differences should be limited

Masculine societies have a tendency to emphasise the differences between the genders, which is not so strange as the differences are often to the benefit of men. In that way, they get their own values presented as the valid ones. Of course, doing that gives power and influence. This means that masculine values such as a competitive mentality, elbow-pushing, self-promotion and being very ambitious are valued more in masculine societies than feminine values such as care, "room for everyone" and obedience are. According to Hofstede, this also means that men in masculine societies behave in more "classically masculine" ways, whereas the women also behave in more "typically feminine" ways. In other words, the women drift towards the kitchen and the family.

If women are to have any hope of success in masculine societies, they therefore often need to behave more like men and put their feminine characteristics on hold. That is precisely what can be seen in Japan and Italy, for example, where a large group of progressive women simply choose not to have children or families and to behave entirely on men's terms. That is why the birth rate is dropping so dramatically in both countries. Neither of the two countries is geared to help career women who also want families. It is the men who have careers and the women who stay at home – unless the career women behave like men. This means that they have to make a conscious choice not to have families, not that they must not *be like* women in appearance. Quite the opposite, because masculine societies are very obsessed with visible gender differences and so women in those societies are decidedly more feminine in their appearance (make-up and clothes which emphasise the female figure) than in the feminine Scandinavian cultures. Just think of the southern European women who would never dream of going down to the corner shop to buy milk without putting their make-up on.

Compared to Japan and Italy, it is much easier in feminine societies such as Denmark to be a woman and also be successful (however, not as easy as it maybe *ought* to be). That is because feminine values also play a role in *general* culture. In other words, values which Danes in general – including men – exhibit as regards being caring and looking after each other rather than focussing only on self-promotion.

In fact, Danish anthropologist Anne Knudsen believes that Denmark has become an extremely feminine society in the past 20 to 30 years, something which is noticeable, for example, in schools.

-----------------------------------------------------------

In Danish schools, any type of competition between pupils off the sports field is looked down on. Even on the sports field, competitions are sometimes changed to just be "collaboration" without any performance requirements (…) the models of how they should be dealt with have all along been identical with what society as a whole connects with femininity. So it can't be any surprise that girls routinely do better than boys at the social aspects of rivalry in school (…) no wonder that two thirds of the boys leave school as soon as they can with a sigh of relief.
Anne Knudsen, *Things are good here, send more money*

-----------------------------------------------------------

The average masculinity index for the Middle East is 52. So it is not at all strange that boys from Middle East societies have such difficulty coping with the Danish school system, as its values are diametrically opposed to those in their families' countries of origin. The strong self-confidence they are instilled with as young boys is completely deflated when they get to a Danish school. People there are not impressed with their cocky attitude, in fact a Danish schoolteacher is more likely to be irritated by their attitude. Middle East girls in Denmark, however, just like Danish girls, do much better than their brothers do.

In masculine societies, people get used to competition right from the outset. So mothers from a masculine cultural background find it quite normal to talk about their sons' (and if necessary daughters') good grades over lunch in the canteen. That works fine in masculine societies, but in a Danish canteen it is easy to be met by a wall of prejudiced silence very quickly. In Denmark, people do not boast or talk about being better than others.

This strong concept of equality is well-suited to smooth feminine cultures where gender differences are not talked about at all. "In reality, we are all the same", people say. So in feminine societies, people try to downplay gender differences and assert that they don't really exist. Internally within Scandinavia, it is also the Swedes who have the most assertive debate about gender roles. The Swedes focus much more on equality than people do in the (in this regard) much more traditional, masculine Denmark.

**External values – what people respect in masculine societies**
- Self-confidence
- Rhetorical abilities and a strong and clear voice
- Smart and expensive clothes – which match your gender
- For men: the ability to impress and preferably oppress women (especially in Latin America and Southern Europe's so-called *macho cultures*).
- Domineering behaviour

**Inner values – what people respect in feminine societies**
- Modesty
- Listening

- Sensible and practical clothes (too much decoration and bling-bling are regarded as vulgar)
- Showing feelings and care (a tear in the eye is not a problem)
- Inclusive behaviour

A classic example of the difference can be seen in Silvio Berlusconi, Italy's former prime minister, who is considered to be vulgar and quite simply "over the top" in Denmark. Almost a comical figure with all his attitude and arm-waving. Conversely, many Italians see the same behaviour as an expression of vigour and certainty (even though many Italians also deplore him and have done so for a very long time!).

I often get Danish participants on my courses to say their full name out loud and clearly. Now! This request is as a rule followed by a rather embarrassing mumble. So I ask them again, clearly and unambiguously, and people say afterwards that it is something that they don't really like; proclaiming their own name in such a way. If they are to cope in masculine societies – which despite everything dominate the world – then that is something Danes need to learn to be better at from the guests who have come to their country from elsewhere. So if you come from a more masculine society than Denmark – and most people do – maybe you could help them a little here?

**Different motivation**

In the example in the introduction, Bill was concentrating on his bonus. His work was a competition between him and all the other hungry wolves, and his need was to get to the finishing line first. In masculine societies, people reward other people (sometimes the group if the masculine society is collectivist, or the individual if the society is individualistic). People take care to emphasise the performance and make it shine. The good performance becomes an example to follow, and people love being rewarded by having others copy them.

In masculine societies, the whole incentive structure is laid out according to this cultural trait. There are pictures of the employee of the month in the canteen and frequent bonus schemes where the winner of the month is announced. No one is ashamed of being singled out for praise.

Benny's Danish world is quite different. To many Danes, there is nothing more anxiety provoking then being singled out in front of others with their name and picture. So rewards are given rather differently in Denmark, with a boss often giving a bonus to the whole department. So it is called a Christmas bonus or is a collective reward for a well-deserved contract which *everyone* can be proud of.

It goes without saying that non-Danish managers who come from masculine cultures have to get used to the fact that they can't just introduce bonus schemes and "employee of the month" into a Danish company, as people will quickly be embarrassed by their own success. In any event, masculine managers need to learn that Danes do not necessarily value public praise and appreciation. Praise has to be given in private. For an Italian or an American who likes to bask in the spotlight and have their results rewarded, Scandinavians appear extremely strange. Which they are.

Conversely, Danes who are managers in masculine societies or are managing primarily masculine staff need to overcome the feminine resistance to rewarding people individually, and instead consider starting competitions among the staff and praising people in public. You simply have to do more arm-waving. "That wasn't so bad", which in Danish means that something is really good, is just not good enough when an American expects to hear that it was "great" or "fantastic". We will look more closely how Danish managers motivate in Chapter 15.

## Meetings of opposites
### Problems for masculine cultures in encounters with more feminine ones

Masculine cultures perceive feminine cultures as weak and without very much consistency. It sometimes appears as if people are more interested in the victims than the strong ones, and it can seem very unjust for people used to masculine values. Men can appear as wimps who are being whipped. From the masculine point of view it can appear that the men have sold out their values and gone for nappy changing, relaxing with the family and demanding to talk about their feelings. That is how Danes in particular appear to many Germans, Americans and people from the Middle East.

Sometimes it can be difficult to see what it is that motivates people in a feminine society when there is so little reward for doing something extra. Income tax for the higher paid is often high in feminine societies – much too high, people in masculine cultures believe.

Another trait of feminine cultures is that people go home from work relatively early and like to maintain a strict work / life balance. In Denmark and the rest of Scandinavia, people therefore go home significantly earlier than in more masculine societies. So leaving the office at 4 pm to collect their children can make Danes seem rather lazy. Which means that Danes working in a masculine culture need to consider whether they want their colleagues' respect or whether they can make different arrangements at home. You can't do both. And definitely not if you are a manager.

Conversely, people in the feminine Danish culture have a heavy responsibility to explain to people from masculine cultures that staying in the office until 6 pm doesn't necessarily get you any bonus points in a Danish company. Especially not if your colleagues *know* that you have family at home. In fact, in Denmark you can lose a lot of respect that way, because Danes do not value people who *seemingly* place their work above spending time with their families. It is a secret code which can often be difficult for masculine *expats* in Denmark to crack.

**Good advice when encountering a feminine culture (for example Denmark)**

- Make sure you tone down all visible signs of status – car, clothing, jewellery etc.
- Avoid being very dominant, and make sure that everyone gets time to speak and is heard.
- Make sure you don't boast too much and talk about yourself a lot – people will find out easily enough whether you are capable and have the right skills. In Denmark, it can be seen as a sign of untrustworthiness if you keep on talking too much about your own achievements.
- Remember to show some self-irony now and again and make fun of yourself.
- If you have done something really good, then remember the Danes will put a high value on you also emphasising that you couldn't have done it without the "whole team".
- For men especially:

- Remember there is nothing unusual about being a woman, having a career and children at the same time. So there is no need to "praise" women for that choice. They would consider that very inappropriate as it is quite natural that there are completely equal conditions for men and women (even though the truth is often different).
- Helping women to their seats, paying the bill in the restaurant and complimenting female staff on their clothes or in any other way emphasising the difference between the genders by gallantry and innocent flirting at work – in general that is unwanted behaviour.

## Problems for feminine cultures in encounters with more masculine ones

Feminine cultures find masculine cultures to be extremely aggressive and self-centred. It seems like they don't see anyone else except themselves. In feminine cultures, people are more afraid of the thought of all the "weak" people who are not looked after by the gorillas of the world. Masculine aspects appear rather "primitive" and concerned with banal status symbols rather than real and inner values. To people with more feminine values, masculine societies seem in general to be more superficial. And it also seems like women are the losers in masculine societies.

### Good advice for encounters with a masculine culture
- Make sure you are smartly dressed and ooze success
- Speak clearly, unambiguously and with authority (with some exceptions, see next chapter)
- Avoid making yourself appear less significant than you are; emphasise your qualities frequently
- You can be rather hard in negotiations
- For men:
  - Don't suddenly stand up during the meeting and say: sorry, I have to go pick up my children (find a different and more macho excuse).
  - You can definitely be extra gallant to women and show in every way that you are a member of the stronger sex and with plenty of energy (because that is how they see you).

### The path to cultural intelligence

Benny should of course have "been macho" and said "yes I am the expert in this particular area so listen to what I am going to tell you to do". That would have given him respect with Bill, because Bill is used to people who aren't really capable of anything saying that they actually are. People oversell themselves.

For Bill it is quite normal for the workers to compete for bonuses and the like – it's all about finishing first. Among proud old Danish workers people would once have been (or maybe still are) called creeps or crawlers if they stuck their neck out too much and worked too hard. That is not how people see things in the USA, where there is no one to inflate your balloon for you – you have to do it yourself.

### Prepare:
- If you are getting a visit from people from more masculine cultures, then prepare some good old masculine pursuits (for the men) for when you are finished, and expect the women to prefer something else (ask them).
- When you send colleagues into masculine societies make sure that they are given "authority" to take with them: business cards, good hotel, expense account – everything has to be top-class (even if they don't perhaps ask for it themselves).
- As a woman who wants to achieve things professionally, consider whether you want to sacrifice time and money on a professional stylist. Travel only in your best clothes, and make sure that your shoes, bags and make up etc. are faultless.
- Consider sending men to negotiations in more masculine societies – if the others do too. I'm sorry, but the choice is between being politically correct or optimising your chances for good results. Choose your battles and remember to send female staff for the tasks where people have a less stereotypical picture of what women can and cannot do – they should not suffer from the fact that not everywhere is as equal as we are in Northern Europe.

### Test the temperature of the water:
- Use the jargon. If there is a lot of positioning and gorilla noise, then find a role for yourself. Do you want to be businesslike and stick to the issue, or beat your chest like a gorilla? Find your own way of doing things and don't do anything you find directly

unpleasant. Conversely – if you want to take part in the status battle, then don't hold back.

- On the other hand, if you find that there is an unpleasant silence if you have spoken far too much and dominated the conversation too much, then hold back and remember to give other people the chance to speak.

**Learn from / explain to:**

- Colleagues from masculine societies have to learn that staff in, for example, Denmark are not impressed by all their qualifications, dangerous little stunts, aggressive behaviour and other status symbols, but at best think it's just a little bit childish. That is one of the most significant reasons why young men from Middle East immigrant families are often considered by many Danes to deserve a clip round the ear. Their constant loud behaviour is necessary for them to gain respect within their own culture. In Denmark, however, they are unfortunately perceived as rude and self-centred. If those types of young guys from masculine cultures don't learn to understand how they appear to others, they will continue to repel people. Both Danes and non-Danes have a responsibility to explain this to each other.

- Ask your local sources what gives respect and impact in their masculine cultures. What impresses people, and what doesn't? Conversely, ask the same question about feminine cultures: what causes trustworthiness and causes people to like you?

# 11

## May I show my feelings?

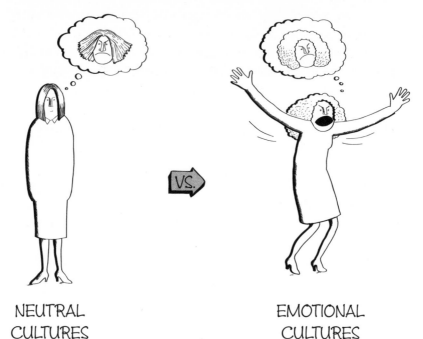

NEUTRAL
CULTURES

VS.

EMOTIONAL
CULTURES

---

**Road Rage in Bangkok**

Jakob has arrived in Bangkok in Thailand the evening before a meeting with a large supplier. He leaves his hotel in plenty of time and climbs into a taxi well prepared and well rested. From that point on, everything goes wrong.

The taxi driver drives like a madman, and the chaotic city that morning is also full of people, animals and large trucks on the way to various different markets, meaning the taxi is just constantly stuck in traffic. So the taxi driver tries lots of different routes which take them a long way away from everything, and meanwhile the meter is still ticking and ticking.

It is clear that the driver couldn't care less that Jakob has repeatedly told him that he will be late for his meeting, and Jakob also suspects that the driver is using the chaotic traffic as an excuse to take an extra long route. The taxi driver keeps saying that he doesn't understand, and Jakob doesn't dare get out of the taxi to find another one for fear of starting from scratch.

When Jakob finally arrives very late at the meeting he is extremely embarrassed, even though the Thais are apparently unconcerned and just smile.

Jacob really wants to express how frustrated he is over the situation and that it definitely isn't his fault. To show how he REALLY wants to apologise, and how much it is the taxi driver's fault, Jakob tells them excitedly about the situation to emphasise that he is REALLY upset by what happened.

Very surprisingly the Thais then say that they think he should just go back to his hotel, lie down and relax. "We'll call you again later." Jakob is rather surprised, but does what they say.

The problem is that they never contact Jakob again. Instead, they cancel all their meetings with him and ask his company to send a different person because – as they say – they are "not comfortable doing business with Jakob."

------------------------------------------------------------

Why do people in the East always smile? Day in and day out? Even if you suddenly fall down in the middle of the street, they still keep smiling and nodding in a friendly way. It is as if nothing bothers people in South East Asia. The same applies to Africa (especially Ethiopia and Somalia). You quickly find out that it's pointless getting annoyed or using capital letters. Things work much better with friendly and understanding smiles. People imply, rather than show what they mean by raising their voices and their body language. They keep their arms down, talk quietly and understandingly and preferably with a lot of long pauses.

So there are big differences between how emotional we are from culture to culture. A small difference at first glance, but a very significant difference when it comes to cultural understanding and inter-cultural communication.

## A question of volume

People differ very greatly in how much they use things other than words to communicate what they mean. Some people use their hands or their tone of voice much more to help get the message across. The differences are large both at the individual level and the regional level. Danes in Jutland generally use their arms much less and pepper their expressions with less emotion than people in Copenhagen do. Just as there are differences between countries, there are also differences within countries.

Such divisions, as I make in this book, can only be rules of thumb, but they are useful rules of thumb and they are always better then knowing nothing.

Here are some of the characteristics of emotionally "expressive" and "neutral" cultures respectively:

------

**Neutral cultures**
- Prefer subdued behaviour and speech
- Limited gesticulations
- (Sometimes) perceive agitation as an indication of mental instability
- Like long pauses
- Can appear tense (to the more expressive)
- Monotone speech
- Self-control rules!
- Can explode emotionally if pushed too hard (tears and fury)

------

------

**Expressive cultures**
- Like expressive behaviour and talking loudly
- Extensive gesticulations
- Agitation is considered a sign of strong commitment
- Feel uncomfortable with long pauses and try to fill them in
- Can appear hysterical
- Varying tone of voice

- Being there rules!
- Constantly "let off steam" so that real outbreaks of anger can be limited

---------------------------------------------------------------

## Self-control versus commitment

In neutral cultures, cool headedness and self-control are the be-all and end-all. You can tell that a person is serious about his ability to curb his feelings and behave in a self controlled manner. So shouting and screaming in a neutral culture can quickly mean that you are perceived as someone about to have a mental breakdown. In such cultures, strong feelings are only made public if you really, really can't keep them under control. Conversely, in expressive societies people believe that feelings are an indication that you are personally committed to something.

One of my colleagues was teaching Danish and had a Thai woman in one of his classes. She repeatedly didn't do her homework or worse, simply did not turn up. At the time, my colleague was unaware of how extremely emotionally shy Thais are, and gave her a serious talking to in front of the whole class. The Thai woman smiled and smiled during the reprimand, and my colleague became more and more provoked by this apparent indifference to the justifiable criticism. Suddenly the facade cracked, and the Thai woman started to cry like a little child.

The change was very sudden and shocking to everyone, but it is very typical for neutral cultures that there is no intermediate stage. People don't want to lose face to the group, and at the same time they are embarrassed when someone does not have the necessary self-control – in this case the Danish teacher. That creates enormous uncertainty, and suddenly they just can't go on. Just like everyone else, neutral people quite naturally also have an emotional life behind the facade. They just don't show it every day. So they almost only have two states: all sluices closed, or all sluices open. People prefer the disarming smile and keeping a large emotional distance. It can seem very provocative, and so it is very important that you don't allow yourself to be provoked and get angry. You should also expect handshakes to be surprisingly limp. That can seem uncommitted and frightful to us. So try to adapt your own handshake so that the difference is not too great.

It is all about what codes you are used to. For a Vietnamese, it seems overkill to use emotions, because they are not necessary. Words are regarded as sufficient. In Latin America people expect emotions as part of the communication, as they back up the words used. If emotions are not shown, the Latin Americans perceive them as "missing".

A particular type of physical behaviour often comes in expressive cultures. People stand closer together, maybe touch each other and are not afraid of giving a friendly pat to the person they are talking to. That is quite normal in Southern Europe and Latin America, and people are not afraid of coming close to each other when talking in the Middle East either.

### Who is what?

It is difficult to graduate parameters such as expressive versus neutral, but it is reasonable to divide things into three categories. An extremely expressive, a moderately expressive and a neutral category. They are summarised here, partly using Richard Gesteland's and Trompenaar's and Hampden-Turner's studies.[6]

| Expressive | Moderately expressive | Neutral |
|---|---|---|
| Italy, Brazil, the Arab world | Russia, Romania, Poland, Germany, Sweden, Denmark, UK, USA, Australia, Pakistan | China, Japan, India, Vietnam |

As can be seen, expressive cultures are particularly widespread in Catholic countries and the Middle East. This does not mean that all Muslim countries are like that, as Indonesia, for example, is excessively emotionally neutral. On the other hand, most Arabic countries are at the top of the scale, and I'm sure that most people have experienced a souvenir trader in an Egyptian or Tunisian bazaar with their aggressive, loud and insisting style of negotiation which seems much too direct and rather unpleasant if you are not from that culture.

It is the middle group which is the most interesting. There, the emotion shown depends on the situation, and what people allow themselves to do and feel happy doing. Compared with *Latinos*,

---

6  Morocco is not included as the data from there is too uncertain.

Danes are of course much colder, but just like Italians they can also enjoy bringing some emotions into a business situation. Swedes, however, think that doing so is not serious enough, as they are slightly more neutral than Danes and keep their feelings more private. Englishmen also like to keep a stiff upper lip professionally, but enjoy heavy irony and sarcastic jokes to interrupt the solemnity, yet still keep their emotional distance.

The Chinese can in fact be expressive in day-to-day life, but they generally remember their traditional "Mianzi" principle. Mianzi tells them that aggression can cause other people to lose face and that it is better to hold back.

In any event, it is important to know that agitation rarely leads to anything in Asia. It is most extreme in Vietnam, Laos, Thailand and other South East Asian countries. Raising your voice very slightly means that they will quickly be afraid that you are angry with them. On the other hand, you often have to prick up your ears in order to hear what they are actually saying in their oh-so-soft voices.

### How do we talk to each other – with and without words

Eye contact is generally important in expressive cultures. If your gaze is not intense enough and directed directly at the person you're talking to, people can quickly feel hurt or think that you are too distant, are hiding something or maybe even upset. In Northern Europe, people are used to not needing to look especially intensely at a shop assistant, or stare into the face of someone they are having a conversation with. In Spain, for example, it can quickly be perceived as rude if you constantly look around elsewhere. When you are having a conversation, you express your presence with your eyes. What is most important is not the words but the whole expression.

Make sure you keep eye contact with people in the Arabic world, the Mediterranean, and in Latin America – at least if they are on the same "level" as you (it can be different with children who have been taught to look down as a sign of respect). More relaxed eye contact, as we know it, is found in most of Northern Europe and North America. In Korea, Thailand and Africa south of the Sahara, there should be less, and in the rest of Asia eye contact is decidedly lacking. A much too direct look there, can simply be regarded as a hostile and aggressive act, so you shouldn't think that people are not interested just because they avoid your gaze. They are doing it purely out of politeness.

Not even the way people speak to each other is the same from one country to another, and again there is a tendency for the differences to have something to do with the emotional commitment. Nancy J. Adler, an American expert in international management, has looked at how we use pauses differently.

For some people, pauses are deadly and embarrassing, and they have to be filled with words as quickly as possible. Others dwell on the silence and do not find it unpleasant. These differences can also be found between cultures.

If you look at the way we talk to each other, it is obvious that the more expressive cultures, such as those in Latin America, like to interrupt and fill the breaks in conversation as soon as they can. Americans, who are at the moderate part of the emotional scale, prefer exchanging conversation without long pauses. But in Asia silence is golden, and people do not look around nervously when no one is saying anything. Such silences are almost physical torture for the more chatty Latinos, and neither do Northern Europeans like too much silence. We immediately think that something is wrong, but that doesn't need to be the case. For example, in Japan people like to say... and well... then wait a long time... just to let the words sink in...

In Adler's graphic presentation, the conversation patterns look like this for the three countries selected:

## SPEECH PATTERNS

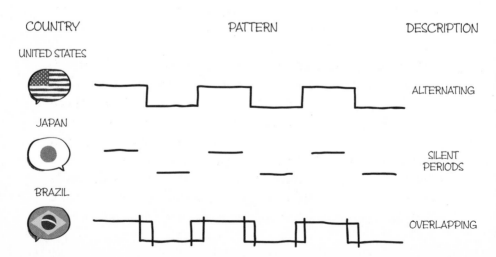

| COUNTRY | PATTERN | DESCRIPTION |
|---|---|---|
| UNITED STATES | | ALTERNATING |
| JAPAN | | SILENT PERIODS |
| BRAZIL | | OVERLAPPING |

Physical contact also varies a lot. In the study above, Brazilians touched each other and their guests on average 4.7 times in a 30-minute conversation. The Japanese and Americans didn't touch each other at all.

If you want to see for yourself, then try watching various different countries' TV programmes and see how their debate programmes are. On Italian and Spanish TV, it is obvious that people like to interrupt and get agitated a lot, but even Danish and Swedish debates are very different from each other. In Sweden, people wait politely just as Americans do (mostly) for the other person to finish, whereas Danes are again the Nordic Italians when it comes to this. Their tone is slightly harder, slightly more theatrical and with a lot more interruptions. There is a shorter route into people's emotions in Denmark than in Sweden.

Gesticulations are a completely independent subject with large variations from country to country. The best thing you can do is to once again look at what other people do and ask what it means *before* you interpret their gestures from your own culture's standpoint. A good example is the head wobbling or bobbling which Indians practice. For the culturally untrained, it can seem to be head shaking, but that is most definitely not what it is. When Indians move their head from side to side it just means: "I hear what you say" or "I'm with you completely". It is an indication of attention and not rejection.

## Meetings of opposites
**Expressive cultures perceive neutral cultures as** cold, unfeeling and slightly boring. In addition, the more expressive cultures quickly fear that someone is bored – and not least that they themselves will get bored. When struck by silence, they can quickly fear that the others have something to hide or that maybe they themselves have said something wrong. Neutral people can appear lacking in imagination and grey and give the impression of being highly disciplined and conforming.

**Neutral cultures perceive expressive cultures as** feigned, possibly aggressive and a little too intrusive. It is difficult to find out how much is facade and theatre and how much they actually really mean. From the carpet trader who appears to be dreadfully hurt that you don't want to buy his fine goods, to the business associate who moans about how high your price is. People from neutral cultures never completely know where they are with their expressive guests or hosts and often end up with a rather cramped smile and a not insignificant amount of scepticism (the latter is not completely wrong, because a lot of it definitely is theatre).

### The path to cultural intelligence

There is no use getting agitated if you want something done in a country like Thailand, so Jakob should have counted to ten and accepted things as they were or ordered the taxi driver to stop so he could have found a new one. It is not at all unusual to be late for a meeting in Thailand, and everyone understands that the traffic in Bangkok can be really dreadful and unpredictable. Jakob thought that his agitation would generate sympathy. He wanted to show that he was really sorry. The Thais did not doubt his sincerity, but they in any case did not become more convinced when he raised his voice.

When we use emotions in communication, it is to underline the importance of what we are saying, but the volume controls are just set a little differently from country to country. The best thing you can do is to listen and ask your informants and other people with local knowledge. When an Arab gets excited about something on the phone, it could very well be much less important to him than it immediately sounds. On the other hand, a slightly insistent Japanese voice can be an indication that there is a really serious problem which requires your attention immediately. The best thing you can do is be aware of the fact that you cannot just listen for the same signals you do when communicating with someone from your own cultural background. Switch off your autopilot and sharpen your awareness.

### Prepare:

- Choose your people culturally intelligently. If you are a manager, then send your staff to the culture that best matches their personality. Some of us are more expressive by nature than others, and we get better results in countries where people are generally more expressive too. So don't send your bad-tempered salesman to Thailand.

**Test the temperature of the water:**
- This is exactly where you do need to test the temperature of the water. Look at how expressive your surroundings are and try to match them as well as you can. Look for:
  - Voice: loud or soft
  - Eye contact: fixed, flickering or completely evasive
  - Touch: (how firm is a handshake, and how long does it last)
  - Distance: (how close do people stand to each other)
- Everyone has different levels for how emotionally they get involved. Notice what other people do *before* you find your own level.
- Respond to expressive cultures with just as much warmth and willingness as they give you (they can quickly withdraw it. You have the right to do the same).

**Learn from / explain to:**
- If you have staff from extremely expressive cultures, then it is a good idea to warn them about how they impact others.
- If you are in any doubt about how close you have got to your very expressive and jovial new "friends" and how sincere they have been, then always ask your informant with local knowledge for an honest answer. He will (if he's good) tell you honestly what is good and bad with even the most immediately open-hearted and close business associate. And what is empty rhetoric and what is genuine.

**Understand**
- Remember that neutral cultures are not cold and unfeeling, they just don't have a particularly well-developed language to communicate emotions in public. So they really don't know how they should show emotions, or deal with people who are more open than they are.
- Remember that expressive cultures are not superficial in their own world. There, they are accommodating and human. They just like there to be something personal and committed in their work. Sometimes it looks as if they are arguing with each other, but that isn't necessarily what they're doing.

# 12

## Is time a limited resource? (tomorrow)

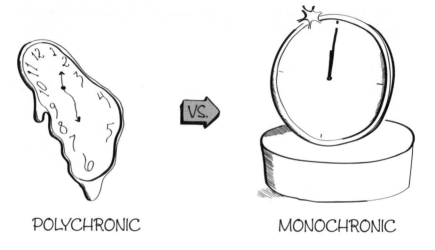

POLYCHRONIC        VS.        MONOCHRONIC

---

### A visit from India

A Danish company which sells precision measuring equipment receives a visit from a salesperson from India. A woman from a good, stable supplier who they have looked forward to seeing. She will be meeting lots of other potential buyers, but her visit to this company is the first meeting on her agenda.

The meeting is scheduled for 10 o'clock in the morning, and everyone is sitting ready and waiting. She doesn't appear, even though they wait several hours for her. By the time it gets to lunchtime and she has still not appeared, those present agree that they will have to carry on with the other meetings planned for that afternoon. But at the very moment everyone is leaving the meeting room, the Indian woman appears.

She explains that she overslept, as she had slept badly because of jet lag. Then she had difficulty finding the address in the car she had hired. The purchasing manager explains to her that unfortunately they have some other meetings now, and that all their diaries are full for the rest of the week, but maybe they could find time at the end of the day on Friday by staying at work a little longer. Unfortunately, that is the day when the Indian salesperson is going home again, so it can't be done.

She doesn't say very much to the Danish buyers, but when she gets home her conclusion from the visit is very clear. "You travel halfway around the world and they don't have time for you just because you're a little bit late. I have never experienced such impolite behaviour before. It's right what they say about Europeans, that they are inflexible and lack decency and politeness".

-----------------------------------------------------------

Doing business outside safe, regulated Scandinavia can be something of a trial when you quickly find out that people regard time in very different ways in different parts of the world. In the chapter about Danes, we saw how their tendency to go by the calendar and precise times can appear very impersonal and flexible to people like the anthropologist Prakash Reddy, who saw things from an Indian perspective. Similarly, the Indian woman above goes back to her own countrymen with the impression of having been grossly under-prioritised.

In her culture, they would have dropped everything else they were doing when something extraordinary happens, and showing such willingness is a mark of respect. It simply doesn't occur to very many people in Asia and South East Asia that an abstract appointment in a calendar cannot simply be moved to a different day because it is given a higher priority than the guest who has just arrived from the other side of the world. Flexibility in their world is an expression for being able to *determine the importance* of events. They are thus able to reprioritise *on an ongoing basis* in India (and as we will soon see, many other places too), when they determine that something – or someone – is more important than what they are doing right now. The latter is especially important in countries where personal relationships are more important than abstract times in a calendar. There, people are willing to change their plans from one moment to the next if someone is shown to be important enough. That is why the Indian woman was so angry. The Danish company showed quite clearly that she wasn't important enough. That shows a lack of respect and means that she lost face. "Why on earth can't they give me a higher priority?" she thinks, and the only answer she can find is that they simply didn't think she was somebody worth doing that for.

## When time goes in circles and doesn't move forward

The American anthropologist Edward T. Hall was the first to describe these two opposing perceptions of time using the terms "polychronic societies" and "monochronic societies". The first of these is better illustrated by circular movement, where the second is more like a straight line.

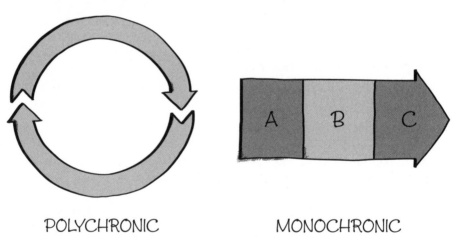

POLYCHRONIC                    MONOCHRONIC

**Polychronic cultures** are characterised by time being perceived as an infinite resource. What you don't get done now can just be done later. More time will come tomorrow, next week or next year. Time renews itself constantly, and the new time that comes along is no different from the time that has passed. In reality, everything just repeats itself[7].

---

7  This perception is, for example, core to Indian Hinduism as well as Buddhism, which is derived from it.

More haste less speed, and tasks don't necessarily have to be completed in the right order. In fact, several tasks can be done simultaneously. People start task A, then C, maybe then B and then back to A again. Getting things done on time is great, but that is not a goal in itself. People don't perceive what happens as being a consequence of what happened earlier to such a great extent. Things just happen, and this very "fatalist" attitude pervades everything they do.

Time is first and foremost dictated by social relationships. That means that things really only happen when someone is present. Periods when you are not together with others are empty periods, where time in effect stops. This also means that people seldom get the feeling of wasting time. Sitting and waiting three or four hours for a train that is late (something not at all abnormal in a polychronic society) is not a waste of time, as nothing actually *happened*. No human interaction = no time used. So polychronic people can seem extremely patient, while monochronic people can conversely appear very stressed to the polychronic: "What are they so busy with? There'll be more time in a moment which they can use instead!"

**Monochronic cultures,** on the other hand, have an almost constant focus on time. People there plan their time and are always aware of how long things must take. They plan almost everything they do, and they try to do everything they can to achieve their goals in the time decided in advance. Arriving late, or not getting things done on time are failures. Visible failures of their ability to plan.

A person's value is to a great extent determined by how punctual they are, and how good they are at getting things done on time. You can't let yourself be distracted by unforeseen events, but should plan for them so there is still time in the event of delays. What people are most nervous about is wasting other people's time.

In monochronic societies, people are very much concerned with consequences and how things not done in the right order are perceived as shoddy work. People there always start at page one. They arrive on time, and leave on time. They make appointments and don't like leaving things to intuition. They know when the meeting starts, and have asked people beforehand about the latest time they will have to leave. If the meeting goes over time, even by a couple of minutes, people start to fidget nervously. That wasn't what we agreed!

To sum up, this is how things look:

------------------------------------------------------------

**Monochronic cultures**
- Prefer to do one thing at a time
- Take schedules and deadlines very seriously
- Follow plans very precisely, especially the planned order of doing things
- Do not like interrupting other people
- Regard time as a limited resource
- Events are related to measurable time such as which year, which date or what time of day something happened

------------------------------------------------------------

------------------------------------------------------------

**Polychronic cultures**
- Can handle lots of things at once
- Are easily distracted
- Follow their intuition and feeling for the "big picture" more than they stick to plans
- Like using time on strengthening personal relationships
- Regard time as an infinite resource
- Events are perceived in regard to their relationship to other events: the year the eldest son was born, when the factory opened, etc.

------------------------------------------------------------

### Mañana

People in southern Europe or Latin America will most definitely know the expression *mañana* – tomorrow. What we haven't managed to get done today, we can do another day. You constantly find people are delayed because something else came up. It's even worse in Africa. There you should be happy if people actually turn up on the same day as agreed.

"Can't they tell the time?" is a typical culturally unintelligent reaction when monochronic people are waiting for someone polychronic to arrive. "Lazy bastards" is another. Of course they can tell the time. It's not because they don't realise that you are waiting for them. It just doesn't occur to them that you feel that the waiting is a waste of time. How can you be wasting time when nothing is happening? More time will be along shortly. Time is measured in people – not seconds, minutes and hours. They also automatically expect you to understand that they have been delayed because their brother called, the neighbour had to be driven to the dentist or because they had been up late the night before and had to catch up on their sleep. Things like that just happen.

Polychronic people do not regard themselves as lazy, just very flexible and human. As mentioned, it's more about who than about when, which is why you can find that meetings with polychronic people have a tendency to be interrupted constantly. In Asia, which is otherwise more and more running to "Western" time in many ways, you can still find that mobile phones ring almost constantly during a meeting and people run in and out of the room all the time. To us it seems disturbing and lacking in respect, but in fact it is what can be called "estimated importance". It is an ongoing evaluation of the importance of things. Maybe it was their daughter who rang and wanted to ask something. Don't you think that the daughter is more important than some random Dane? Of course she is. Always.

It's the same for you – regardless of which type of society you come from. Your daughter (or son, sister, father etc) is of course more important to you, but if you are monochronic you will argue that right now you are dealing with task A (holding a meeting) and that you can only find time for task B (returning your daughter's call) once you are finished with task A. That is not how polychronic people think – they prioritise here and now. So if you have become so culturally integrated into Denmark that your child has to be picked up from day care right now, then use that as an explanation to your polychronic partners from abroad. They will understand it more than you think. In any case, it is foolish to say that you have to do lots of other things (go to the dentist, shopping or whatever). They will not be able to understand that concept to the same extent. Unless you are a man and sitting with polychronic people with a very high masculinity score.

The journalist Louise Windfeld-Høeberg lives in Zimbabwe, and has hired a young woman, Tracy, to teach her about African culture. Including something about how people regard time in Africa:

African time is like an elastic band. You can wind it forward or backwards. You can stretch it or let it spring back. Boredom, being forced to do something or worst of all waiting and being forced to kill time, none of that happens. In Africa, you can not have too much or too little time.

The bus doesn't leave at 10:57, it leaves when it is full.

The meeting doesn't begin at 9 o'clock as it says on the invitation, the meeting begins when everyone has arrived. When nothing is happening, it is impossible for time to be wasted. Arriving too late has nothing to do with a lack of respect for other people. You come when you're ready.

"In the West, time controls you. In Africa, we control time," said Tracy. "Ask a white man if he's hungry, and he will look at his watch instead of feeling his stomach."

It really doesn't matter whether it is November or December. What matters is whether the rainy season has started or not, so you can get started with sowing your crops.

Quite. If only we could hold our summer holidays in Denmark according to the same principle. It doesn't matter if it's raining buckets during your holidays in July. You have to take your holidays at that time instead of staying at work. You can't wait for the sun to come out to decide to take time off.

- - - - - - - - - - - - - - - - - - - - - - - - - - - - - - - - - - - - - - - - - - - - - - - - - - -

## The art of planning

When I hold workshops for Danes, I don't always get everything covered I had planned to do. Because dialogue is very important and because there should always be time for unanticipated questions, time often runs out. It is also because, in my heart of hearts, I am myself slightly polychronic. Despite my own Danish background, adapting and prioritising people rather than the calendar and the time of day is simply easier for my own values to handle. Maybe that is why I never get to the last slides in my PowerPoint presentations. I never find teaching people from abroad who are from polychronic countries to be a problem. I can be sure that Danes will include in their evaluation of the course that it was disappointing that we didn't get through all the material. This is of course a complaint (as always in Denmark, one that is written between the lines). Something went wrong with my prioritisation.

I have to say that I usually get most things done on time, but sometimes there are a lot of very good questions or examples from the participants on a particular day. They don't have a particularly good understanding for that type of excuse, yet maybe the only reason they realised we missed something was that they could see in the handouts that there were a few slides that we didn't manage to go through.

Sometimes it is easy to sympathise with polychronic people who are much more realistic about determining what can actually be achieved. On the one hand, Danish participants expect the course leader to take questions, allow debate, input and examples, but on the other hand we also have to be finished exactly on time just as we would on a day when no one said or asked anything. It's not so surprising that we stress each other so much at work in the Nordic countries. We demand both precision and adaptability from our staff…

In polychronic cultures you can find people who seriously believe that they can have a conversation on the phone, deal with clients, put nail polish on and solve a crossword all at the same time. The same phenomenon can sometimes be seen here in Denmark among teenage girls working in bakeries, but otherwise it is something very characteristic of polychronic cultures. In Denmark, this behaviour only occurs when the boss has his back turned. In monochronic cultures, people look down on that type of behaviour. Concentrate on your work, young lady!

But if in fact she *can* get things done in that way, surely that's okay?

## Who is who?

Polychronic cultures are by far the most common in the world. According to Edward T. Hall, monochronic cultures are first and foremost a product of industrialisation, but Protestantism has also played a part. According to the German sociologist Max Weber (1864-1920), its focus on virtue, diligence and asceticism meant that Protestantism was the prerequisite for industrialisation and capitalism being able to appeal to people at all. Protestantism's focus on individual responsibility and the demands of industrial capitalism on people to arrive at the factory on time caused a completely new culture of time and obligation to be ingrained into the souls of people from Scandinavia, Germany, the Netherlands, Britain and America. The Catholic Church does not rear its members with a work and obligations ethic in the same way. People are not promised religious salvation in return for hard work, and in southern Europe many companies have found that it is difficult to get people to come to work on time, and difficult to get them to feel a sense of obligation to their work.

It may be that the working week is shorter in Protestant countries than in other places in the world, but if you don't do anything, you have a weak character. That type of behaviour is perceived as directly amoral in those parts of the world which have been most affected by protestant work ethics. "Hard work is its own reward", as people say, and "idle hands are the Devil's tools".

The experience of polychronic cultures is that they never really have control of things anyway, so they just shrug their shoulders when things go wrong. "Inshallah", as they say in the Middle East – "God's will". It can seem a little provocative to be met by this attitude when trying to do a deal. It's fate, or the will of God. So there is no point in always blaming individuals. The Lord works in mysterious ways, and what has happened has happened.

| How fast is your city? The average time (in seconds) it takes to walk 60 feet (18.3 metres), from the fastest to the slowest | |
|---|---|
| Singapore | 10.55 |
| Copenhagen | 10.82 |
| Madrid (Spain) | 10.89 |
| Guangzhou (China) | 10.94 |
| Dublin (Ireland) | 11.03 |
| Curitiba (Brazil) | 11.13 |
| Berlin (Germany) | 11.16 |

| How fast is your city? The average time (in seconds) it takes to walk 60 feet (18.3 metres), from the fastest to the slowest | |
| --- | --- |
| New York (USA) | 12.00 |
| Utrecht (Netherlands) | 12.04 |
| Vienna (Austria) | 12.06 |
| Warsaw (Poland) | 12.07 |
| London (UK) | 12.17 |
| Zagreb (Croatia) | 12.20 |
| Prag (Czech Republic) | 12.35 |
| Wellington (New Zealand) | 12.62 |
| Paris (France) | 12.65 |
| Stockholm (Sweden) | 12.75 |
| Ljubljana (Slovenia) | 12.76 |
| Tokyo (Japan) | 12.83 |
| Ottawa (Canada) | 13.72 |
| Harare (Zimbabwe) | 13.92 |
| Sofia (Bulgaria) | 13.96 |
| Taipei (Taiwan) | 14.00 |
| Cairo (Egypt) | 14.18 |
| Sana'a (Yemen) | 14.29 |
| Bucharest (Romania) | 14.36 |
| Dubai (United Arab Emirates) | 14.64 |
| Damascus (Syria) | 14.94 |
| Amman (Jordan) | 15.95 |
| Bern (Switzerland) | 17.37 |
| Manama (Bahrain) | 17.69 |
| Blantyre (Malawi) | 31.60 |

In short, monochronic cultures are to be found in those parts of the world where Protestantism dominates, whereas Catholic countries, and broadly speaking all other cultures in the world, are predominantly polychronic. When I say predominantly, it is important to remember that many traditionally polychronic cultures have learned to adapt to (north) Western conditions, as they have also gone through industrialisation and needed to clock in and out at work. Asia has come very far with this, and there you can be quite sure that meetings will start on time. In southern Europe, Latin America and to the greatest extent Africa, you will still find that time is treated much more loosely. Or as the cultural researcher Richard Gesteland puts it: "The closer you get to the Equator, the slower the clock seems to run".

Out of our 18 countries, the decidedly monochronic countries are thus (as well as Denmark): Sweden, USA, UK, Poland, Germany and Australia. The rest are polychronic to a greater or lesser degree. In countries such as Japan, people tend to keep to their appointments, but the general polychronic spirit is maintained because people still in principle regard time as circular and keep to social time, yet they have also imported linear monochronic time into their working life, transport and a number of other areas. That sort of behaviour is of course extra sneaky, because the apparent monochronic Japanese suddenly, without warning, exhibit typical polychronic behaviour by prioritising family and relationships just as we thought we were dealing with something quite different. So things are rather more complicated...

### In the details

One thing is the country you come from or are in at a given moment, another thing is the specific context you are in in the particular country. Of course there are big differences between making an appointment for a meeting with several participants and an official agenda – in such cases, people in Asia, for example, will turn up on time. But it's much worse with unofficial socialising. The party, the reception or the private invitation. In such cases, it is normal for people to turn up very late, or that you are the only one to arrive at the agreed time.

In the Middle East, southern Europe and Latin America it is more the rule than the exception that a party you're invited to for 7 pm doesn't really get going until just before 10. It is only then that the guests start to arrive. If you come at the agreed time, you can easily risk the host not being dressed or not having started getting ready for the party. It would in fact be very inappropriate to turn up at the "agreed time".

In countries such as China, most people would arrive on time, and (well educated) Chinese have like Westerners, gained an understanding that you can "steal" and "waste" people's time. The problem there is more a question of confirming appointments repeatedly. If you have an agreed pick-up time with a dry cleaner's or an appointment with a restaurant for 2 pm, it is a good idea to call a couple times and get it confirmed. Once the day before, and once on the day itself. Asians are still not used to organising time in the same zealous way that we are, and so they can quickly "forget" an appointment.

### The path to cultural intelligence

As a rule, the worst misunderstandings between polychronic and monochronic cultures occur once the damage is done, and one side perceives the other as undisciplined and lazy (that is usually the perception of the monochronic ones), whereas the other party is taken aback by the lack of flexibility and the rigid attitude to schedules. In such situations, it is important to understand that these are just different views about what is important when people interact with each other.

Remember that polychronic societies also have a tendency to be societies where relationships mean a lot, so they are surprised that monochronic people are constantly looking at the time. "We are having a nice time, why does it seem like they're always wanting to leave?". In monochronic societies, people are used to constantly looking at the time. That doesn't mean that they're not enjoying themselves in your company. Sometimes they can be really upset to have to go, but they just have another appointment. Polychronic people would be more likely to drop the other appointment, whereas monochronic people do not feel they can. They feel so obligated, and they would scarcely admit that they had allowed too little time. Poor planning is a deadly sin in monochronic societies.

Of course, the Danish company in the example in the introduction could have *prepared* for meeting a potential polychronic culture. Booking up the rest of the week wasn't a very smart thing to do when they were trying to match the flexibility of an Indian. It would also have been a good idea to have offered to collect the Indian woman from her hotel.

**Prepare:**
- Allow plenty of time when visiting polychronic cultures for meetings
- Be flexible when dealing with polychronic people, allow plenty of extra time in your calendar if they are coming to visit you – make sure alternative times are available
- If you are travelling to polychronic countries, then have some other work with you to fill in the waiting time. Monochronic people get more annoyed at having to wait if they have nothing else to do.
- In monochronic societies such as Denmark, it is very important to keep appointments and deadlines. You can be very sure that someone who wants to have something ready at a particular time expects to receive things on time. No matter what. You cannot expect especially great flexibility so be realistic with the time you allow, otherwise you risk losing trust points.

**Test the temperature of the water:**
- Be aware of how detailed the schedule is that you are given. If there are precise times on everything, then you are in a monochronic society where the times must be followed. Don't get irritated by people not turning up when you expect them to, and just seemingly arriving when they feel like it. Try to see the relaxed pace as something calming – there is nothing you can do about it anyway.
- Pay attention to how people deal with delays and follow their example. For example, note whether people apologise for being late. Is it when they are three minutes late (the norm in Germany) five to ten minutes late (the norm in Scandinavia) or only when they turn up two to three hours late (the norm in numerous polychronic societies). Or when they don't arrive until the following day. Maybe. (Africa).

**Learn from / explain to:**
- If in doubt, then ask when they expect you to arrive. Limit this to private events and always make sure to turn up on time to

business meetings (remember that people in polychronic societies know that people like you arrive on time. What they expect *from each other* is something else).

- If you have polychronic staff, pupils or clients who arrive late or do not get work done on time, then explain to them why it is not a good idea. You can either argue rationally: There is a schedule which everyone expects everyone else to follow, and it makes other people's work difficult if you don't stick to it. In the long-term, you can't fit in well into a monochronic society if you don't learn to arrive on time. Alternatively, you can also get good results by making the argument personal: explaining why it means something to you that he or she delivers on time. Remember that polychronic societies are predominantly human and relationship oriented. They have more respect for the personal relationship to you than an abstract deadline.
- Argue overall for linear time with social time, understood as such that in reality it is about giving a high priority to other people (colleagues, clients, etc.) when getting things done on time or arriving on time.

**Understand:**
- Are you polychronic, then try to understand how much of this discipline is fundamentally human: namely concern about wasting other people's time. Monochronic people are enormously concerned about being efficient and as a rule, they will achieve far more in half an hour than polychronic people – even though the price of this is stress and overwork.
- If you are monochronic, then try to consider whether it might be nicer to be more interested in human relationships than clock-watching. Looking at it from the outside, you can quickly become ashamed of the somewhat stiff and blunt system in monochronic cultures, where spontaneous social opportunities are rejected just because they weren't planned. In principle, it's quite true that *"more time* will be along tomorrow". It's seldom that people on their death beds regret not having worked hard enough – usually people regret not having had enough time for friends and family.

# Part 3

## Bridging differences

In this part of the book, we will look at how we can collaborate despite our differences. Those are the active elements of cultural intelligence, where we convert our knowledge to better planning and better communication. Once again, with a particular regard for precisely how Danes behave.

# 13

## Use cultural knowledge in the right way

It is so much easier to deal with the diversity there is in the world once you have mapped it out a little. The Americans are informal, mildly hierarchic, mildly emotionally expressive, extremely individualistic and live in a low-context culture. If you come across one who doesn't match this profile, then you can have the money you paid for this book back.[8]

Unfortunately, it's not that easy. The second part of this book was about *mapping*, which is an attempt to dissect a very complex reality. But *mapping* only paints a picture of an average, which is why the whole house of cards doesn't collapse just because one or two individuals suddenly behave in a way we weren't expecting. So we absolutely have to proceed with caution if we want to be culturally intelligent. It is important to *prepare* but not to *expect*. If you expect, you will often be disappointed. If, however, you are prepared, then you will be ready to encounter both what you had counted on, and hopefully also ready to handle the unexpected. You definitely should be prepared for that, as people don't behave like clockwork. We are affected by so many things that it is never possible to predict our behaviour precisely. As we know, that is what personality is about, and no one is a clone of anyone else.

So: if you use your cultural knowledge as an expectation, then you risk only seeing precisely what you had expected to see. So your knowledge becomes self-fulfilling prophecies, which means it is useless as knowledge. Your knowledge has instead become a *preju-*

---

8  Danish irony

*dice.* But what actually is the difference between knowing something more general about other people, and being prejudiced towards them?

## What are stereotypes?

"I'm like my mother, I stereotype. It's faster." says George Clooney in his role as Ryan Bingham in the film *Up in the Air* (2009) when he has to explain why he always picks the queue with the Japanese. They travel lighter, so they have less to unpack at security. And he is right – right that it *is* faster to create a stereotype. And everyone does that. Even our mothers.

Stereotypes are simple models for how we perceive others around us. Stereotypes can, in the example above, be useful, but they are often imprecise and so too often lead to prejudices. Prejudices are attitudes, whereas stereotypes are a type of model for our knowledge.

We all have stereotypes. They often survive from generation to generation and even though they change, they often have a core which remains unchanged over time. That is of course because there is a grain of truth in all stereotypes, but also because they get reproduced in our upbringing, in culture and especially in popular culture. Stereotypes are easy to understand, easy to communicate and often funny. They also tell a story we like, and which I will come back to later.

Try for a moment to forget the nuanced view of culture I have tried to plead for in this book, and imagine instead a prototypical Frenchman, German, Swede and American (if you come from one of these countries, then try to recall what you have heard people say about your countrymen). Try to turn your inner thoughts into words and write a few things down about each group. Focus on what we all know is prejudice and which we are not very proud of when it comes to thinking about other people.

It's highly probable that the words you will choose for these people are like these:

| Germans | Frenchmen | Swedes | Americans |
|---|---|---|---|
| Stiff | Snobbish | Boring | Shallow |
| Orthodox | Self-obsessed | "Prohibitionis-tic" | Unintelligent |
| Commanding | Nationally chauvenistic | Snotty | Oversized |

This is reasonably stable across all the courses I have given, and as regards Germans, Frenchmen and Americans it also matches quite well to other studies of prejudices among both Danes and non-Danes. However, it is important to remember that you only get these characteristics coming up when Frenchmen, Swedes and Americans are judged by *outsiders*. The words don't match at all what those countries' people mention when they are judging themselves. It's maybe not surprising that there is a trend of people saying lots of positive things about their own group while highlighting negative things about others.

What is interesting is that stereotypes don't have very much to do with specific *experience*. They are to a great extent "cultural constructions". In other words, they are ideas embedded in culture and which are recreated when we talk about them. For example, if you think about the German, French, Swedish or American friends, acquaintances or colleagues you have, do you think these expressions fit them? Most likely you will say no. It's not at all unusual to hear Danes say "I think Germans are very stiff" and then quickly add "but the ones I know are not that bad".

In other words as a Dane, I have lots of ideas about how other people are but they are not in any way based on my own experience, they are just something I have heard somewhere else. They are ideas embedded in my own culture and which people repeat uncritically. That matches the typical statement you sometimes hear in Denmark: "You can't trust those Muslims – but Ahmed down at the greengrocer, he's okay, he's not like the others". Well, maybe "the others" aren't like "the others" either. That's also a possibility.

## Why stereotypes?

If the German, the Frenchman, the Swede and the American in the list here don't have so much in common with reality, then why on earth do we have such misleading ideas? The explanation could be that when we're dealing with stereotypes it's not about "the others", but that we're really just talking about ourselves. We consciously select negative characteristics in others in order to emphasise positive characteristics in our own culture.

If we take the opposites of all those hard words, could we have found some characteristics which we like to use about ourselves? Let's try:

| Germans | Frenchmen | Swedes | Americans |
|---------|-----------|--------|-----------|
| Stiff | Snobbish | Boring | Shallow |
| Orthodox | Self-obsessed | "Prohibitionis-tic" | Unintelligent |
| Commanding | Nationally chauvenistic | Snotty | Oversized |

| Danes | Danes | Danes | Danes |
|-------|-------|-------|-------|
| Easy-going | Laid-back | Funny | Thorough |
| Independent | Open | Free | Intelligent |
| Inclusive | International | Plain | Slim |

This is very likely a good match with your own self-image. In any event, it matches surprisingly well to Danes' self-image and the characteristics are typically positive ones that Danes emphasise about themselves. So opposite contrasts to others also include good, positive characteristics which maybe don't cover the whole truth about yourself, but which in any event express an idea about who you are and what you or your group believe to be positive.

Who you like to build and maintain stereotypes about is of course very different from culture to culture. The reason why Frenchmen, Americans, Swedes and Germans were chosen above is because this book is a translation of an original Danish book for Danish readers, who have very highly developed prejudices about these four groups. They are either geographically or culturally very close to Denmark and so will typically be the nationalities that Danes have lots of prejudices about. You very likely recognise this from your own society. If you are Indian, you have prejudice about Pakistanis, if you are a Spaniard, you like to emphasise how different you are from the Italians and Canadians use most of their waking hours to emphasise why they are not Americans.

The reason for this is that you have a greater need to differentiate yourself from a culture which is very close to your own. In that way, we make sure that there is no doubt about who we are. As the Norwegian anthropologist Fredrik Barth concluded, it is at borders where, more than anywhere else, we use time and energy to explain who we are, and who the others are. The more people resemble us, the more need we have to explain how "strange" the others are.

## The best protection against stereotypes is *real* knowledge

As mentioned, stereotypes very often get deflated when you come into contact with reality. The Germans, Americans, Indians and Chinese you know yourself – of course they don't match the stereotype. It is not easy to change your perceptions and prejudices because the ideas can be difficult to change.

What we see of course affects our ideas, but our ideas are to a great extent controlled by what we see. This has been known for a long time in cognitive psychology, and a very good way of illustrating the problem has been developed by American psychologist Ulric Neisser.

# HOW TO CHANGE MENTAL MODELS

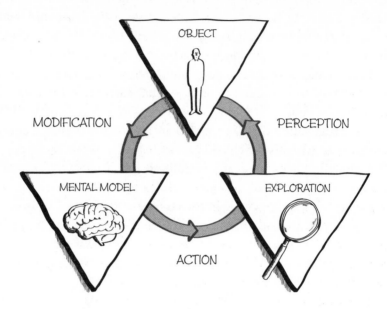

Neisser's point with the model is that as humans we have a large number of mental models which make up our knowledge and not least our expectations to our surroundings. We have a lot of experience which helps us very much to interpret and determine what we see. For example, we can recognise something very quickly if we have seen it before. However, new experiences take longer. That also means that we have a special "readiness" to reality, so we often end up seeing what we expect to see. Not just because we interpret what we see with the help of our knowledge ("perception" in the model), but also because we often pay attention to what we know and ignore things we have no experience of ("action" and "exploration" in the model). This means that we unconsciously end up confirming what we already know because we don't see what we don't know.

So we all need to look in different directions than we otherwise would have done. We have to challenge what we believe and what we know and say "look at that" – look at what we didn't realise we *couldn't* see. In the cultural field, it is about allowing yourself to be surprised and forcing yourself to pay attention to what you hadn't expected. It is about challenging the "mental model" of the world by "modification" every time you encounter a reality different from what you expect.

So it was good advice to *share your knowledge* and it is *more important to share the surprises than to share what you were already agreeing about last time.* In any culturally intelligent process the steps are to:

- *Acquire knowledge about what can generally be said of the others through exchange of experience, literature, informants* (I will deal with the latter later).
- Then challenge each other about the knowledge when exchanging experiences: *who has experienced something DIFFERENT to what was expected? Something DIFFERENT to what you usually see.*

The final step requires effort and knowledge. It requires you to be aware that all knowledge is temporary and simply a chart for navigating reality. It is only once you are sure about *what* you know (but not whether it is necessarily right), that you start challenging all the "truths".

For example, the eternal problem with Chinese diversity. China is so enormous that it is actually extremely difficult to make very definite predictions about the behaviour of Chinese people. According to certain books, the Chinese are typically emotionally neutral and nervous about showing too many emotions, but there is also widespread experience that many people find that the Chinese can in fact be extremely vociferous and aggressive in certain situations. So which is correct?

Again, it depends on where you are, what the context is, who you're talking to, which culture you yourself come from and 117 other things. Ideas about Chinese emotional extraversion are thus weighed down with a certain amount of uncertainty, and their extraversion is maybe something which it is very difficult to be specific about. Dealing with the Chinese and their emotions is very complex. That is in fact a very good conclusion to reach in certain cases, because we shouldn't try to force real people or nationalities into categories they do not fit into very well.

Models about other people which don't hold up should always be challenged so that you can find out whether it is simply a case of exceptions, or whether there actually is a problem with the "truth" that you were accepting as such. Try making a game out of finding examples of the opposite. You can only gain from it.

Knowledge which doesn't fit can't be used for anything. It just gives a false sense of security.

## Control your expectations

It's good to have knowledge, but even better to test the temperature of the water. For example, just imagine what would happen if you expect that your visitors will come half an hour late because you know they are polychronic, but they actually arrive on time because they know you are monochronic. So suddenly *you* are the one who appears lacking in respect, because they were so aware of how shameful being half an hour late is in your country. If in your mistaken attempt to adapt to their culture, you arrive far too late, then you are simply considered to be treating them with complete disrespect.

It was the same in the episode with the Indian vegetarian in the chapter about the lack of religiousness among Danes. His Danish colleagues had decided that it had to be his religion which did not allow him to eat meat. They thought they were right because that is what their mental model told them. The same goes for the manager who asked a Muslim woman when interviewing her for a job: "How many children do you have?" or "Your husband doesn't mind you going out to work, does he?" Once again, we can only conclude that the cultural card came before the individual being addressed. Such a conversation most definitely starts out with so many prejudices that the poor woman became more ethnic than she was human. A problem we will look at more in the next chapter.

Test the temperature of the situation first. Don't *react before you see*. Your knowledge is your backup, your tool to understand what you see, but the immediate practical and human handling of your surroundings is more important than anything else. You look around and take the map out before you depart and when there is something you don't understand. Otherwise, just make sure to keep your eyes and ears open.

# 14

## How to choose your cultural battles

A Danish couple is walking through a Turkish bazaar. They have been on holiday for almost a week, surrounded by strange cultures and people, and the smells and atmosphere in this exotic market-place imbibe them with strange impressions. They are a long way from home, both geographically as well as culturally.

Suddenly they hear two well-known voices through the myriad of shoppers. Or rather, they hear a familiar language. Danish. Another couple is standing very close to them. The man is bargaining for some cheap safran which his wife says is "guaranteed to be cheaper here than it is at home". "I think you're right" the first couple says to the surprise of the other, who thought they were the only Danes there. The conversation continues. The first couple are called Bent and Vibeke and come from Bjerringbro. The other two are Niels and Jannie from Slagelse. They have doubtless never seen each other before and had they been standing at the frozen food counter in the local supermarket one Thursday, it would have been unthinkable for them suddenly, quite out of the blue, to have initiated a long chat about themselves with complete strangers. So what is the difference here?

### Surroundings create people

The difference is the surroundings, because the surroundings mean everything when people have to find out whether they want contact with each other. Some situations are more "socially integrating" than others. For example, as previously mentioned, it is much easier to approach someone you don't know during a hurricane, or if you have both just witnessed a traffic accident. There is suddenly a common frame of reference which is unusual, and so you're quite happy to talk to each other. Because normally, as we know (at least in Denmark), we like to keep ourselves to ourselves. But things are different abroad. When one Dane happens to find another representative of the "Danish Family", they are quite happy to have a chat with people they otherwise never would have given a second glance. Remember that Denmark is precisely the type of tribal society where people almost feel they are related to everyone else. Not all nations will experience the same situation as that described above. But for most societies it will definitely not be something unusual.

Because for Niels, Jannie, Bent and Vibeke what was crucial for their meeting was that they were Danish and a long way from Denmark. They would of course be just as Danish if they had met in the supermarket, but they would scarcely be aware of the fact. In Turkey, they quickly noticed that both couples had *something in common* – being Danish – and so therefore they had an excuse to talk to each other simply for that reason. Because, when you are abroad, your national identity clearly comes to the fore.

They compare the locals with how things are in Denmark, how things smell in Denmark, how service is in Denmark and how close people stand to each other compared to what they do in Denmark. Yes, Danes are in imminent danger of becoming much more Danish when they are abroad. To a great extent that is the difference that makes a difference, so that difference becomes even more obvious than it actually needs to be.

## Where do I belong?

*On an individual level we are all involved in identities of various different types in disparate contexts, in our own respective lives and as a consequence of background, connections, social activities or whatever. The same person can, for example, be a British citizen, of Malaysian origin, with Chinese racial characteristics, a stockbroker, a non-vegetarian, an asthmatic, a linguist, a bodybuilder, a poet, an opponent of abortion, a bird-watcher, an astrologer, and one who believes that God created Darwin to test the gullible.*

Professor Amartya Sen, Harvard University, Nobel Laureate, born in India.

Amartya Sen's observations about complex identity are of course more valid in some parts of the world than others. In more traditional societies, identity is often connected to the relationships people have (family, employer, friendships) whereas modern societies have far more identities which are connected to the categories people are in. Groups which are also good at marking themselves out with categories for special interests or a particular community (nationality, sexuality, language, gender, ethnicity, ideology). So there are rather more strings to the bow in more complex modern societies, and it was precisely one of Amartya Sen's points that countries which allow their members to have many different identities are also countries with growth.

People don't just have one single identity but many, something which is nothing new in anthropology. The English anthropologist E. E. Evans Pritchard studied the Sudanese Nuer tribe in the 1930s, and today his study is regarded as a classic. The same applies to his study of their "associative relationships" – what we today would call identity but which Evans-Pritchard used other words for. He also discovered that who you are, depends on where you are and who you are with. In order to understand this, Evans-Pritchard created a useful model of concentric circles where each circle represents a level of identity.

For the Nuers it looked like this:

## MODEL OF RELATIONS

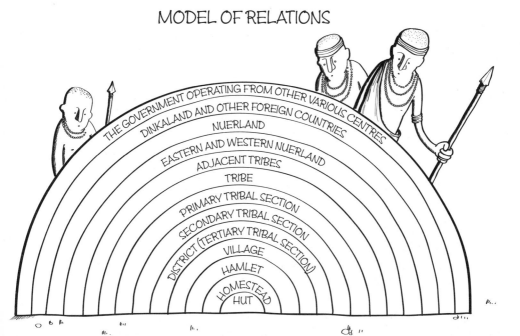

THE GOVERNMENT OPERATING FROM OTHER VARIOUS CENTRES
DINKALAND AND OTHER FOREIGN COUNTRIES
NUERLAND
EASTERN AND WESTERN NUERLAND
ADJACENT TRIBES
TRIBE
PRIMARY TRIBAL SECTION
SECONDARY TRIBAL SECTION
DISTRICT (TERTIARY TRIBAL SECTION)
VILLAGE
HAMLET
HOMESTEAD
HUT

Even traditional peoples such as the Nuers have complex identities. When encountering a Dinka (another ethnic group in the area), then they became very aware of the fact that they themselves were Nuers, and a Nuer in Dinkaland would have the same experience as the Danes in the Turkish bazaar when meeting another Nuer.

It can be very useful to draw such a *segment model* of your own identities. Maybe it could look like this:

## WHO AM I?

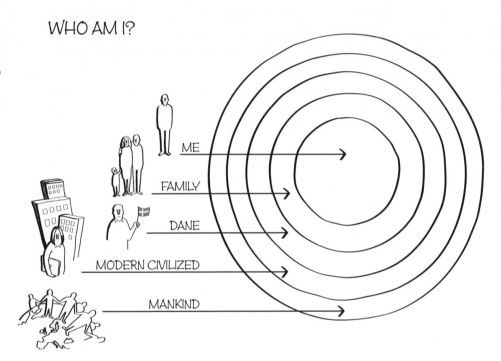

ME

FAMILY

DANE

MODERN CIVILIZED

MANKIND

Where as a Dane I could write Jute, Scandinavian, European and lots of others, an American would put some completely different identities. The point is that you are much more than your national identity and that who you are, is only determined by the situation.

## We are definitely *not* like the others

When that is so important it is because we all have to try and stop talking so much about our national culture when we are out among "the others". Yes, that can seem to be a paradox in a book which is taking very many pages to tell the reader that culture plays a very large role. But nevertheless it's very sensible.

Culture *plays* a very large role but only as large a role as you want it to. In any event, you can turn the "volume" of your own culture up or down by changing your behaviour and thinking about what you do. So culture cannot be used as a bad excuse for everything if you don't try to make an effort to accommodate other people and think about what you do. More about that later.

It is just as important to remember that people are much more than just their national culture. Hardly anyone goes around feeling enormously German, Spanish or Argentinian on a day-to-day basis. We feel lots of other things, but it is only when we encounter people who do not share our national identity or are in a country outside our own that national identity is something we begin to think about. That is like culture being a headwind on the cycle path. In other words, it is the contrast that makes us aware of who we are. Or "at the border", as Fredrik Barth described in the previous chapter.

Why is all this so important? It is enormously important because it means that when we encounter other people, we focus on the differences between us to a much greater extent. This means that the differences can be self-fulfilling prophecies, just as the problems can be because we focus on them, which means that national identity stands in the way of everything else we could have in common.

What if we dug a little deeper into our identities, or looked at one of the other rings? Could there be something there that we have in common? Well it could be a bit pompous to start talking about how it is to be a world citizen or a citizen in a UN country, so let's make a different list of who we are.

## Who am I?

Take a look at the quote from Amartya Sen again. Could that just as easily be you? Well maybe not exactly, but maybe *some* of the identities he mentions could apply to you, surely? Not vegetarian or maybe asthmatic?

Try to make a list of all the roles and identities you have. It will quickly start to include words such as: brother/sister, colleague, father/mother, golf player, amateur musician, Christian, atheist, Michael Jackson fan or something completely different. As well as your national, ethnic, religious or regional identity. Underline the identity which is most important for you.

My experience is that people underline "parent" and maybe their profession. But I have never had anyone underline "Danish". Never.

In other words, there are many other things that you can talk to Danish and non-Danish colleagues, friends or guests from abroad about than what is different. You can find out whether people have exciting leisure interests before you start looking for confirmation of how strange and weird they are in your culture. Because if you look for the differences, then you will only ever see differences. If you are looking for similarities, then they are there to be found. Believe me, you'll find the differences – they will appear all of their own accord. It is the similarities you have to look further for. Not because the similarities are not there, but because our brains first look for the obvious differences. Because it is the difference which is most relevant for a stone age brain, which is always looking for someone to go and hunt a gnu with without there being any fatal misunderstandings during the hunt. So we are aware of all the differences immediately, because we are on the lookout for them.

So keep hold of your complex identity, have a look at the long list and remember the strangest ones for later. You'll need to explain the differences when they appear, but why steer directly towards them when there is so much else you have in common?

Remember too what we went through in Chapter 1 – what everyone in the world has in common. If you put these "primary human similarities" into the model with all the "secondary human identities" which we potentially can have in common with other people (and which I just went through), then yes – what differentiates us actually doesn't seem very significant.

## Inner differences are often greater than national differences

You often hear that we are becoming more and more similar as the world becomes more and more globalised. That is a truth with modifications. In fact, many people have spoken of an increased localisation (or glocalisation) because people more than ever are getting the opportunity to pursue their niche interests with each other. In World of Warcraft, which is a computer game on the Internet, no one asks what nationality you are. It is a secondary characteristic, because here you are a wizard or a warrior or something completely different. The game has become widespread throughout almost the whole world, and thus we have become more similar to each other. But also more dissimilar, because previously we were just a small group within one country who knew about this game and created a community around it. This cultural breakout group has developed because of new technological possibilities which have led to globalisation. So in fact, more cultures rather than fewer have appeared. The number of possible identities has greatly increased, not decreased.

This also means that we have things in common across borders more than ever before. In fact, communities inside traditional national borders are being challenged by new communities which are just as strong or stronger. Or in any case often more relevant. If you are working for the Red Cross or for Maersk, there are lots of other people in the world you have something in common with. They will give you things to talk about and build bridges across the cultural gap.

You will often be much closer to people who do the same as you abroad than you will with your home help, chicken breeder, musician or fisherman from your own country if those are not trades you yourself are involved in. This applies to some professions more than to others. The sociologist Henrik Dahl has described how doctors and architects in particular have almost brotherly relationships to each other where they share a large number of tasks in their day-to-day life and therefore also have the same views on lots of issues. I can add that the same applies to anthropologists.

## Management and leadership across borders

"I have never felt myself to be so ethnic as when I joined this diversity project". This statement is from a new member of staff in a company which put diversity leadership on the agenda and made no secret of the fact that cultural, ethnic and national differences were part of reality. I will touch on diversity leadership in a moment, but the example can already be used now to show what you risk if you use too much energy talking about differences and too little energy focusing on each other as individuals.

In any event, here is someone who was not allowed to do anything else than be a walking ethnic insert into the company. Who on earth in the long-term wants to be the "exotic" one who is never asked who he thinks will win X-factor – but who on the other hand always gets asked whether people get student grants in his home country "just like we do in Denmark" or whether he is "allowed to eat pork" where he comes from.

As humans, we have a tendency to treat people from other countries as one large homogeneous mass. This includes having difficulty seeing the differences in their faces. People from Asia or Africa "all look the same" to white people, and conversely Europeans easily all look the same to an African. That's unfortunate, but that is the way stone age brains are made. That means it is easier for us to see them as a group than as individuals (and as mentioned, they do the same to us). So it is very important to ask the others as "individuals" rather than ask about everything they have in common with the other Pakistanis, Germans or Poles etc. Otherwise we will just continue strengthening the assertion that all "the others" are the same.

As a manager or colleague in a company which either has workers from abroad or branches abroad, it is therefore important to do as follows:

- Be aware of conversations being "ethnic", or whether they are also about other things than just culture. Help to find and start conversation subjects which are not ethnic (just as you would do with your countrymen).
- Ask staff questions which do not automatically assume lots of cultural things from the outset ("do you have three or four children?").
- Don't do as expected: Make other people aware of, and mention it when "others" *don't* behave in the way you had expected them to do in that culture.
- Give people work according to what they *say* they can do, rather than what you believe that "someone like *them* is going to be good at".
- Motivate them to follow some of the popular culture of the country they are in (TV and gossip) – studies clearly show that being able to join in such conversations improves integration.

## Diversity leadership – in a good and a bad way

Active diverse citizenship is a pre-requisite for us benefiting from the advantages of cultural diversity and not ending up at the wrong end of the curve I presented in the introduction. It requires that knowledge be shared about differences, and that an open and tolerant environment be created. In other words, it is about creating a culturally intelligent workplace and emphasising the principles and approaches which have been presented in this book.

Fundamentally, it is about respecting but also encouraging differences in the company, avoiding discrimination, actively applying diversity as a resource and forming teams with large differences as regards gender, ethnicity, religion, handicap, age and sexuality.

Or as defined in the book *Diversity at work*: "Diversity leadership is […] a strategic process of targeted efforts to create development and results through the creation and leadership of a diverse workforce which possesses a broad range of skills, perspectives and personalities".

That is excellent and required and the whole point of this book is surely that this is what you should do? The problem occurs when diversity leadership starts to be about dealing with differences and when diversity is something you want purely for the sake of diversity. For example when

- Ethnic/cultural makeup becomes just as important (or maybe even more important) than actual qualifications.
- Positive discrimination, where an ethnic, handicapped or older person gets the job because of their minority status, where you risk that this position is automatically regarded as less burdened and his or her work as of less value.
- Special groups get special work responsibilities because you feel that they are especially good at those particular tasks (without actually asking them first).
- Not everyone gets the same rights, some are allowed to pray during working hours or have time off during Ramadan, but you have to have that special culture in order for that to be permitted.

The problem with that type of misunderstood diversity leadership occurs when there is too much fixation on differences. It ends up not seeming as dynamic as its supporters would themselves want. Because is it particularly dynamic to determine right from the start which groups there should be more of? It is a quota mentality where you hire people based on a top-down planning model where you potentially exclude lots of qualified people who unfortunately are not second-generation immigrants, handicapped, older or maybe even women.

But it's especially serious when you risk holding onto differences and spelling them out for everyone whereby we indirectly ask people to carry on doing what "people like you do so well". It is a leadership form which does not require development, but requires that staff fulfil the diverse ideas management has about that specific group. You never leave the role of being "the other one", but are kept in it more than ever. You become your culture.

------------------------------------------------

### Dream management in Scandinavia

According to Swedish business consultant Anita Ekwall, you can put together a powerful winning organisation with a Scandinavian foundation by putting the various countries' representatives into specific jobs according to cultural characteristics. This would look like this:

*Chief Executive: Swedish. Because Swedes are masters at getting teams to work and explain to everyone where we're going.*

*Marketing Director: Danish. Because Danes can sell everything, including themselves, can move fast and like to have cards hidden up their sleeve.*

*Finance director: Norwegian. Because Norwegians are very capable of analysing and holding onto money.*

*Technical director: Finnish. Because Finns dare to have weird ideas and are very capable when it comes to technological innovation.*

------------------------------------------------

The above suggestions are of course extreme and meant as a joke, but it is not completely unproblematic to talk so directly about differences all the time – even though they may show themselves to be relevant; instead of talking about differences as explanations mostly *when* problems and misunderstandings occur, culture suddenly shows itself to be important. When culture gives us a concrete challenge, or when a particular group of Chinese prove to be very good at a particular task and we cannot avoid asking ourselves the question: *could* that have anything to do with culture?

We have to keep culture in the back of our minds all the time, but if it constantly stays right at the top of our minds, then there will no longer be a place for pure culture. And then culture would be an unavoidable fate.

## Cultural openness and consciousness rather than diversity planning

To take the example with the dream Scandinavian leadership, a culturally intelligent way of handling recruiting can be (let's just call it a type of compromise) that you do not exclude in advance but maybe actually actively seek out some particular cultural groups because you believe that they could have culturally specific abilities you need. That is to say that you might advertise the job in Sweden knowing that Swedish managers are often good and effective, not that you specifically go after a particular *quota* of Swedes in the company, or decide specifically to *want* to hire a Swede. So it is still the qualifications which determine *who* you hire, but you use your cultural knowledge – your mapping – to work out that maybe you should look outside the normal little national box you are in. In large companies with heavyweight leadership positions it is quite normal to look abroad, but maybe you should also think about that at the lower levels of the company and in all types of company.

So this type of prioritisation is only maybe a bad idea. It depends on what you attach to it and how culturally intelligent you are. Not only accounting for culture, but also letting culture play a sensible role. Not as an all-dominating and determining factor, because then you will get an ethnic goat market of a workplace. No matter how politically incorrect it is, it is sociological fact that *large cultural differences can lead to reduced trust*. It is difficult to control the stone age brain. So the more a company uses its efforts to talk up irrelevant differences and emphasise differences in self-serving speeches, the more it risks reducing trust among staff…

## Your rules or mine?

Another problem with overdoing diversity is that you can't agree on rules because everyone has different rules. You end up suspending the important and very intuitive rule we all have which is "when in Rome, do as the Romans". Those are the rules of the location, which are the starting point (and I emphasise *starting point* – which does not mean that it is valid for all eternity).

If you take diversity too seriously you can start to argue in favour of special rules. That can be a dangerous slippery slope because it forces staff apart, so you constantly have to evaluate whether cultural arguments bring people together more than they force them apart. Maybe it is in fact best to justify what the organisation or company has to do by referring to the bottom line, to safety, staff satisfaction or health?

The bottom line or safety can sound like boring and sensible reasons, but maybe they are the easiest ones for the staff to deal with, regardless of what their culture is. We are all interested in a workplace surviving, nobody likes getting hit on the head by heavy objects, and we all want to maintain a healthy workplace. Don't you?

My point is that if *at the outset* you focus a little more on the similarities and less on the differences when you are working with people, then it is much easier to generate a feeling of belonging regardless of the differences. So you can live with the differences which attract our stone age brains' constant attention for the "dangerous and different", but which often don't mean anything in particular – and instead critically attack the differences which actually really hinder people from working constructively together.

That all sounds very good, but what does it mean in practice? I would like to give some very specific examples of that, because there are simple tools which can be used in (almost) all cultural disagreements – unless you are a negotiator somewhere abroad subject to others' mercy and conditions. If you have subsidiaries abroad with foreign staff, or if you have an ethnically diverse group of staff in Denmark, then there are in fact good, objective ways of solving cultural disagreements.

## Where should you draw the limits of diversity?

"That's just how we do things in Denmark". That's how you sometimes hear people argue for a special practice or special value, which for one reason or another people can't find out how to justify in any other way than referring to tradition: that's how we've always done it here.

Sometimes it's not easy to find better explanations than that. As we saw in Chapter 3, we can, for example, come up with very good explanations as to why we celebrate Shrove Tuesday, or why some people build "pepper mills" outside people's houses on their 30th birthday. When we ask why, we sometimes get really poor answers. That's how it is with heavily symbolic things such as rituals and strong cultural traditions. But it doesn't have to be too much like that in a workplace. Maybe you can come up with especially good explanations why the queue at the salad bar always starts from the left, but everything else practical in a company should really have a more profound rational justification. Why do we wear safety helmets, and why do we arrive on time? Wouldn't it be wrong to justify that by saying it's just an old tradition or maybe just a special Danish way of working?

The fact is that the Dane and the Pakistani would get just as bad a bang on the head if they weren't wearing a safety helmet so it would be pointless to refer to Danish safety traditions when explaining to a Pakistani or anyone else for that matter about why they should be worn. Safety helmets, and a large number of other things, should therefore not be justified by traditions, because then we exclude people who do not necessarily share those traditions. Other norms and traditions have literally no rational reason for being practised, but they are part of a complex social game which it is useful to learn how to follow anyway. For example shaking hands with everyone regardless of their gender. There is no rational justification why it is good to shake hands in the same way as it is good to wear a safety helmet, but it is definitely rational to have a good relationship to one's colleagues, and so it is therefore advisable to shake hands with everyone regardless of their gender. In Denmark, a well-functioning workplace is characterised by trust and honesty. That is due to Danish values and traditions, but also because Danes make a living by finding creative and complex solutions in knowledge-heavy organisations, and don't just copy other people's work. So these norms and values are important to communicate to new staff and also important for those new staff to learn.

Fundamentally, it is about common rules for everyone as a basis. Regardless of which minority background, gender or nationality anyone may have. It is this fundamental equality which is important, and which you have to be very careful not to endanger if diversity leadership suddenly means special rules for some staff instead of others.

My experience is that very many difficulties of integrating different cultures at work stem from not having made it clear from the outset what is acceptable and *why* things should be as they are. Not doing that creates a number of problems later on, which occur again and again:

- People with special cultural demands which management do not know whether to reject without getting a discrimination case against them.
- Not knowing which arguments can and may be used when people play the "cultural card".
- Because there is not a fixed procedure (because culture is sometimes rather taboo) then you end up fighting the same battle again and again because no precedent has been set for what to do.
- Using far too much time discussing completely open and shut cases (things that really ought to be allowed, or ought to be forbidden) rather than discussing the more interesting grey areas, where it is always difficult to say yes or no.

The easiest thing to do is simply to draw a line at the start and justify what may and may not be done in a very simple rule:

*We are here to make our company/organisation function, and we have some daily objectives and long-term objectives. If you choose to behave in a way which comes into conflict with those objectives, then you need to consider changing your behaviour or finding somewhere else to work.*

I'm deliberately emphasising the words "choose to behave" because you can of course not place the same demands on disabled or chronically ill people as you can on others. *But culture is, broadly speaking, the choice you make – culture is not fate.* If culture becomes fate, then you let culture take power over people and that can never be the intention. The intention is that people should have power over culture, *use* their culture and *change* or *modify* culture in such a way that it can fulfil our needs. Culture is a tool we have developed to make things easier – it is not an *obligation*.

# Moving from culture as an essence to culture as a process

*It is not the strongest of the species that survive – nor the most intelligent ones, but the ones that are most receptive to change.*
Charles Darwin

Culture changes, and must therefore always have the opportunity to be changed. Because if we rigidly hold onto traditions, we risk having culture no longer serving us, and we would start to serve culture instead.

That can seem rather abstract, but culture was something stone age people developed and which gave them new opportunities to share perspectives and ideas, so collaboration, communication and development could go much faster for us than for other organisms. We could invent things and share them with each other. If we are so pleased with what we have invented that we think that it is "treason" against our culture to modify and change our inventions, then we have become slaves to our own ideas and our traditions. If now and again we don't want to change our language, rituals, culture, traditions or tools because we are afraid of losing our identity, then it is guaranteed that we are going to run aground. It has happened several times in history that large empires have disappeared because they refused to develop. They were so nostalgically preoccupied by their own past and traditions that the dynamic potential completely froze.

- - - - - - - - - - - - - - - - - - - - - - - - - - - - - - - - - - - - - - - - - - - - - - -

### The Easter Islands – when culture fails

The Easter Islands are in the Pacific Ocean and are a puzzling place. There are no trees of any significance and all over the island there are tall stone figures. Erected by a people no longer to be found on the island.

Archaeologists believe that the lack of trees and the statues are part of one and the same story. The statues and the attempts to build them played such a central role in the culture that they led to the felling of all the trees on the island. The trees were namely important for the transport and erection of the statues.

Without trees, there was no fuel for heating in winter and nothing to keep the soil in place during heavy rain. According to author and ecologist Jared Diamond, the inhabitants of the Easter Islands caused an ecological catastrophe because of a very bad cultural tradition. And the Easter Islands are not the only civilisation lost because someone forgot to change, because they got a bad idea and because the word "usually" wouldn't die. Diamond's point is that civilisations often die because of their own self-chosen values and habits. It is difficult to change your culture but if you want to survive in the long term then there is no alternative to change.

------------------------------------------------------------

We must set demands on our culture and we must always consider whether we have new needs – and at the same time we must naturally respect our own and others' needs to follow some strange, special and not immediately understandable or rational ideas, habits, norms or traditions. Culture is not an essence but a process which is about deciding which traditions to keep because they are meaningful to us and which traditions oppose the change we also need. For example because they are in conflict with the need we have for collaboration with other people. It is that balance between tradition and development which is so incredibly difficult, but we can in fact get better at balancing if we constantly challenge ourselves and our culture. Not changing for the sake of change, but having the courage to think in new ways where culture, norms, traditions, prejudices et cetera block beneficial development. In order to do that we need cool, rational consideration about what our *common* goals are. These considerations can help to challenge what has to be challenged, and leave untouched what just has to be as it has always been – even if we can't justify *why* it should be so.


## The three box principle

Think for a moment about how you bring up your children. There is almost certainly lots of things that they mustn't do under any circumstances. For example, crossing the road by themselves (if they are still too young) or talk to strangers. There is no need to have a discussion, it's always forbidden. And so there are things which are always OK. "Can I play with my Lego bricks?" Yes, if there isn't anything else Junior has to do, then of course he can play with them. Children don't need to come and ask every time. And then there is the final category: "Perhaps". Can Junior have an ice cream? Yes, it depends. In this case, the child has to ask each time, or we can come to an agreement. "Perhaps" is negotiable. "Never allowed" and "always allowed" are not. We can put the three situations into three separate boxes:

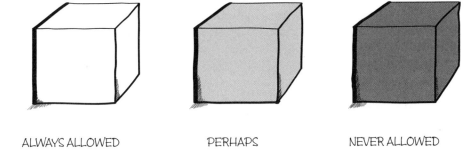

ALWAYS ALLOWED        PERHAPS        NEVER ALLOWED

They set the framework for bringing up children. There are objectives and goals which cannot be compromised, and which determine what belongs in which box. The more you put into the "maybe" box, the more you have to accept the child asking about and being unsure of. Slightly clearer limits are easier to work with and less time-consuming. All children need clear limits.

The same goes for staff at work. Unfortunately, far too many cultural questions end up in the "maybe" box, either because no one dares to confront cultural questions, or because people think their arguments are not good enough for either always allowing or always forbidding.

But the argument can be made easier: your culture must not come into conflict with your work. If it does, then you need to find another place to work. Maybe you don't have a completely free choice about your culture, but you can choose how to practice it. Culture is not set in stone, it is set by people, and people can be flexible and adapt.

Take a look at the following cultural conflicts and try to decide for yourself which box to put them in. A member of staff:

1. Does not want to shake hands with the opposite sex
2. Chews Khat (a psychedelic substance in leaves and twigs particularly used by east Africans)
3. Insists on time off during Ramadan because "working is not allowed then"
4. Will not eat pork
5. Is a Sikh and therefore wears a turban – he refuses to wear a safety helmet
6. Wears a burka
7. Consistently arrives late
8. Has a habit of inviting colleagues to private family parties – something which causes embarrassment to Danish staff in particular
9. Refuses to work for a woman
10. Refuses to ask questions out of fear of you losing face
11. Tells his colleagues at lunchtime about the good grades his children got at school
12. Declines to drink alcohol at the Christmas party

There is nothing absolutely wrong or right here, but there are good and bad arguments because some things have greater, lesser or absolutely no significance for doing the job or not. In addition, it also depends on what values a company has: should we just enjoy working here, should we respect human rights, is it important for the company to project diversity or to do the opposite?

I would say immediately that 4 and 12 clearly belong in the white box. In these cases we are talking about a fight there is no reason to take up. Unless there is a cultural learning project as an objective, in other words, unless you feel that all staff should be the same. If so, you should seriously consider whether you are suitable to be a manager at all, because no one can dictate what other people should eat or drink!

The other things are situations where it is important for the company to have a position, because they can potentially threaten good teamwork. They are areas where you have to have a position and cannot just ignore the problem. Some most certainly belong in the black box: here I am thinking specifically of 2, 5, 7 and 10. Psychedelic substances are quite naturally forbidden, regardless of the arguments that "they are my culture". Safety rules are safety rules, and regardless of whether the health and safety inspectors come along or not, a turban is no excuse. Polychronic time perception can be useful, as it makes for flexible staff, but as a minimum you must be able to demand a minimum of punctuality. And last but not least, it is necessary, especially in a Danish workplace, to have staff who are comfortable with asking questions. It is a value which Danes rate very highly, and which is expected of all, because the Danish way of working depends on people thinking for themselves and asking when in doubt.

These are my personal suggestions and arguments. You don't have to agree with all of them.

For the others, you could argue that the belong in the "maybe" box. That is to say that you decide according to:

- What sort of tasks does the member of staff have and in what circumstances?
- Can we find a compromise?
- Do the problems occur so rarely that we can decide on a case-by-case basis? Is it a question of the cultural majority among the staff taking a critical look at their own culture – is the problem due to limited cultural intelligence on the part of the majority or perhaps even on "both sides"?
- And then of course the culturally intelligent communication about what the disagreement is about: how does the member of staff justify the behaviour which is causing problems? How does his or her cultural world look? Ask about each other's perceptions, look into the different perspectives and try to understand what the goal of the behaviour is. Broaden the perspective so that most people will feel that the behaviour of the others has a pleasant basis as a rule.

**The circumstances** can vary dramatically. It's not really a problem that a member of staff declines to shake hands with the opposite sex (or work under a woman), if the company almost only consists of people of one sex. Or if the work involves so little contact with other people that it is completely unnecessary to greet each other by shaking hands (maybe you only shake hands on the day you're hired and then never do it again). You can have all sorts of principles, but the question is simply whether the principles should be applied to this particular member of staff; whether you can keep your cultural horses in the stable and instead focus on what really counts: can the member of staff do the work or not?

**Compromise** is not shameful to strive for in areas where both parties clearly can benefit from giving a little. A burka or a niqab may be extreme, so if the woman could manage with at least having her face uncovered, then maybe we have a solution (again, depending on the job). And maybe the member of staff can have a week off, but the whole of Ramadan (which after all lasts 30 days) is completely out of the question. On the other hand it could be that he or she is very happy to work over Christmas, when many ethnic Danes prefer to have time off.

If we assume that the company is Danish, then the Danish workers also need to show a little tolerance for behaviour they are not used to. People from very masculine cultures can seem irritating to the modest Danes who are used to subdued behaviour without too much boasting. But here the question is whether the Danes have to learn to accept some small differences. As long as it doesn't mean anything for getting the job done, then they have to live with the fact that not everyone can or has to be the same. Some people simply make more of a fuss than others.

Danes, and very certainly many others too, can be embarrassed when they receive a wedding invitation from a colleague they have only known for two weeks, but we need to remember that such an invitation can have a different meaning to him than for you. He maybe sent invitations out to a broader range of people than you are used to doing. In this case, it is the manager's task to determine the expectations of both sides to each other. Colleagues must be informed about who they all are. We should know something about each other's cultures. From that point on, colleagues have to fend for themselves. It can't go in either the black or the white box because it is something that always depends upon the circumstances. But it requires *knowledge,* so that the member of staff *understands what* is happening and makes a decision on that basis.

It is very seldom that people deliberately want to embarrass others, but it is pointless to forbid cultural misunderstandings. Because misunderstandings occur all the time. But it is okay to say to your staff that they are *obliged* to act when there are misunderstandings. Not just ignore them and hope that someone one day stops practising their own culture. Instead, they must explain and learn from each other. Companies and organisations must permit people to talk about culture. Otherwise, collaboration will break down into unspoken frustrations and incorrect interpretations.

## There is an elephant in the room and its name is "Culture"

"An elephant in the room" is often used as a metaphor for there being something that the group is well aware of and which is very important to their work but which no one dares mention or draw attention to. It is a little bit like when someone has a scrap of food between their teeth, and everyone can see it but no one dares say anything. The one who finally plucked up the courage to tell you about it is the hero of the day, because even though it causes momentary embarrassment around the table, the pressure is off and everyone else can relax again. And the person who had the spinach stuck between their front teeth is of course also relieved.

With culture it is often the same. You're sitting in a meeting and someone says something that everyone realises is due to their cultural background. The cultural outsider is maybe aware of something completely different from the majority, and maybe there is a deadlock. Sometimes the unease is due to the person concerned, just like with the scrap of food, not being aware that he or she is doing something the others know is very culturally specific, but that he himself is not aware of being so (because it's perfectly normal for him). It is a large elephant in the room called culture, which someone has their back to, but which the others are staring in the face – but nevertheless we are often all in agreement that we are not going to talk about it.

However, you can in fact bring all the cultural problems back into play. As long as people are willing to reflect on their own culture, as long as people are open to the fact that cultural differences are something that are okay to be aware of and as long as people know where the differences are (in other words that cultural training has been given to the staff). If those things are present, then it is perfectly possible to talk about it respectfully and without prejudices when an obvious difference crops up. If someone says yes but means no, when a quite relaxed attitude to time shines through, or when a Danish manager thinks that everybody has to be heard even though it drags the meeting on forever (more about that later). In other words, it is a good idea to put words to the cultural difference when it crops up and when it is relevant. However, it is not constructive to start out in advance by talking about how "tribe 1" in the room differs from "tribe 2" before it actually becomes relevant.

Naturally, we should take care not to make personal differences between staff into cultural differences, but nevertheless it is quite possible to be in a meeting with a small group of Swedish or German staff who all react in a very "Swedish" or "German" way. So then it might be the right time to puncture the taboo and ask whether the disagreement is based on something cultural, and with that I mean ask about what they feel is important and significant. Then the difference is on the table, and for many people it is a relief the problem is not personal, but cultural. So it's not personal with Göran from Sweden, it's just because he's used to doing things differently there. From that point on, it is easy to argue for some people having a tough one to swallow. Because maybe Göran is taking account of something he doesn't need to, is concerned about situations which won't occur anyway, or is waiting for a signal which will never come.

Culture often presents itself as an enormous problem, but often the biggest problem is not being allowed to talk about it. The cultural problems can often be fixed because people find out that they are reacting to something because of a particular *norm* which could just as easily be something completely different. There may be no fundamental differences between how people see things, but there is a superficial variation in behaviour which is always interpreted in lots of different and often incorrect ways by lots of different people. People think, for example, that a particular argument is important but suddenly understand that if they had grown up in the other person's culture, it would be a completely different argument that was just as important.

With cultural intelligence people become more willing to give up the battles that are impossible to win and instead get on with the job.

- - - - - - - - - - - - - - - - - - - - - - - - - - - - - - - - - - - - - - - - - - - - - -

**When culture causes planes to crash**
In 1979, a Korean Air plane crashed in Seoul. A jumbo jet. In 1982, another one crashed at Sakhalin in Russia. In 1987, it

was a Boeing 707 which crashed into the Andaman Sea, and in 1989 there was a crash in Tripoli and another in Seoul. In 1994 in Cheiu in South Korea and again, another jumbo jet, a Boeing 747. All planes with experienced pilots. All in perfectly good condition. The rate of loss for Korean Air in the period was 4.79 accidents per million departures. By comparison, Scandinavian Airlines' figure is 0.57.

That wasn't good, and in 2000, Korean Air consequently hired an expert from Delta Airlines, David Greenberg, to examine and fix what the real problem was: Korean culture.

In an attempt to fix the problem, Greenberg got access to the voice recordings from the planes' black boxes. This is an extract from the dialogue on board flight 801 which crashed in 1997 with 228 fatalities. The background is that the weather was very bad, but nevertheless the captain had decided to do a visual approach to the airport in Guam even though doing so required good visibility.

Captain: *Err... I'm really tired...*
First Officer: *That's obvious... Don't you think it seems like the rain is getting heavier? In this area?*
No answer. They break through the clouds and can see light ahead
Flight engineer: *Is that Guam?... That's Guam that's Guam!*
Captain: *That's good.*
Flight engineer: *Captain: The weather radar has really been a big help*
Captain: *Yes it's very useful*
Shortly after an electronic voice can be heard from the terrain warning system.
First Officer: *Let's do a missed approach*

Seven seconds later flight 801 crashes into a mountainside on Nimitz Hill, barely 5 km from the airport. The technicians later determined that the accident could have been avoided if the first officer had pulled up (executed a missed approach) when he himself suggested it. At that point the ground was barely 100 m beneath the plane.

The problem was that the captain was not questioned. First the first officer tried to say that they were flying into bad weather and perhaps should give up the visual approach. Later, the flight engineer tried to please the captain when he thought he had spotted the airport, but that was wishful thinking. A bit later he again tried to draw the captain's attention to the weather radar which clearly showed that it had become impossible to execute a proper visual approach further ahead. But nothing was said directly (Korea is also a country with high context communication). The first officer finally *suggested* the action which could have saved them all. But he did not do it himself. Because it was the captain who decided.

People have attempted to compare the number of serious plane crashes a country experiences with the country's position on Geert Hofstede's parameter for power distance several times, and in fact there has been shown to be a clear connection between power distance and plane crashes. The cultural norms are so strong that they can cause people to act completely madly and irresponsibly. Several studies of communication in planes from hierarchical societies have shown many disturbing examples of how incompetent people have behaved out of fear of embarrassing an even more incompetent (or maybe rather tired and unsuitable) superior.

But planes should not crash. It is part of the *job* that they should be kept up in the sky until they land in a controlled manner. So the culture at Korean Air had to change. An old culture which was not just the airline's, but also the whole of South Korea's.

They succeeded. David Greenberg forced them to change their culture. And he went after the junior officers in a strong way:

"They were the sort of guys who had worked hard in the old system for more than fifteen years. They had long ago accepted the role of junior. They were at the bottom of the ladder. We retrained them and put them together with Western pilots. Since then, it's been a real success story. They all changed their style. They take initiative. They bear their share of the workload. They don't wait for someone else to take charge. They are experienced *people over 50 with a long background in Asian culture, who have been retrained and now work effectively and successfully in a Western context. We reset them as regards their culture and gave them a new starting point".*

Today, Korean Air is just as safe as any other airline. Member of the prestigious SkyTeam Alliance and with a virtually accident-free record since 1999. So when people say that culture is ingrained and cannot be changed then they are simply wrong. Korean Air is the example which proves the opposite.

When you are a guest in other people's countries other rules naturally apply, but when you are working together with people from other cultures for a longer or a shorter time (here at home but also sometimes abroad), there is no reason not to challenge the others' culture as long as you do so respectfully and as long as you are also in a position to challenge your own. The next chapter is about the latter. We will look at what people from abroad often experience in their encounters with the "weird Danes" and how people can perhaps themselves challenge the Danish way of managing and working because they understand the background for what it is they want to achieve and together can find a compromise that everyone can be happy with. If they don't themselves become so happy with the "Danish model" that they let themselves be completely integrated into this very special culture.

# 15

## What everyone should know about cultural encounters with the Danes

Denmark (and also the rest of Scandinavia) is an extreme. Yes, it is not completely factually incorrect to say that they are very strange, which probably also matches the experiences readers of this book have had. If you look back at the way we dealt with cultural differences in the second part of the book, you will quickly discover that with the exception of the parameter about emotional commitment, then Denmark is usually at the top or the bottom of the scale. They are among the most egalitarian in the world, the most "feminine" (according to Hofstede's understanding), the most uncertainty avoiding, the ones with the lowest context, they are extremely monochronic and they are also relatively strong individualists.

In addition, as we saw in Chapter 4, they maybe have the lowest level of religiousness in the whole world, the highest degree of trust and the most informal way of dealing with each other. Yes, they're really something special up there in Scandinavia.

This is of course due to some very special historical conditions, the small size of the country, a low rate of immigration and the political decision to change an agricultural society with independent farmers into a very modern and self-conscious nation, and later a welfare society which quietly took functions away from families and assimilated everything from care to religion. A very special history creating a very special culture.

This means that Danes, more than any others in the world, have to be extremely culturally intelligent, but most certainly that they also require a portion of patience and insight from those who are going to work together with them. Both because their country is so small that they cannot avoid coming into contact with other countries and nationalities, but also because they simply don't fit into categories. Most of the world is still relatively traditionally oriented as regards hierarchies, relationships and collectives such as family and religion. The whole of the West, compared to the rest of the world's population, is still a strange minority, and that applies to the greatest extent in the Nordic countries.

In this chapter – which in many ways builds on the insights from Chapter 4 about Danes, added to what we now know from Part 2 of the book about everyone else – we will look at how things often go very wrong in encounters between Danes and non-Danes and how we can all maybe solve some of the worst problems.

## Trust is good but control is better

Danes can appear naive in their almost limitless trust of each other. That is maybe why the country has been hit by spectacular financial fraud affairs on several occasions, where con artists have been able to generate excitement, backing and not least investment for projects which have only been sold because of a particular person without the slightest evidence of that person having anything of substance to sell. The most well-known affair is this spectacular IT Factory or Stein Bagger case where I at one point heard an economist say that such a case is very typically Danish. Because Danes trust each other so much. Con artists and fraudsters such as Stein Bagger make good use of the fact that no one bothers to check their CV, contacts or contracts thoroughly.

When encountering others, Danes have to learn to be just as sceptical as others are and non-Danes have to help by reminding Danes about that. Danes who suddenly realise that the agreement they signed in India or China is not worth the paper it is written on learn it the hard way. Trust is not something which comes easily, but something which has to be worked on. I have spoken to several advisers for Danes who, on hearing that Danes thought that a contract negotiation was almost complete when it in fact had only just begun had to shake their heads in despair, because in their naiveness the Danes thought that well-meaning and positive indications of intent actually meant something definite and certain. They just don't always do.

In a leadership context that means that someone is used to having someone looking over their shoulder all the time, whereas the Danes are used to trust and become uncomfortable with control and monitoring. So when encountering Danish management, you will find that there is very little monitoring of what you do and you will only get feedback when you specifically ask for it. Elsewhere, maybe in your own country, people more often work from the motto that trust is good but control is better.

Danes work by the motto: Freedom with responsibility. And they say that frequently and with great pride.

## A delicate balance

Lots of trust of course also means lots of influence. Compared to many others, Danes are very autonomous. It is expected that they will find new tasks on their own (not just sit and wait for the boss to bring them), that they find out how to do the job on their own and that generally Danes are surrounded by high levels of trust at work.

Here is an example from anthropologist Susanne Ekman's field work in a modern Danish company, where there is plenty of room for flexibility and independent thinking and thus, as we will see, plenty of room for confusion for everyone too:

------------------------------------------------

**Danish double pressure**

Henriette is a middle manager in a large media company. She is responsible for 15 staff and also has to deal with the rest of the management group and the executive. That same executive told her three weeks ago that the absolute top priority was to complete her department's strategic plan. It had to be delivered on time. As a conscientious middle manager, Henriette threw herself into the task.

Three weeks later, her manager comes over to her looking very displeased. "Why haven't you done anything about new business now that our competitor is cutting back?!", he asks. Henrietta is baffled: "But you wanted me to get you the strategic plan on time!" The senior manager is equally baffled: "Henriette, this company makes its money from clients. It's obvious that when we have the opportunity to acquire more of them, then the strategic plan has to take second place!"

------------------------------------------------

According to Ekman, the problem is that the manager in his first approach talks like a classical manager giving an order down the hierarchical ladder (Danish workplaces are not completely anarchic, and of course, Danes know that the bosses are actually bosses). Henriette has to do what she is told and on time. But the second time he comes to her, he is dissatisfied because Henriette has not been independent enough and put the task he gave her to one side; of course, she should think for herself and not just do what she's told, but do what *should* be done.

Many people will surely recognise this situation, and Danish workplaces have a lot of this schizophrenic balancing. "Double pressure" as Ekman calls it. Henriette forgot this ambiguity even though she almost certainly is aware of it. She grew up in Denmark with the concept of "freedom with responsibility" and all that.

The problem is that many staff who are not Danish – at least all of those who come from countries outside Scandinavia – are completely lost in this situation. They simply don't know what to do.

For them, things seem chaotic and anarchic and extremely contradictory. Because even though they quickly understand that they are supposed to find things out for themselves, that doesn't mean that everything is allowed.

Independence is required from staff, but in order for that to work there needs to be openness, trust and easy access to management. That is the formula which works in a Danish company, and if you take some of the parts away then the whole thing will collapse. That is why a Danish company can be something of a trial if you come from outside. You have to have control of everything and learn everything:

- Learn to ask questions
- Learn that it is okay to go to your boss if you are in doubt, but not constantly and not about every detail
- Learn that you must and may admit mistakes and report them
- Learn to find your own solutions and your own tasks
- Learn that your boss will rarely give you feedback unless you ask for it

Those are the five points you have to be particularly aware of if you are working for Danish management. They are areas where it pays to adapt to Danish expectations, but where it is also a good idea to explain that you are maybe used to doing things differently. That applies especially if you come from a culture where you have a tendency to think that asking questions is a sign of impoliteness, where admitting mistakes means losing face or where management is quite simply unapproachable and communication is always top-down and not bottom up. You can start to unlearn these ideas immediately. Because that's not how things work in Denmark.

So you need to be aware of:

- Understand and be at the forefront of this double pressure and thinking for yourself – so always decide what benefits the issue more than what you were told to do – but do discuss with your manager your interpretation of what is right or wrong to do, as long as you don't ask him about too many details in your work.
- You are expected to ask questions if you're in doubt. Especially when it is about the extent to which you should do something as you were told or what you feel is necessary. Everything which Danes believe you can find out for yourself, which you maybe have not learned, is your responsibility or decision.
- An absent manager is not a manager who doesn't care about staff, but just a manager who shows trust by not watching over people all the time. It is an expression of trust and not disinterest.

------------------------------------------------------------

**How Danes are perceived by foreigners working in Denmark**
*Study by Oxford Research in 2010*
83% of over 1500 respondents in the study answered that they find the way of doing things in Denmark to be informal, and in 2006 only 27% of Danes answered that they show great respect for their superiors (there are no figures for 2010). And as it says in the report in 2006: "This is positive to the extent that it is connected to the majority of respondents (56%) believing the Danish work culture encourages creativity and independence". In 2010, the figure had incidentally risen to 61%.

------------------------------------------------------------

## Danish management – when the manager is not the expert

Having lots of levels of hierarchy is not common in Danish companies, but that does not mean that there are no differences between people. There are most definitely differences, but whereas in countries outside Scandinavia they are vertical differences, the internal differences in Denmark are often horizontal. People are namely part of various different specialist groups. People are technicians, engineers, clerical and shopworkers, human resource people, accountants or managers, etc. All these groups are from a formal point of view equal.

The latter is very important. In many Danish workplaces, people like the fact that the difference between people is about different interests, specialisms and working areas. Put bluntly, that means that the director is just an expert at being a director, whereas the engineer is just an expert at being an engineer. From a formal point of view they are all equal with different skills. This, of course, doesn't last in the long run (the director earns significantly more, his words have more weight, his power is significantly greater etc), but in Denmark, it is important that at least the official way of thinking is so.

That type of attitude is completely unnecessary in Japan or China. Of course the director there is better than me. He is the best one of all of us, the only reason he doesn't do everything is because he doesn't have 2000 hands. But there can actually be something to this attitude. Maybe the Chinese manager is in many ways the most capable overall. People are promoted to management positions for other reasons in that part of the world.

In Denmark, many managers are generalists and not specialists. They are good at leading because that is what they have been trained to do. In other and often more traditional countries' companies, the boss is a man who has fought his way up through the system and who maybe started as an engineer among other engineers. Such a person has a lot of knowledge about what people lower down in the hierarchy actually do. If he's a middle manager on the way up, he will often be the one, people go to, to find out what is right or wrong. He is without a doubt "the best" of them all.

Things seldom work like that in Danish companies[9]. The specialisation in the individual specialist groups is simply too great. It can't be taken as given that the manager can answer questions about what is right or wrong. Staff are hired to think for themselves and not sit and wait for orders: "I don't know how you should do this job, that's what I hired *you* to do".

In other words, a Danish manager doesn't necessarily know what staff are actually doing right now, neither does he go around monitoring and checking whether they do the job properly. The manager is not a kind of super-worker who does everything right, he is just a good manager. Hopefully.

Managers in more hierarchical organisations will, however, often know in detail what their staff are actually doing and will be ready to answer yes or no if one of them has a specific question about how the job should be done. The manager will know the "truth" and the "right answer", and staff will sometimes have to guess what the manager wants and do things that way. Staff should not necessarily do what they themselves believe is right, but instead follow orders from the capable specialist manager. Nobody comes up with new suggestions because that would be equivalent to saying that the procedure the manager has set is not good enough.

Therefore staff in more hierarchical societies also think that their boss has the answer to everything and can be very disappointed if, for example, a Danish manager doesn't grasp why he should have an opinion about a particularly tricky technical question. A group of French researchers tried to demonstrate this difference a few years ago by asking staff in a number of different countries how important it was for their boss to have "precise answers to most questions which staff could have about their work". You can see below how many that was.

---

9  An important exception is of course very small companies and not least very traditional public sector workplaces such as hospitals, universities and of course the military. There, the manager is preferably a (senior) doctor, an academic (professor) or the highest ranking military officer who has made his way up through the hierarchy. But these specialist areas also have an increasing need to move towards professional management. "MBA-ification", as it is rather disdainfully called in the old, traditional power bases.

## Percentages who prefer precise answers

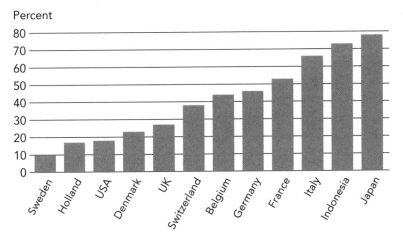

Percent

So we don't have to go very far south of Denmark before it is expected that the boss to a much greater degree knows exactly what staff are doing and what they need. There, people expect that managers check on their staff regularly, correct their work and answer questions. Bosses are just as much knowledge resources as they are managers.

In Denmark, generalists are hired to management positions. Capable people who can develop people's skills and competencies, challenge them, get them to do their best and establish good teams, etc. But these generalists do not necessarily have any specialist knowledge about what people are actually doing down on the factory floor or in the marketing department.

Maybe the reader can see the problem with what happens when Danes try to manage people who:

- think that the Danish manager is the best specialist in the team and will therefore lose face if they follow their own intuition rather than waiting for the manager's precise instructions
- sit and wait for specific orders, guidelines and instructions
- have difficulty making suggestions
- expect that right and wrong is something the manager will judge and not something to work out for themselves on an ongoing basis
- expect the manager to know exactly what staff are doing at any given moment

The Danish generalist can thus quickly lose respect from the people who are used to a manager knowing everything, if they are not aware of the fact that in Denmark, it is the individual member of staff who is expert in his or her own field. That is what they have been trained and hired to do. The manager is therefore quite rightly, as they insist, hired only to manage. It is his area of work and in principle makes him a member of staff in the same way as anyone else.

It can be difficult to understand if you are used to things being done differently. You most certainly know more than your Danish boss does, and he or she most certainly has absolutely no problem with that at all.

## Lead by challenging – lead by rewarding

If you won so much money in the lottery that you could afford not to work for the rest of your life, could be completely financially independent and quit your job with a good conscience, would you do it?

Danes would usually say no. 56.5% would continue working despite the fact that they didn't need the money, according to a recent study undertaken by Rambøll Management / Analyse Danmark and the newspaper Jyllands-Posten. Only 17.7% would stop working. In a previous study undertaken by the University of Aalborg, the numbers were even more pronounced. 78% of Danes agreed or strongly agreed with the statement that they would prefer paid employment even if they didn't need the money. 47% strongly agreed. Which is noticeably higher than the "second place", Sweden, with only 14%.

|         | Strongly agree | Agree | Neither nor | Disagree or strongly disagree | Respond-ents |
|---------|----------------|-------|-------------|-------------------------------|--------------|
| Denmark | 47             | 31    | 6           | 16                            | 1015         |
| Sweden  | 14             | 61    | 13          | 12                            | 1244         |
| Norway  | 13             | 61    | 13          | 14                            | 2061         |
| UK      | 7              | 47    | 18          | 28                            | 972          |

|  | Strongly agree | Agree | Neither nor | Disagree or strongly disagree | Respond-ents |
|---|---|---|---|---|---|
| Holland | 8 | 44 | 18 | 31 | 2015 |
| Italy | 13 | 39 | 13 | 35 | 1007 |
| Spain | 10 | 42 | 11 | 37 | 1162 |
| USA | 10 | 50 | 16 | 25 | 1162 |

So Danes go to work for more than just their salary, and even though this may not be something unique, it is definitely a good example of an attitude which is particularly northern European, according to economic lecturer Christian Bjørnskov: "Pleasure in doing a good job applies all over the world where we have looked. But the Protestant work ethic means that the job is a little bit more important for North Europeans". As previously mentioned, the Protestant work ethic was discovered by German sociologist Max Weber almost 100 years ago. In his work about *The Protestant Ethnic and the Spirit of Capitalism*, Weber showed countries with a long tradition of Protestant Christianity perceived work as a virtue and hard working morals as an expression of an ability to ignore oneself and one's own needs. People didn't earn money to be rich, but to put money into circulation and create more money.

"Work itself is the reward" as people at these latitudes say. Conversely, this concept is less recognised in southern Europe and not at all in Asian countries, where work is not about self-realisation but to a much greater extent about prestige and money. In countries where individualism is low, words, such as self-development and a desire to find personal challenges which give personal benefits in the form of increased self-awareness, are relatively unknown. Why on earth go through all this personal development if it's not something *anyone else* can see? If it doesn't give more prestige, more public reward, stars on your shoulder or first and foremost a bigger pay packet? In those countries people don't work for their own personal development, they work so that their family and social network will be proud.

So it is important to remember that when you come from cultures where people don't have very much – as opposed to the relatively rich Scandinavia – then money naturally means more. It is money and wealth which are so lacking. So culture is not the *whole* explanation.

A good manager working with Danes knows that he has to manage by *motivating*. By finding good and *challenging* work for his employees to make sure that they are not bored. He has to *develop* them and make sure that they *grow*. A Danish employee who goes to work to find out "who he is" has less need for financial reward and more need for being rewarded with tasks. The study above tells a very clear story here.

If you hate your job in Denmark, you get another one. Danes can very quickly drop everything and go somewhere else. Whereas for example in India, people to a great extent accept the fact that they don't find their jobs particularly interesting. It is not a question of living to work, but working to live.

This of course has big significance for how you are treated by your Danish manager and how he or she tries to motivate you at work.

If the company is willing to recognise that people are motivated for different reasons and should therefore be treated differently, then this is a good basis for you and your Danish boss agreeing expectations to how you would like to be rewarded for your work.

If you have a high need to focus on visible reward (and that doesn't of course have to have anything to do with culture, we are all different from each other) then you could find that your Danish boss thinks you are working for the "wrong reasons". In such a case you need to mobilise your efforts to get your Danish boss to be more culturally intelligent and focus instead on whether you are doing your work well rather than how you are rewarded and with what.

Remember that when a Danish manager says he wants to give you some more challenges, it is not meant as a test, but most likely as a well-meant attempt to give you new exciting tasks. Because that is what his Danish staff prefer.

As I said, the culture surrounding "work is itself the reward" is particularly North European and so you can expect opposition to this reward mentality among staff from outside this region. For example from more collectivist cultures or more masculine cultures where people expect *visible* signs that they are valued. In such cases, people only want more exciting and challenging work if it means a higher salary or a better job title. Danes, however, seldom experience anything other than embarrassment at being rewarded visibly.

## Drop the formalities

Can you remember the way people talk to each other in Denmark? The informal and direct way Danes talk to their boss, the relaxed dress code, the relaxed attitude and the lack of classic politeness? Sometimes you have to remind Danes to "get their act together" a bit when they are talking to people from outside the tribe, just as other people have to make sure not to appear too "stiff" and formal when talking to Danes.

This phenomenon is due to Danes regarding other Danes as part of the "family", and their level of politeness therefore quickly matches that. Just as you maybe don't say "excuse me" when reaching in front of someone for the salt at a family dinner, but do say it to people you don't know, Danes are much more nonchalant and relaxed about dealing with their own "tribe". All the time. When you feel at home, have your slippers on and don't need to keep up appearances. When Danes feel at home among other Danes they can very quickly slip into the same relaxed attitude.

Other nations are used to not knowing each other quite so well. The countries are larger, and trust limited to their immediate sphere and family. They expect that people maintain the form, say things less directly and show respect for others by dressing nicely. That is why Danes can sometimes perceive very friendly and polite mails as irritating and over the top. "Crawler" they think perhaps, or "why is she talking down to me in that way"? But that reaction shows the Danes haven't really understood that other people have different codes from them so it is always a good idea to take note of how Danes reply to you.

A Brazilian woman I once had on a training course was taken to task very directly by her colleagues about her e-mails. They were angry over her friendliness and said that she was "writing to them as if they were small children". It is difficult to keep people happy if they are surrounded by people who think that old-fashioned politeness is very suspicious: "Why is she treating us with kid gloves?" Is what many Danes think when they receive a request wrapped up in reams of politeness. They themselves would just have asked directly without beating about the bush.

Americans especially can often get on Danes' nerves a little with their (from the Danes' point of view) superficial politeness or over-the-top gratitude. Danes would mostly make do with a short thank you or a brief smile. They are not used to having to make people feel special. They are not used to praising people to the skies or receiving praise.

## Being reserved and the careful approach

There is no doubt that one of the greatest intercultural challenges for Danes is their shy, reserved manner. Their lack of tendency to invite people to their homes, lack of spontaneity in social matters and their embarrassed way of dealing with other people's invitations.

Can anything be done about this? Is it just how it is? As a foreigner, do you have any way of getting Danes to open up more?

Of course you have! There are lots of small tricks you can use, but first and foremost it is about removing masses of misunderstandings.

**Danes don't like other Danes either.** First of all, foreigners need to understand that the reserved behaviour of Danes is not due to them not liking foreigners. They behave the same way to other Danes. They don't even open up very much to their own Danish colleagues. They think they've got enough friends and acquaintances already. Danes don't all go off to a secret club when they leave work at 4 pm. They go home to their families. It's important for foreigners to understand that. Because in my experience they take it very personally and misinterpret it as some sort of xenophobia.

**It's not dangerous to be invited, but dangerous to invite.** Remember the story about the fallen apples which Prakash Reddy had experienced in Hvilsager (Chapter 4). The old man didn't dare to approach his neighbours and give them the apples directly out of *respect for their private life*. Because when you give something to somebody, then they owe you something in return. Gifts are not free. It is a universal principle which Marcel Mauss was the first to write about in his book *The Gift*, which I have mentioned previously.

That is why it is intrusive for the Danes to invite people to come to dinner, accept apples or offer to help someone with something. They don't want to bring the other person into an embarrassing situation, because what would happen if *that person* didn't want anything to do with you? So it is rude to come with lots of offers which they would feel obliged to reciprocate later. The solution to this is of course: that Danes don't usually make that offer.

Here is my hypothesis: Danes do in fact want more contact with other people, but they don't dare to ask. I can't provide any sort of scientific documentation, but I'm just basing this on all the times I have seen Danes give invitations to something in a very clumsy way that shows how much they don't want to impose: "it would be great if we could meet over something other than work", "we'll have to find something to do together one day", "we should get better at seeing each other here on the street" – are all completely innocuous "invitations" left hanging in the air waiting to be accepted. They are careful feelers resulting from an enormous need to see more of other people, but also of an extreme *modesty* with regards to being the one to ask first. Maybe that is why Facebook quickly became, and still is, so popular in Denmark. It is a delightfully arm's-length and non-committal way of being "friends" with people and it is easy to make and decline invitations with just a click. So remember to invite your colleagues as Facebook friends if that is the norm where you work (or not, as the case may be).

Having children is often a good opening to other's private lives. "I think Anne would love to play with Jesper", says one parent to another. Because children are so innocent and don't know anything about personal boundaries as parents do. In reality, it may actually be Anne's parents who have a burning desire to get to know Jesper's parents, but they just don't dare to say so directly. But using the children as a Trojan horse, they can come over into the neighbour's garden and share a cup of coffee on the patio while they watch the children play. Children (and dogs!) are the perfect excuse, and many people find that they make new friends through their children. Doing so is entirely risk-free.

So what can we – or they – learn from that?
- Foreigners need to learn to read these small signals and invitations-which-are-not-really-invitations-but-nevertheless-are-real-invitations. It is about understanding the tribe's almost hidden communication signals. Listen to what is being said when Danes are fishing for an invitation – or ask them directly what they mean.

- You have to dare to be more seeking yourself. To put it bluntly: *If you sit and wait for them to invite you, then you'll wait a very long time!* And very many Danes actually *want* other people to invite them, but they are just too modest to do it themselves out of respect for you.
- Use children as social grease. If you haven't got any, then get some. It's also fun to have kids.
- It is quite okay to "frame" social activities with clear expectations. Precise start and finishing times are quite normal in the country where people formalise their social life more than they formalise their work.
- As Danish homes are difficult to get into and as a rule reserved for close friends, then it is a good idea to invite several people (or couples) when you invite Danes round. That feels less like an attempt to force yourself upon them, and Danes find it easier to "hide" in a slightly larger dinner party group. You never know, they may get the courage to invite you to something more intimate later on.

## Meetings without decisions – talk without action

According to the large Expat Study from Oxford Research in 2010, Danes have nothing to write home about when it comes to making fast decisions. 45% of those asked perceive decision-making processes as either slow (31%) or extremely slow (14%) whereas only 25% have the opposite perception. Not impressive, even though it depends on the nationality of the respondent (which unfortunately cannot be determined from the study), and it shows Danes' preconceptions (about them being the most effective Nordic country and being able to make immediate decisions as opposed to the more foot-dragging, polychronic and relationship–focussed foreigners from the South and East) maybe need a reality check.

It's quite right that Danes can make independent decisions and thus make decision-making more efficient, and it is also true that they are fast negotiators because the great amount of trust they have in each other means that they do not need to take a lot of time to get to know the other party before they close a deal. So if that is the case, how can it be that so many directly say that Danes are extremely slow?

The study itself concludes that "it can be felt that a democratic decision-making culture in Danish workplaces is perhaps time-consuming compared to more hierarchic working cultures" and that matches very well what I hear from foreigners working in Denmark. If there is one thing which foreigners in a Danish company fear more than anything else, it is the very many meetings.

Denmark may be an individualist society, but as a society it has a very strong equality norm. The low hierarchy and the feminine "listening culture" encourage everyone to be heard and everyone to have to say something. You are not allowed to not join in. In addition, their very independent way of working makes it necessary for Danes to meet – simply in order to find out about what the others are doing. There are many good reasons for holding meetings in Denmark. They just don't hold very good meetings.

The research group from the Danish University of Education, under the leadership of lecturer Ib Ravn, started to study meeting culture at seven large Danish companies, both public and private, in 2004. The result was that those asked felt on average that every fifth minute spent in meetings was a waste of time. 20% of the time was simply unnecessary.

---

The meeting started 10 minutes too late. It was unclear what the meeting was about, because we just get together once a week. There was no actual meeting leader, the most suitable person didn't take charge. Suddenly the discussion gets going. It quickly loses focus as people jump on their hobby horses. A few people talk too much, some don't make any contribution at all. When the debate fizzles out, no one concludes. Who should do what? No one knows. The meeting goes over time by half an hour, and afterwards the participants ask themselves: Was that meeting actually necessary?
Ib Ravn, lecturer at the Danish University of Education

---

The problem is that few people take responsibility for the meeting, there is no proper agenda, no proper minutes, and seldom very much control of the meeting's purpose. What should they decide? When do they know it's been decided? And who will actually do the work? Why are they starting to discuss again what they already decided in the last meeting?

The flat structure definitely has part of the blame, but is also Danes' inclusive (feminine) manner which doubtless plays a role – where everyone has to be heard and where the few must not dominate too much.

It is not only foreigners who get frustrated about the bad meeting culture. Danes do too. But when other nationalities take part in the meetings it becomes even more important to do something about the problem. Because if there is something you need when you are new to an organisation, it is structure. The completely esoteric meeting culture where the meeting has become a kind of ritual and where the agenda and the schedule (if they even actually exist) are even more difficult for those outside the tribe to understand. *In other words, Danes need to get control of their meetings before they invite more people to them.*

It is a question of culture. In Sweden, meetings are possibly even slower than in Denmark because Swedish culture may possibly be even more consensus oriented than Danish. Everyone has to be heard, and in fact Swedes often find that Danish meetings go too fast.

In reality, there are some simple rules to follow which make meetings easier for both Danes and foreigners, and which definitely remove some of the esoteric aspects which bother non-Danes so much.

- Start on time and agree when you want to be finished.
- Appoint a chair for the meeting who will keep the speaker list.
- Agree the agenda, because changes should be agreed before starting.
- Find out from the start what the expectations are to the subjects on the agenda: is point A something where there has to be a decision? Is point B simply information? Is point C for discussion, but actually without any formal decision at this point?
- One thing at a time: The meeting chair has responsibility for the discussion staying on track and not suddenly going off at a tangent.
- Make sure that each point is concluded – and the minutes are taken, particularly as to *who* will do *what*.
- Give recognition to the meeting participants' opinions and ideas.

- Feel free to finish earlier than scheduled, because that gives a fantastic feeling of having been very efficient.

You could also consider whether you really need to hear everyone and not just carry on the meeting until everyone has said something. That is the responsibility of those concerned. There must be limits to equality!

When Danes themselves are aware that meeting discipline is poor and that discussions often go in ritual circles then the presence of foreigners can often be a useful reason to try something new. So try to challenge Danes about their meeting culture and meeting leadership. As I said, most Danes themselves know it is awful, but they are so tied up with their own inherited cultural practice that it can be difficult for them to think outside their ingrained habits. As an outsider you don't have that problem so you can be precisely the opportunity to do something new which everyone is waiting for (without actually knowing it). It is precisely why intercultural situations can lead to so many improvements, because new cultural input can do something about dysfunctional habits which everyone unfortunately thinks is the only way to do things. So feel free to inspire the Danes to try something new.

## The language problem

When people are asked for the first time what problems they have working in another culture, most of them will say "the language".

That says something about how important a cultural *marker* language is, and it says something about how much culture in reality is all about communication. We focus so much on language that hardly any of us can function as well in a foreign language as in our own. In fact, I will suggest (and I do that with a background in neuro-scientific studies of languages) that those who say they can communicate just as well in two languages are always exaggerating a lot. It is *not* the same as not being able to learn new languages, of course people can do that. But they never become as good at them as the first language they learned as a child no matter how hard they try.

It's very smart to be just as good at English as at Danish, but in reality it's extremely rare. To do so requires having learned both languages from the cradle. Then you really are bilingual, but it is only a very few who have had that opportunity.

In Denmark there are many people who use English as their first foreign language, and that means that none of them can speak it as well as they can Danish, even though the level of English in Denmark is generally very high. That means that Danes also make mistakes.

It is my impression that Danes are very proud of their language, and that they also speak it well. As Indian Triloki Nath Sharma wrote: "Danish is not just Danish. The language is much more closely connected with Danishness compared to how most other people's languages are connected with their national identity, precisely because Denmark is a tribal nation to a great extent." That means there are a lot of phrases and strange expressions which are often spoken very fast, and where the endings are swallowed or where the whole sentence is simply squashed together. As a non-Danish person (I don't remember from where) said: "what does båpåbløb mean"? This is what Danes almost always say when they come to pay by card in a shop. "Båpåbløb" is just "bare på beløbet" spoken extremely fast. It means that the person concerned merely wants to pay the exact amount by card rather than also have some cash back in addition. Languages confined to small geographic areas (in this case Denmark) develop such codes and expressions much more easily and faster than languages which are more widely spread.

- - - - - - - - - - - - - - - - - - - - - - - - - - - - - - - - - - - - - - - - - - -

**Should I learn Danish?**
No one can force anyone to learn a language, but for immigrants who don't expect to leave the country again it is of course a good idea to learn Danish. If you really want to take part in the life of the country, then Danish is a necessity. For your own sake.

It's a bit different if you only expect to stay here for three or four years. First and foremost, it depends where you come from. A Chinese person will learn the language more slowly than a Dutchman, so the Chinese need to make a decision about whether to learn it. My advice to the Dutchman (and Germans, French and English) is: get on with it.

Danes will not be pleased if you don't make the effort. It is a difficult language spoken by few people so learning it gives respect and pride.

On the other hand, Danes have to be *much* better at being patient with foreigners. Danish is one of the world's most difficult languages, and as beginners say, one which take the longest time to understand. This is partly due to the language's vowel sounds. They do not have that many more vowels than others, but the vowels have different *sounds* according to context. Just take a word such as dør (which means door) but also die (as in the last thing you do in life). If you know the language a little you can try to pronounce them. There is a tiny difference in the vowels which only the trained voice can pronounce. Danish is full of that sort of thing. Depending on how you count them, there are between 40 and 50 different vowel sounds. That is more than most other languages in the world. And typical for a small tribe such as Denmark.

This means that Danes must be patient with beginners, something they are not very often particularly good at. Most Danes speak such good English that they switch over to it when someone's Danish pronunciation is not quite perfect. They think it makes things easier. Danes are lazy at languages. But how on earth should anyone manage to learn Danish if everyone keeps replying to them in English? So make sure you insist that people speak Danish to you so that you can learn to understand it. Most people will be very understanding. They are only switching to English to make things easier for you.

------------------------------------------------

Once you have learned the language, you will also quickly find out that Danish is full of phrases that mean something completely different from what they actually appear to. I'm telling you this to explain why Danes prefer to speak their own language and often completely forget that the foreigners present probably don't understand a single word. Danes are also limited by their level of English because they cannot make the same in-jokes in a foreign language. They can do so many advanced things with their own language that it reminds us of high context and homogenous societies such as Japan where people don't need to use very many words either in order to understand each other.

So make sure that your managers support having an inclusive language policy in your company. Let the Danes speak Danish now and again but make it very clear when English should be used. For example, you could experiment with having tables in the canteen where only English or only Danish is spoken, and have them marked with small signs so that people can decide where to sit. This is an excellent solution I have seen work well in many places.

## Moral self-overvaluation and German-Danes

Danish perception of Denmark as a role model which everyone should follow has its downsides. Firstly because it can be terribly exhausting for other people to constantly have to hear conceited Danes talking about their own country at the expense of others, and

secondly because it probably won't end up impressing anyone anyway. People will go a long way in support of their country regardless of how bad things are. But not all of them do it as much as Danes and a few other nations do.

This can also give serious management problems (and mean you miss out on important input) if Danes are convinced that their way of doing things is always better than everyone else's. And researchers know this, because it's been documented several times.

This is something which is especially seen when Danes go abroad and for example buy a company there. The attitude can quickly become that the foreigners should think themselves lucky that they have been bought by a Danish company.

If the attitude from the Danish side is that people should be happy to work for a Danish company because it is decent, democratic, fair, ethical and professional (which of course all Danish companies are), then it can be easy to treat the staff badly because "they are of course used to something worse". So the Danish managers can always hide behind the fact that they are a Danish manager and so almost by definition a level above everyone else in the world. That is a dangerous bed to lie on. It means that the Danish manager is automatically vaccinated against having a critical eye for how he or she is really behaving. Again, as the example in the box shows, their very high degree of moral self-awareness can give Danes a blind spot.

Researchers Jakob Lauring and Jan Selmer from Aarhus Business School undertook a study a couple of years ago about how foreigners in branches of a Danish company in Saudi Arabia were treated by the Danish managers. It is troubling to read. The Danish managers simply decided that the Danish style of listening and including just didn't work on that sort of people, so instead they decided to have a management strategy which was autocratic and far too firm.

As a Danish manager in Saudi Arabia describes it in the study: "To begin with, you are probably a bit too ambitious or too Danish. You start out involving the other nationalities too much and then eventually you conclude that it doesn't work. Then you learn not to waste your time. You know, the Danish way can get you far but there is no point dragging on to the bitter end. So it ends up with you just telling people to do this and do that – and that is how it has to be".

Maybe that sort of thing doesn't happen because of the moral self-overvaluation and a rather provincial idea that Danish is best. Maybe it is just because Danes lack a feeling for how hierarchical societies function. Remember that our stone-age brains, and also Danes' stone-age brains, have difficulty seeing other cultures as just "different". We all tend to evaluate them as "bad" from a moral point of view. In the same way that Danes are brought up to believe that hierarchies are bad, oppressive and just plain evil, and maybe therefore think that hierarchical management is mostly about being an unreasonable dictator who treats his staff with disdain and barks orders at them. "Because that's how people are used to being treated down there. Otherwise they won't understand anything!".

But it's not at all certain that they are right. It is rather that that type of management is a Danish caricature of a hierarchical management style, which reveals above all that many Danes have a prejudicial and stereotyped idea of what management is like outside Scandinavia. Managers who have grown up in hierarchical societies are quite naturally used to people respecting them, but being a hierarchical manager is not the same as treating people badly. A "born hierarchical manager" knows how to earn respect, and leads with a good feeling of what is expected of them. They manage according to the rules, which creates respect even though it is not inclusive. It does not give too much room for independent thinking, but on the other hand is precise and impossible to misunderstand. That is something Danes have difficulty understanding as they were brought up to think that everyone who thinks they are better than other people is a stupid idiot.

When Danes in management positions have to navigate hierarchical societies, or are faced with staff from more hierarchical cultures, they lack the same finely-tuned navigational equipment which the "born" leaders have. They do not know the rules for hierarchical societies and so sometimes end up being a tragic parody of a manager. It ends up being a bit like having to play a football match only having learnt that it's about getting the ball into the goal, but not knowing anything about penalty kicks, offside rules or that you're not allowed to touch the ball with your hands.

Instead many Danish managers, not least abroad, can benefit from taking the temperature of the water and if possible learning from local managers through observation, questioning and obedience.

Jakob Lauring describes among other things how Danish managers in an English context were nicknamed "German Danes" because the English experienced an authoritarian and shouting management style from the Danes which they normally only see from Germans. But shouldn't those Danes have been democratic, listened and focussed on equality?

So if you see Danes behaving inappropriately and as caricatures when among more hierarchically-oriented people, it is a good idea to give them a little advice about handling the situation. They are playing the match on an "away pitch" and often only have their own rather prejudiced ideas about what is required of them.

## And everything else:
### Religion
- Be careful about starting conversations on religious subjects with Danes and avoid asking them about their own beliefs. Most

Danes are Christians but that does not necessarily mean that they are religious or even believe in God. Their rather strange religious behaviour can only be maintained if they don't talk openly about that contradiction, so this means that they simply don't talk about religion very much.

- If Danes say that they don't believe, that doesn't mean that they consider themselves to be atheists. So they will rarely introduce themselves as such. Maybe you think that that's what they are, but avoid using labels and you will find it much easier to deal with them.
- If you find that the Danes are prejudiced about your religion but your beliefs are in fact just as relaxed as theirs are, then try to explain that to them. Danes often believe that others are fundamentally more religious because they are so aware that they themselves have so few beliefs.

## Humour

- Danes use irony and sarcasm to deflate status. Both for themselves and each other. If you think that is unpleasant then say so because Danes are very well aware that they are rather special where this is concerned. They don't mean any lack of respect when they make fun of each other, quite the contrary – including people in humour is a way of showing recognition in Denmark.
- If you are in doubt about whether Danes mean something sarcastically or ironically then ask. They will be more than happy to answer the question.
- In the same way, it is a good idea to warn Danes when you can hear that they are about to make fun of themselves or others. Sometimes they only realise it when it's too late. If you want to see how badly things can go then watch the clip of Danish film director Lars von Trier and especially his leading actress Kirsten Dunst tying herself in knots in embarrassment at a press conference during the Cannes Film Festival in 2011. Von Trier only realises when it is too late to make fun of himself because Danes can go much further before being embarrassed about what they do. http://www.youtube.com/watch?v=LayW8aq4GLw.

## Permissive behaviour

Danes have a very liberal attitude to many things. Alcohol, drugs, homosexuals, abortion, women's rights and a long list of other things. That is protected by Danes' large amount of respect for people's private lives and the right to live in your own way as long as it doesn't affect other people.

So it's a good idea to keep quiet if you have very strong conservative views about some of these areas. Danes perceive themselves as being "ahead" of others in these areas, and often see people from more southern skies, and also Americans, as rather backward and having an illiberal attitude to such things. Because Denmark used to be more conservative, their current attitude is seen as "progress" and for the same reason they conclude that more critical reactionary attitudes are something that belong in the past.

## Alcohol

The Danish alcohol culture is a chapter all on its own. In Denmark, alcohol plays a big part when people are socialising and relaxing. The average alcohol consumption per person is almost 10 litres a year. That puts Danes as number 9 in Europe. A nice position.

In Denmark, alcohol is used in particular to let go of inhibitions, and in a relatively inhibited population such as Denmark's there is clearly a need to let go now and again. It can definitely be said that that's what they do. Christmas parties are very good for getting an impression of what Danes otherwise hide. The ketchup bottle suddenly explodes with all their embarrassing and intimate details. It is generally accepted because contrary to the way things happen in more southern parts of Europe, people believe that when you are drunk then you are more or less absolved of guilt. What you do when you're drunk doesn't really count and it is simply not done to talk about people's embarrassing behaviour once everybody is sober again. What happens when Danes are drunk is a strange kind of exceptional situation where ordinary rules about guilt and morals are temporarily suspended (unless you do something really serious, dangerous or illegal). What happened at the office Christmas party stays at the Christmas party – no one wants to hear anyone recall the embarrassing episodes again once they get back to the office.

Drinking yourself senseless is not completely unknown in other cultures because it is often connected with poverty, social outcasts and worse. Things which are quite rare in Denmark, so people can be very drunk to all the parties you see them at without anyone dreaming of saying that they have a problem with alcohol. Very often Danes will not even bother to keep quiet about how drunk they were. Again, because it is very difficult to lose face in Denmark.

They drink very often to get into a very drunken situation and so you will often find that Danes decline a drink or two with a foreigner because they "have to work tomorrow". Now, it is not strictly speaking necessary to end up completely drunk every time you sit on a bar stool. But for many Danes that is the point of starting to drink, and therefore Danes can sometimes seem to be rejecting personal contact just because they want to avoid being in a situation which can sometimes end up being inappropriate if they really do want to be fresh for work the next day.

## Work ethics

One of the most tenacious myths about Danes among foreigners they work and live together with is that Danes don't work very hard. Yes, they're just lazy. It stems from the fact that foreigners see Danes leave work at 4 pm and rush out of a meeting before it is over because they have to pick up the children from day care. All things that belong to a culture such as Denmark's, and which score low on the masculinity index. Danes also take longer holidays than many other people. Until quite recently you could find official advice on the Foreign Ministry's website about doing business in Denmark. It was a long description of how difficult it is to find Danes in the office during the summer holidays, between Christmas and New Year, in the spring and autumn school half-term holidays and how people leave work even earlier on Fridays. It's been removed from the website now because even the ministry could see that even though it was true, maybe wasn't the best advert for Danish efficiency.

Nevertheless it is not true that Danes are lazier than so many other people, and it should be something which any culturally intelligent visitor should research in depth before making a superficial judgement. Because it maybe does look like Danes organise their working day differently to many other people, but that is not a reason to judge them on first impressions.

For example, Danes have very short lunch breaks which they take together with their colleagues, and this is something where non-Danish staff need to understand that it is considered very anti-social in Denmark to eat your lunch alone in the office. In many other countries, for example in big cities such as London or New York, it is quite normal to go out for lunch on your own and stay away for at least an hour.

In addition, many Danes work from home in the evening once the children have gone to bed. If you add it all up, then their working hours actually begin to look like those of many other countries. That can be very difficult for other people to see if they do not have it explained to them and only judge by what they can actually see.

If you really want to confirm that, then you can check the OECD survey of working hours where Denmark comes out as the fourth hardest working country among OECD countries. So it is true that they have a lot of holidays, waste a lot of time in meetings, and of course work a lot less than the Chinese or Indians, but they're not really that bad.

# 16

## Communications and negotiation

*You know that you are culturally intelligent when you get the reactions you expect again and again over time.*
Martha Maznevski

This last part of the book covers what we do in practice in cultural encounters. As we have already been through some of it, we will not put much more information on the table. Instead, we will just look at how to operationalise further by using some very simple models of how we can deal with other people and how we, so to say, can get "on their side" when we communicate and negotiate.

### It takes (at least) two to communicate

A very banal observation of course, but nevertheless absolutely essential to remember. It means that there are also at least two stories present.

Many of us often believe that there is only one story present, namely the message to be given from person A to person B. It is in person A's interest to pass the information on intact, and if person B doesn't agree, it is just because he hasn't understood yet. So it just has to be made clearer.

But in fact, there is the information to be communicated, the context it is to be communicated in, and then there is the sender's knowledge and expectations and the recipient's knowledge and expectations. Four stories in all, which will have to come together if the communication is to succeed.

The first is called the transmission model, the second the social constructivist model; it is the social situation which, so to say, constructs the communication.

So there are several worlds present in the room, but we ignore them all too often. That is because a lot more happens in communication than just the information which moves around. People get an impression of each other, and themselves create an impression. They build a relationship to each other and try to confirm what they understand about that relationship.

### The transmission model

- Information must be clear
- Information must be heard
- Information must be precise
- The objective is to reduce uncertainty
- The objective is to obtain an answer to a question
- The objective is to solve a problem

### The social constructivist model

- I must be aware of the context I create with my communication
- What spoken actions do we generate?
- What relationships do we create?
- What identities do we create?
- How do we investigate each other's worlds?

The transmission model definitely has many good intentions but it is not sufficient to ensure good communication. Especially when there is a cultural gap between the parties in the communication. So it is not just a question of saying things more clearly, more unambiguously and more precisely.

The two models were established by the American communications researcher Barnett Pearce who says: "I'm not interested in entering into a discussion about to what extent the transmission model is correct or not. I'm satisfied with pointing out that it works best in conversations between people who have common deeply held perceptions of what is true, morally correct and politically intelligent beforehand". In short, in conversations which cross cultural gaps we have to look at more than just the actual transmission.

In the social constructivist model we don't look quite so much at what we should *do*, but what we *create* together. People are aware of everything else that happens when several people are present.

I tend to say that the transmission model runs on autopilot. This means that people expect that the other person is an open tub into which information should just be thrown, so you just have to keep trying on different channels and frequencies until the right "clunk" sound comes from the tub indicating that you have hit the right spot.

You have no idea which channels to use. Person A just tosses a few different strategies in and has already decided when *he* will be satisfied because he has an expectation of what the *right* reaction from person B should be (the "clunk" in the tub). But people are convinced that there is a way through, and if they don't get there immediately they just have to push a bit harder, try and increase the speed, talk more slowly, higher or whatever. Instead, they could consider whether they need to look a bit more at *who* it is they are trying to force their opinion on to, and which *worlds* they each live in.

## Pakistani prunes

A fun exercise in communication is called "Pakistani Prunes". Two people negotiate with each other on the right to bid for a bunch of Pakistani prunes at an auction. Each participant in the exercise gets a piece of paper describing his role. The roles are Dr Rubio Sanchez, medicines researcher at the UN, and Dr Kim Wilson, product developer for a large biopharmaceutical firm. Dr Sanchez needs to use the prunes to develop a substance which when added to soil can reduce the amount of water it is necessary to add to the soil in order to get plants to grow. Dr Wilson's research team has on the other hand discovered that the same prunes can reduce cholesterol levels dramatically and thus make a major contribution to improving the quality of life for up to 20,000 seriously or potentially seriously ill people. They can both only bid on this crop.

Two good issues, aren't they? So who should have the prunes? Naturally, both Wilson and Sanchez will speak in favour of their own issue. Their papers will also have informed them who the other is and both have a feeling that their opponent is entering into this negotiation with almost unlimited means. Each believes that the

UN and the large biopharmaceutical firm respectively have almost limitless funds. They have also been told that the other is a very hard negotiator. So both parties very quickly begin to try and convince the other about the necessity of their own project, and their willingness to listen to what the other party is saying quickly proves to be very limited.

Of course, these prunes are a specially delicate resource which only grows in one place and where the soil also has to lie fallow for at least a year before more prunes can be planted. The opportunity of finding an artificial alternative to the prunes is a long way off in the future.

Some way into the discussion (sometimes earlier but actually mostly never) they discover, however, that each only needs part of the prunes. Wilson needs the flesh and Sanchez needs the stones. Things should be solved now, they can just divide the prunes up and just agree how they get the flesh and the stones transported to each factory respectively. Unfortunately, by this time so much bad faith and negative ideas have been generated that neither really trusts the other. When will you deliver to us, who should get what first, and how do we know for sure that you will stick to your part of the agreement?

## What was it all about?

The negotiation about the Pakistani prunes was about two people who each entered into a communication with a background, and together created a completely new context whilst they were sitting together. Each had a very clear agenda. There was a reality to each agenda, but they also each had a perception of what the other's reality was. In the conversation between them, they talk from that starting point. They don't ask about what they assume in advance, they both have their own information and stick to it.

From the outset, they create an idea about it being a competition between them because they see it as a zero sum game where there is only one winner. That assumption is completely wrong. They could in fact have reached an agreement if they had been more interested in what the reality of the other *actually looked like*, rather than the "story" about the other one which they had been given. That story ends up filling the space between them and makes it impossible for them to learn anything about each other. There is a large risk for their conversation shaping and supporting the story they were given about the situation. The story they were given is about the other being a hard negotiator only interested in his own project and that that project makes the other objective impossible to meet.

So they play their cards very close to their chest and pass on very little of the information they possess. That's annoying enough because if they had been more open about what and how they needed to use the product, they would quickly have been able to find out that each needed a separate part of the fruit – problem solved!

The relationship they build is therefore dominated by mistrust and the negotiations they have are designed to get the other to understand that his requirements are completely unreasonable and wrong. The identities which are stuck to are that the issue each has is the only correct one and that what the other person is doing is therefore wrong. So a lot is "created" in such a situation, but they forget because they are focussed on getting their "message" across to the other person.

Even though they eventually realise that their needs are different, the agreement that follows about how they share the stones and flesh will often be made in such a tense situation of mistrust, creating an unnecessarily complicated and restrictive agreement. Once they have built up a conversation with a very clear story, it is difficult to challenge that story back. If the other person's story is not recognised as legitimate right from the outset, then the fight will simply just continue using other means.

That is in any event what happens most often when the game of "Pakistani Prunes" is played.

## What could have been done?

First and foremost they could have considered the question I put in the box with the social constructivist model. That is the preparation which causes us to focus on what happens during the conversation. It becomes a focus about creating the right process (and through that achieving our goals) rather than constantly focussing on a goal we ourselves have, and on the conversation as something which is to be "won".

What is the conversation about and how is it shaped? With those questions we become aware of when our conversations end up on a particular track which often ends in a dead end. Pearce called these the conversation's "fork points".

We can choose to follow the fork which continues to confirm our story, or we can do what is actually more difficult, which is take the path which recognises that the other person can have a point but that he or she for one reason or another is not stating the point we want them to. All conversations follow a script in our heads. As we know, the stone-age brain would like to be able to predict every communication, and has almost always decided in advance what answers it wants to hear and which answers are correct and valid. If the other person doesn't answer exactly in the way that the stone-age brain expects then we are disappointed, trust drops and we get no further.

Unless people *dare* to let the other person answer differently and thus dare to enter into the other person's world. "Tell me right from the outset what you want to use the prunes for". That question rewinds the film right to the start and most certainly surprises everyone. Because what is interesting is not the other person's story, but the objective of the conversation: who is going to get the prunes? In any event, that is how we think.

Most of us prefer a conversation which runs on autopilot and we get confused if we suddenly don't get an answer which suits the context we are talking inside. But that is precisely what happens in situations where people have different cultural backgrounds. That is why we prefer giving a lot of information and then getting the other person to answer whether they agree or not. Yes or no.

It requires a lot to dare to ask the other person to give information and tell us about their agenda. And we often think that we know what the other person's agenda is; that as we have seen several times in this book; that is exactly what it is dangerous to assume.

"Fork points" are the areas where the conversation can steer around the story we have written in advance and which we are predictably fulfilling the roles for. A story which we continue to write while we talk but without realising that that is what we are doing.

Dr Rubio Sanchez from the UN plays his role as the fearless defender of a warm-hearted good project and has thus already decided to be the moral winner. If he could just understand for a moment what moral story the other person has to offer, then he could maybe understand the equalities and thus also help lower the level of mistrust which is making their mutual solution complicated, difficult, time-consuming and something they are unlikely to look back on as good collaboration.

The fork point consists of challenging the story and being open to the other person telling a different story. "Tell me Dr. Wilson, what will happen if you don't get the prunes". Suddenly, information isn't from the script that you had with you, but from the other person. Now there is only one thing to do, and that is to listen and understand. In other words, you are constantly open to challenging what you should believe, what you know and that you want the other person to provide full information. That requires that you learn:

## The art of asking the right questions

To avoid everyone playing according to their own script, you have to learn to ask questions which challenge the autopilot. That requires us to start finding out about the other person's story and the story we are going to create together.

In Chapter 8, in the section about Asians' difficulties with saying no, we saw open questions which could not be answered with a simple yes or no. Questions which force you to elaborate on your answers because the question demands it.

Those sort of questions are not just essential in the East, they are actually a general tool which is useful for opening lots of dialogues across *all* cultural boundaries.

Fundamentally, we can say that *information should be contained in the answer and not in the question.* Here are two completely different examples of information being found in the question

1. Are you happy working with management who expect that you proactively find your own tasks to a great extent?
2. The computer error you mentioned. Is that an error that occurs often when you are running several programmes at the same time, and if you let your computer go onto standby rather than restarting it?

In both cases, the questioner has a number of expectations. In the first question, the questioner knows what the employee will have to be able to do and has imagined two types of answer. People who like that kind of management, and people who don't. So we only have two possible answers rather than the diversity of answers we could have got if we had asked: "What type of management do you prefer?" If you ask in that way, you have created a fork point in the conversation, and rather than there only being two possible answers you have now opened up for a veritable pot-pourri of possible responses.

With that type of question, the information has to come from the other person, but we often ask questions heavy with information because we much prefer own story, our own project and want to steer the conversation. We want our information across and over into the tub with the right "clunk". We want so much to be able to plot the course of the conversation, because then it is easier to navigate. On the other hand, we risk only seeing part of the picture. Out of concern for getting too much information, we unfortunately get too little. And misunderstand each other. If not right now, then later on.

Similarly, the accommodating IT expert also has a clear script he is following. He knows about a common error. Of course he wants to solve the problem. He wants to have something achieved rather than listening for whether there were other stories. It is fine for the IT guy to try to get to the core of the problem by looking for various different symptoms, but if there are too many of those sorts of questions, he will end up having defined the problem (and the solution) in advance.

All the people in these examples of course want the best. They think they are helping by giving so much information, but in fact, they are creating a very narrow horizon for the conversation where the various different stories, objectives, wishes, ideas, experiences, agendas, emotions, background knowledge, concerns and everything else necessary are not allowed a look in. Because the conversation has been set on autopilot.

Ask short and open questions which demand something of the responder, and then listen. Avoid thinking that you *know* what the answer is in advance. Avoid finishing people's sentences or concluding based on their words before you have heard them several times. There is no shame in asking people to "replay" in more or different words. That way you can be more sure that you are not hearing what you *want* to hear, but what is in fact being said.

This is difficult in high context cultures, where the relationship plays such a large role, and a lot is understood between the lines. In such cases, you have to be aware of what is being repeated (this is where the real message can be found), you have to encourage them to tell you more, and instead of guessing about what they want, simply ask (politely). It's for their own sake, because of course you want the best for them.

## Not a question of clear messages but clear contexts

It is about understanding the social world which your conversation partner is taking part in and a lot of that is about the preparation we looked at in the second part of this book. But the rest has to be cleared up in the situation. It is the context you are sitting in. The rest is a question about how you ask, and whether you can manage to show interest for and have time to see what reality your conversation partner is dealing with.

As the picture tries to illustrate, the problem occurs when people constantly try to confirm that they have been understood instead of

ensuring that they have been understood by asking about what is actually happening in the other person's head.

Cultural understanding and cultural communication are about reaching out over what is already understood and trying to be better at explaining what you mean, using more words when you are asked and fewer words when you yourself are doing the asking. Expressing your wishes (without it being at the expense of the polite phrases which various cultures value) and if necessary repeating them and rephrasing them.

- Ask questions which *assume as little as possible*
  - Open (exploratory) questions
  - Few or no closed questions (yes/no questions)
  - Information should be contained in the answer and not in the question.
- Listen (be careful not to assume too much)
- Switch the auto pilot off and go over to manual control.
- Get your wishes known by talking about your agenda – spread your world out as well as possible (your agenda, intentions, wishes, values and priorities). Let them look over your shoulder as regards the script that you are following.[10] Ask for the same from your conversation partner.
- Make sure you adress the elephant in the room. The more openness there is about the context of what you are saying, the easier it becomes to understand the meaning of what is being said. For example, "in Denmark we like to have a schedule in advance and follow it, that gives us certainty." So at least they know where you stand and you can take things from there.

### E-mails and phone calls – so easy yet so difficult
Humans are adapted to life on the African Savannah around 200,000 years ago. There were no telephones, e-mails or texts. It's easy to see that when we communicate today...

We simply function best in face-to-face relationships because a significant part of our communication takes place with body

---

10 But be aware that it can be counter-productive in some negotiations across cultural boundaries, where it is not good to be too honest. For example, when buying or selling, and you don't need to be to open about the price you would be willing to accept if under pressure.

language and facial expressions. I don't want to suggest an unjustified percentage because it has become somewhat of a sport to suggest that anything between 60% and 95% of our language is body language, and to be completely honest it is impossible to say and totally dependent on culture (a Finn does not say as much with their body as an Italian, that much I can guarantee). But it is a significant part of our communication that takes place other than verbally.

When talking across cultural boundaries in particular and having to start something which resembles a negotiation, a serious or personal conversation, bad news or other important situations the best thing to do is pick up the phone, start a videoconference or simply meet face-to-face. Good videoconference equipment can really be worth the investment and if you are in daily contact with your own or other companies abroad it is really worth thinking about.

E-mails and texts are literally only for short messages about tasks and brief exchanges of opinion. That is how they are used in many other places in the world. But especially in the past few years, e-mails and texts have replaced cards and letters to such an extent that it is even possible to receive warm-hearted and personal text messages. So it can suddenly be a surprise that people in other countries rarely start with "Hi" or conversely do finish off with their "best regards" and full name. Because e-mails are short impersonal messages. If you want more from me, give me a call.

Misunderstandings about what something means, how intensely something should be understood and how polite you should be in an e-mail can often be the first short step to a spiral of mistrust. So, many companies can benefit from a "code of conversation", especially in virtual teams where, together with colleagues from abroad – or whoever they are – they can agree about some simple things:

- How to start an e-mail: "Dear", "Hi" or nothing?
- How to finish an e-mail: "Best regards" as a minimum or just "B.R."?
- Do all e-mails require an answer unless you write that an answer is not necessary?
- How much time may pass before answering?

- May smileys be used, or should there be a rule that if you need to put faces in your message then it is because the message really requires a phone call or face-to-face meeting so you can express the feeling you are worried that the text itself will not be able to express?

Difficult? Definitely, but it can without a doubt be necessary. Even with a small merger "at home". If you know the rules of communication and agree about them, then you avoid guesswork. Guesswork is a sure way to misunderstandings, because the guess is always dependent upon the script for the conversation which you yourself bring in to your encounter with the other person.

Try to avoid guessing. Asking instead of guessing is a fantastically culturally intelligent communications rule.

So if you suddenly have almost daily contact with the company abroad, have a chat about what you expect from the various different forms of communication. Because all these electronic opportunities are fantastic if only they are used with care and if everyone agrees what they are to be used for, or at least what the others are using them for.

# 17

## Informants – nothing beats local knowledge

### The informant

As we saw in Chapter 13, you should always think twice and never blindly trust the information about other people you get from a book. Not even a book like this one. Stories, myths and stereotypes often play a large role, and ideas which are wrong have a tendency to live on if no one questions them.

One way to get over this problem is to have local sources. In anthropology we call them "informants", and they are a significant source for our studies because anthropologists mostly deal with *qualitative studies* and so do not use questionnaires and the like so much. Informants are the local sources of knowledge. They are the ones we ask about everything.

However, as we saw in the last chapter any dialogue is an interpretation, where people adjust to each other, guess what the other one wants to hear and sometimes focus more on the conversation than the reality to be talked about. The same problem can occur when you talk to your local sources. So no anthropologist can rely completely on informants alone. We also have to observe whether people *actually do what they say they do.* We say that we could never imagine breaking the Highway Code, shouting at our children or being unfaithful. But often that's just not true. So we can't rely on *everything* we *say*, we also have to compare it with *what we do*.

### Who are your informants?

Who your informants are can be determined by two things: their job and their personality.

The people we often find as informants are people we come into contact with because of their jobs. They come into contact with us and come into contact with people we want to know about. Typically they are interpreters, colleagues (maybe with a particular mentoring responsibility) or local people from the organisation or company currently functioning as "our man out there".

The other thing which determines if someone is to become an informant is quite banal, namely whether or not we actually like the person. Is it someone who reminds us of good colleagues or friends, or someone we have interests in common with. Remember the long list of all the other things which we have in addition to our nationality: playing golf, being fans of the same football team or mothers of children in the same swimming club (maybe for the same number of children and of the same sex) or liking cooking. You have to spend a lot of time with your informant if you seriously want to get into a culture, so it is best to find out if you share interests with that person.

Informants are not people you have negotiations with. They are people who are there to give information because of their work (as interpreters, mentors or people who the company organisation has sent to simply be your local representative), or the people who are doing the same work as you do – in other words a colleague. As an exception, they can also be friends of friends or maybe even family you have abroad. The reason for this is that you have to be able to rely on your informant and play your cards openly, and that's not quite so easy if you are buying or selling from each other. That is another type of game.

## What can informants help you with?

The short answer is: everything! That is why it is so important to have them. An enormous amount of culture lies inside the second layer of the "culture onion" as we saw in Chapter 1; all the norms that are left unsaid or are secret. How to greet people, whether you mean something ironically, how far into the morning you should say good morning, how to sit on the bus or signal that you have finished eating. All the secret codes which make up so much of culture, but which we never talk about.

**In high context cultures/relationship-focussed cultures**

It is especially necessary to have informants in the typically relationship-focussed cultures such as Asian cultures. These cultures are characterised by a lot of understood knowledge which only circulates in personal relationships and networks. Relationships and context are everything when you seldom rely on people outside your network. You have to get inside the network, and this is where the informant is often an admission ticket.

If you have to go into an Indian passport office to have your visa extended, it may be a good idea to approach someone from a higher caste rather than the person who just happens to be sitting at the closest desk (as I was told by one of our Indian experts). But without insider knowledge, you have no idea who that might be. The local informant has a much better nose for that type of thing and will know who to talk to, what should be said and maybe even what time of day it is most likely that you will get the service you need. In a relationship-focussed high context society there are fixed procedures and clear rules. It's all a question of knowing the right people and knowing the unwritten rules. Informants are simply unavoidable in countries such as India, China, a large number of Eastern and Middle Eastern countries and of course Africa.

**In hierarchical cultures**

In hierarchical cultures it is crucial *who* you talk to. In order not to waste time talking to people without the power to make decisions, you need to be guided to the right place. This can be easier said than done, because people's titles can be difficult to understand, and the name alone doesn't say very much. If the local informant can do some research for you, then he or she can find out who to talk to and about what.

## Choosing your informant

An informant should be able to tell you everything about what goes unsaid and put words to the local culture. An informant should be able to give specific instructions and answer questions when there is something you're not sure about. That requires an informant who is also reasonably culturally intelligent. The culturally unintelligent are characterised by not understanding that someone can perceive their own culture as something strange. The culturally intelligent can on the other hand always see their own culture from the point of view of an outsider. So if an informant appears culturally unintelligent, talks other cultures down or does not make any effort to understand your point of view, then you should consider finding a different one.

The best thing you can do is to use the same intuition you use when spotting someone you feel is someone you would like to "hang out with". But there are nevertheless a few small things to remember:

- Be careful with outsiders. It is a well-known fact among anthropologists that the first person who approaches you and wants to be your "friend" out in the field is the one no one else wants to talk to. The nerd or the outsider desperately looking for someone's company. Like in the school playground. So pay attention to whether they are often alone or whether they have people with them. You don't want an informant who is socially isolated. It's often because they themselves don't *understand the codes* that they end up being outcasts. You need someone who knows the codes like the back of their hand.
- Be generous and accept invitations and gifts (but not gifts which are suspiciously expensive).
- Position in hierarchical societies is everything, so if your informant is very low down in the hierarchy you can risk having someone who cannot be used as an entrance ticket to the powerful and influential. You also risk having *him* lower *your* status. In many societies you are who you are seen together with. People do not socialise outside their class (or caste, professional group etc.).
- You have to be honest with each other. Informants should have the courage to tell you when you're doing something wrong. It is important that you explain that you would rather know if you're doing something wrong than lose face in front of others. Strive for honesty (it can be especially difficult for Asians to say something which can embarrass you about your behaviour, but try and see if you can build up enough honesty).

## How to look after an informant
Your informant can be or become a friend, but remember that the definition of friends varies from culture to culture. Perhaps he calls

you his friend, but you may be more likely to call him a good acquaintance. In Denmark, the opposite would very likely be the case. Your Danish informant would maybe not use the word friend, and will likely not need to call your relationship anything at all. That's perfectly okay. Often it's just the words that are different. You can very easily just say: a loyal person you know you can be honest with who feels obliged to inform and help you in the culture which is foreign to you. That is the definition of a good acquaintance, a good friend and also a good informant.

Just as with all good friends and acquaintances, the relationship needs maintenance. That means you need to remember to write now and again and ask how things are going. Remember birthdays and children's birthdays. Send Christmas cards (even if your informant doesn't celebrate Christmas) or phone them.

I can't tell you precisely *where* people expect a little more effort, so the best you can do is always pay attention to your informants. It takes half a minute to send an electronic card to an informant in China, and he will love that. If you have got to know them well, Danes do not demand so much maintenance. You could be out of contact for years, but when you get back in touch it's just like the good old days again.

And remember: don't forget what his wife and children are called, how old they are, whether they have started school et cetera. Write it down in your address book if you are like me and simply can't remember that sort of thing.

**Other good things to ask your informant about:**

- Politeness and customs and use (requires you to be honest with each other and that they point out mistakes).
- The price of things – from goods you will buy, to how much you should pay your chauffeur.
- Clothes. What is a proper and correct dress code?
- Gossip, not because gossip is that nice but because it is an unavoidable source of knowledge of the surroundings. We use a lot more time on gossip than we are willing to admit to, because we use it to update our knowledge of each other which is necessary for our stone-age brains to know whether they can still trust our social surroundings.

- What is happening in popular culture in the country. Which music and film stars are being talked about? How is the country's football team doing (or whatever other sport the country concerned gets its honour and self-respect from)? Which books are good to read? In short, the informant needs to teach you to hold your own in small talk.

# 18

## What have I learned and how do I move on from here?

This book is a self-help book, so looking at it as a whole, it is a number of suggestions for actions and ways of thinking which will help you and those you work with to think and act culturally intelligently. If you still believe that you lack a short summary, then I have listed what I think is most significant for you to remember in order to stay culturally intelligent and keep your stone-age brain on temporary stand by. It is a mental checklist of the most important things in encounters with both Danes and with anyone else.

Cultural understanding is about changing mindsets, it is about switching the autopilot off when you approach things, thinking differently and expanding your models for explanation and understanding. It is a question of habits and discipline, of making a bit more effort to understand your surroundings, expand your horizons and your frame of reference. It requires knowledge but also the will, because the hundred-thousand year old tribal-oriented stone-age brain often stands in the way.

Cultural understanding, as summarised below, can be instrumental, but it is not just something you do from one day to the next. It is something you slowly understand more and more if you allow yourself to be challenged, if you dare to be critical about your own understanding and your own culture and if you are willing to seek more knowledge about the diversity of "rules of play" and values there are in the world. So it should be maintained and refreshed regularly, and so it is important to spread the message among your colleagues, staff and others like you. The more you agree about thinking differently and the more common references you have to terms such as cultural intelligence, and the more knowledgeable you are together, the more you can help each other with the difficult task which is tolerating, understanding, predicting, negotiating, planning and working with Danes and everyone else who is not quite the same as you are.

## You are going to be a colleague of or manage people who come to Danish culture

- Tell them about the country they have come to. Give them a qualified insight into Danish culture.
- Give your Danish staff insight into the culture they will receive people from and make them aware of what you yourself think has been challenging when encountering their culture.
- Give your Danish staff insight into their own cultural baggage. Together with particular regard to the "difference that makes a difference" in relation to precisely the people they will be encountering. Look at the comparisons in the second part of the book in order to find out about the greatest contrasts.
- Talk about your foreign staff's cultural challenges together with them and give them a free pass to let off steam – avoid steering around what is taboo by only talking about professional issues. Avoid "Dane Bashing" where you just complain constantly and accuse Danes of everything under the sun, but instead listen and try to explain Danish behaviour to them, and put it in context.
- Talk about cultural differences if and when they occur and become a problem.
- Encourage your Danish staff to take part in social events with expats and make sure that those sorts of events are organised.
- Go out of your way to make decision processes, relationships and other structural conditions much more explicit than normal – and if necessary prepare job descriptions for people.
- Make sure you have properly structured meeting leadership.
- Be aware of the need to reward people differently, and respect it if someone is used to a different type of reward than you are used to using for yourself or Danes – diversity leadership is about recognising differences in the needs of staff – different forms of recognition and motivation.
- Agree expectations of the Danish company's or your own ideas about (good) management with staff.

## You are going to work in a culturally diverse environment

- Take a look at your own culture and how your culture and your habits are seen by others. Consider whether there is anything you need to change or modify.
- Remember to ask questions about things you don't understand and explain norms when you see someone making themselves look stupid.
- You must encourage others to do the same.
- Try to acquire knowledge about the other people's culture. Update it regularly and remember to challenge stereotypes – you shouldn't guess, you should know.
- Look for similarities rather than differences.
- Make sure that a language everyone understands is spoken.
- Try accepting invitations and giving invitations back.
- Always argue based on the task in hand and not based on traditions (choose your battles carefully).
- Make an effort to understand why the opposite do what they do (it is not the same as loving them for it).
- Offer to be an informant.

## You are to be sent abroad

- Test the temperature of the water: think before you speak, and observe before you conclude.
- Prepare for the culture you are to encounter by reading about it, and find out which parameters differ from your Danish background.
- Find an informant.
- Remember that you are sitting at their table, and that it is their rules which are the starting point for negotiations about how you are going to work together.
- Try to fit in so as not to attract much attention by finding your own style without completely copying others'.
- Remember, it is quite normal to get a culture shock, and then it can be months before you feel that you are in any way integrated.
- Prepare yourself just as much on the return home – the culture shock you will experience when you get home again is often much worse than the one you had when you left.

## Remember the weaknesses of the stone-age brain:

- We believe all too often that people do things for the same reasons we ourselves do them, and misinterpret others' actions as a result. So we think of all sorts of reasons without actually asking them first.
- Our brains seek cause and effect, we automatically see motives and intentions for everything – even when there are none. Consider whether you have interpreted something deliberate about something which is in fact merely a coincidence.
- We focus too much on cultural differences and too little on what we have in common when we encounter others' cultures.

- We believe that trivial and superficial differences in norms say something fundamental about the other people's morals and ethics.
- Our stone-age brains still believe that cultural differences are dangerous – because collaboration across cultural differences which were too great, was too risky in the Stone Age – quite the opposite to today!
- We create stereotypes which really tell us more about how we see ourselves rather than the other people.
- We have a tendency to look for things that confirm our stereotypes about other people.
- Remember that what is foreign seems worse than what you have in your own culture, and maybe isn't quite so bad.

# Bibliography

## Introduction

Edward T. Hall and Mildred Reed Hall (1987) *Hidden Differences— Doing Business with the Japanese.* Doubleday. The quote is from the foreword page xvii.

The Danish Foreign Ministry (2005) *Det nationale kompetenceregnskab (The Danish National Skills Audit) – main report* p. 103.

The Danish Research and Innovation Agency (2007) *Innovation og mangfoldighed – Ny viden og erfaringer med medarbejderdreven innovation (Innovation and diversity – new knowledge and experience with employee-driven innovation)* Damvad.

Economist Intelligence Unit 2012 – The study can be read here: http://www.jku.at/zsp/content/e48784/e164612/Competing_across_borders.pdf.

Carol Kovach's study was examined at Nancy Adler (2008) *International Dimensions of organizational behavior.* Cengage Learning.

Sally Khallash (2012) *Send flere indvandrere, tak (Send more immigrants, please).* Gyldendal Business (quote from p. 74).

American consulting firm Accenture published an in-depth study of whether cultural training actually works and increased turnover in 2006: It does. In international companies who have outsourced parts of their activities abroad, they experience an increase in productivity with on average 26% compared to firms in the same situation but which have not invested in cultural training programs:http://newsroom.accenture.com/article_display.cfm?article_id=4376.

The division in cultural understanding, mapping and bridging can be found inter alia from the Canadian professor in international business Martha Maznevski. From the American Andrés Tapia this can be found in another form, where the first level, in addition to general cultural understanding, also contains the significant element of self-understanding.

Maznevski, Martha og Joseph DiStefano. 2004. "Synergy from Individual Differences: Map, Bridge and Integrate (MBI)". In: *IMD – Perspectives for Managers*. No. 108, March 2004.

Andrés Tapia (2009), *The Inclusion paradox: The Obama Era and the Transformation of Global Diversity*. Hewitt Associates.

Studies of how cultural training works and what is most difficult to learn has been obtained from: Mark E. Mendenhall and others (2004) "Evaluation Studies of Cross-Cultural Training Programs" in Dan Landis m.fl. *Handbook of intercultural training*. Sage Publications.

## 1. Culture and collision

Tor Bomann-Larsen (1995). *Roald Amundsen – a biography*. Oslo: Cappelen.

Berton, Pierre. *The Arctic Grail The Quest for the North West Passage and the North Pole, 1818-1909*. New York: Viking, 1988. And the theory about the Franklin expedition's lead poisoning was presented by Owen Beattie in *Frozen in Time* (2004).

The slogan "Grasp the Natives' Point of View" comes from field work pioneer: Bronislaw Malinowski. 1922. *Argonauts of the Western Pacific*. London: Routledge.

Stocking, George W. 1993. *The Ethnographer's Magic: And Other Essays in the History of Anthropology*. University of Wisconsin Press.

The example with the pocket handkerchief comes from Gary Ferraro (2008) *Cultural Anthropology*. Thomas Wadsworth, p. 15.

One of the kings of studies about how our daily behaviour is controlled by a large set of unwritten rules (so-called micro-sociology), and how embarrassing situations are caused when someone suddenly departs from those rules is Erving Goffman: *Behavior in Public Places. Notes on the Social Organization of Gathering* (1966). New York: Free Press.

The structure of the brain-Panksepp, Jaak 1998 *Affective Neuroscience: The foundations of Human and animal Emotions*. Oxford. NY: Oxford University Press.

I have described more precisely elsewhere the development humans have gone through and how their suspicion of outside cultures has developed in Nørmark, Dennis and Lars Andreassen 2007. *Det Virkelige Menneske – sjælens og kulturens naturhistorie (The Human Reality – the natural history of soul and culture)*. People's Press.

The Mere Exposure Effect was described for the first time by R. B. Zajonc (1968) "Attitudinal effects of mere exposure" in the *Journal of Personality and Social Psychology*. 9, p. 1-27.

The quote from Mellon is from the book *Og gamle Danmark* (And Old Denmark) (1992), Copenhagen. published by Forlaget Centrum.

Research about whether trust was a particular virtue among Vikings is still underway, but has been been presented here (among other places): Christian Bjørnskov: "Holdånd – har vikingerne gjort os lykkelige?" (Team spirit – did the Vikings make us happy?) In: *Politiken*, 4.5.2008.

Research into immigration into Denmark from Hans Kornø Rasmussen's *Den Danske Stamme* (The Danish Tribe) (2008), published by Politikens Forlag.

For more information about trust and how it functions as a resource see Francis Fukuyama (1995) *Trust.*

Or Robert Putnam's classic *Bowling Alone* (1995) His study with the newest data is also summarised in *Scandinavian Political Studies.* Putnam, R. "Diversity and community in the twenty-first Century" 2006. Vol. 30, no. 2, pp. 137-174.

Further experimental confirmation of the hypothesis that we trust people who look like us: Edward L. Glaeser et al "Measuring Trust" in *The Quarterly Journal of Economics.* (2000), Vol 115 (3), , p. 811-846 and Alberto Alesina and Eliana La Ferrara (2002) "Who trusts others?" i *Journal of Public Economics,* vol. 85 (2) p. 207-234.

For ideas about what hypersocial means, read: Jill Byrnit 2007: *Mennesket – det hypersociale dyr (Humans – hypersocial animals)* Dansk Psykologisk Forlag (Danish Psychological Publishers).

Marcel Mauss 2000 [1922] *Gaven (The Gift).* Spectrum.

This fundamental division between ethics, morals and norms is elaborated upon and is also argued for in my and Lars Andreassen's book (see above). References can also be found there to literature which supports common human morals and ethics.

The attempt to give people red and blue shirts and see what happens refers to the British Channel Four TV programme "The Human Zoo", and the story of the school buses arriving at different times is from the famous "Robbers Cave Experiment"

which you can read more about in Sherif, Muzafer, O.J. Harvey, B.J. White, W.A. Hood, C.W. Sherif. 1961. *Intergroup conflict and cooperation: the Robbers Cave experiment.* University of Oklahoma Press, Norman.

Studies about social capital and especially Danish conditions are not presented better anywhere else than: Gert T. Svendsen and Gunnar L. H. Svendsen (2006) *Social Kapital – En introduktion (Social Capital – an Introduction).* Copenhagen: Hans Reitzels Forlag (Publishers).

Klaus Rothstein's and Mikael Rothstein's book *Bomben i turbanen,* Tiderne Skifter (The Bomb in the Turban) (2006) summarises very well the two very different perspectives of the Mohammed cartoon conflict from south and north.

Regarding the headscarf: Interview with Maria Mawla where she herself denies that she is especially opressed or supports opression: In: *B.T. newspaper* 21.07.2009.

Catinét study referred to in *Kristeligt Dagblad (Christian Daily Newspaper),* 12.3.2008 and the study of women's own attitudes to the headscarf has also been investigated in a qualitative study by Camilla Elg (2005): *Set og overset (Seen and overseen). Young women with immigrant backgrounds in Denmark.* Aalborg: AMID/AAU.

The spiral of mistrust is a mixture of my own experience, but it is almost identical to what researchers have found to be the basis for the escalation of ethnic conflicts and wars among people who otherwise live peacefully and tolerate each other. Lake, David A. and Rothchild, Donald 1996. "Containing Fear: The

Origins and Management of Ethnic Conflict". In: *International Security*, vol. 21, no. 2, p. 41-75. That is why the spiral of mistrust is very definitely a very applicable model for cultural conflicts overall. And Bjørn Nygaard's book *Kulturmødet på arbejdspladsen (Cultural Encounters in the Workplace)* (2010) from Gyldendal Business, includes an excellent summary in Chapter 1 (p. 75-107) of a similar model for conflict escalation.

## 2. Cultural Intelligence

Elisabeth Plum 2008. *CI Cultural Intelligence – the art of leading cultural complexity.* Middlesex University Press.

I obtained information about Indian attitudes to modesty and the difference between the castes from personal communication with the Indian expert in my institute.

Scientific articles and books about CQ and their ability to predict performance:

M. E. Sharpe (2008) *The Handbook of Cultural Intelligence;* Kok-Yee Ng, Linn Van Dyne & Soon Ang (2009), "From experience to experiential learning: Cultural Intelligence as a learning capability for global leader development" in *Academy of Management Learning & Education*, vol. 8, no. 4, p. 511-526; Ang et al. (2007) "Cultural Intelligence: Its measurement and effects on Cultural Judgment and Decision Making, Cultural Adaptation and Taks Performance" in: *Management and Organization Review*, 3:3, p. 335-371.

For a more popular and business-oriented style I can recommend

David Livermore (2011) *The Cultural Intelligence Difference,* AMACOM.

That people behave "conformingly" in groups with a different majority has been confirmed by psychological experiement. Henrich, J. and R. Boyd (1998). "The evolution of conformist transmission and between-group differences". *Evolution and Human Behavior,* no. 19, 215–242.

Hans Magnus Enzensberger describes his train compartment metaphor in the book *Den Store Vandring (The Great Migration),* Gyldendal, (1993: 9).

Richard Gesteland (2006) *Cross-Cultural Business Behavior.* Copenhagen: CBS Press (quote on p.17).

Interview with Asmaa Abdol-Hamid: Christina Hilstrøm: "Asmaas håndtryk" (Asmaa's handshake) In: *Berlingske Tidende newspaper.* 25.4.2007.

Thomas Bredsdorff and Lasse Horne Kjældgaard. 2008. *Tolerance – eller hvordan man lærer at leve med dem, man hader. (Tolerance – or how to learn to live with those you hate)* Gyldendal.

## 3. Cultural Understanding

The quote from Bronislaw Malinowski is from his main work *Argonauts of the Western Pacific.* 1922, p. 25.

Danes' perception of equality is described in particular depth in Peter Gundelach's large value studies. For more information, see the reference list for Chapter 4.

Regarding management in Scandinavia / Denmark: Kirsten Weiss *Når Vikinger Slås (When the Vikings fight)* (2006), Jette Schramm-Nielsen, Peter Lawrence and Karl Henrik Sivesind. *Management in Scandinavia.* (2004).

Specifically about egalitarianism in Scandinavia: E. Fivelsdal and J. Schramm-Nielsen: "Egalitarianism at work: management in Denmark", from: D. J. Hickson (1993). *Management in Western Europe.*

Smith, P. B., Andersen, J. A., Ekelund, B., Graversen, G., and Ropo, A.(2003). "In Search of Nordic Management Styles" In: *Scandinavian Journal of Management, 19: 491-507.*

Perlitz, M., and Seger, F. (2004). "European Cultures and Management Styles", In: *International Journal of Asian Management, 3: 1-26.*

The fact that in Denmark, knowledge workers in particular find it a paradox that they are required to be independent and also to a certain extent follow their manager's orders, but often don't know when to do what, is decribed well in: Ekman, Susanne (2010). *Authority and autonomy – paradoxes of modern knowledge work.* Copenhagen Business School.

Examinations of the pros and cons of hierarchical management are taken from Hofstede and Hofstede *Cultures and Organizations – software of the mind.* (2005: 55-58). It is also shown there that there are no sure indicators that one type of management is necessarily more effective than the other.

Among books documenting Asian progress and the special but effective hierarchical management style, I can recommend Jan Lund's and Jørgen Ørstrøm Møller's *Asien Buldrer – og sådan undgår Danmark at sakke agterud (Asia is Storming – how Denmark can avoid being left behind)* (2007) and a direct comparison

between Scandinavian and Chinese management styles can be found in Verner Worm's (1997) *Vikings and Mandarins: Sino-Scandinavian Business Cooperation in Cross-Cultural Settings.*

The problem with division of responsibility and decision-making in Denmark has been studied in the large *Expat Study* from 2010 (Oxford Research). 45% of the expats in Denmark questioned judged decision-making processes in Denmark as slow (with only 25% believing the opposite). They also mentioned that flat structures with lots of working in teams helped to dilute responsibility and decision-making ability.

About community and meaning: Anthony P. Cohen *The Symbolic Construction of Community* (1985).

The sotory of the Koma people can be read in: Bjarke Paarup-Laursen 1998. "Liv og fortolkning. En Analyse af rationalet bag et ritual hos Koma i Nigeria" (Life and Interpretation. An Analysis of a Ritual of the Koma People in Nigeria), in Kirsten Hastrup and K. Ramløv (ed.): *Cultural Analysis.* Copenhagen.

And the tendency for anthropologists' informants often bringing "post hoc rationalisations" and thus not particularly analytically satisfying explanations of their own rituals and way of living is described very well by Maurice Bloch in (1998) *How we think they think.* Boulder/Oxford: Westview Press.

## 4. Why do Danes do what they do?

I have used a broad range of anthropological and sociological studies of

Danish values and cultural characteristics, with most of them being in Danish. In addition, one particular one gives more general observations. The main works referred to are:

Prakash Reddy (1993) *Danes are Like That* and *Danske Dilemmaer (Danish Dilemmas)* (1998) both published by Grevas.

Richard Jenkins (2011) *Being Danish – Paradoxes of Identity in Everyday Life.* Museum Tusculanum Press.

Peter Gundelach, Hans Raun Iversen and Margit Warburg. (2008) *I hjertet af Danmark (In the Heart of Denmark).* Hans Reitzels Forlag (Publishers).

Peter Gundelach (ed.) (2002) *Danskernes Værdier 1891-1999 (Danish Values 1891-1999).* Hans Reitzels Forlag (Publishers).

Peter Gundelach (ed.) (2004) *Danskernes Særpræg (Special Characteristics of Danes).* Hans Reitzels Forlag (Publishers).

Peter Gundelach (2002) *Det er dansk (That is Danish).* Hans Reitzels Forlag (Publishers).

Bent Jensen and Torben Tranæs (2011) *Vi der bor i Danmark – Hvem er vi – og hvordan lever vi? (We who live in Denmark – who are we and how do we live?)* Gyldendal.

Patrick Kingsley (2012) *How to be Danish.* Short Books.

Flemming Lundgreen-Nielsen (1992). *På sporet af dansk identitet (Seeking the Danish Identity).* Spektrum.

Mehmet Yüksekkaya. (2007) *Uskrevne regler på det danske arbejdsmarked (Unwritten rules in Danish workplaces).* People's Press.

Triloki Nath Sharma. (2008) *Danskerne – Portræt af et bemær-kelsesværdigt folk. (Danes – Portrait of a strange nation).* Forlaget Klim (publishers).

Tone Saugstad Gabrielsen and Marie-Alice Séférian (1991) *Hvor danske er danskerne? (How Danish are the Danes?)* Forlaget Amanda (Publishers).

*Equality*
Robert Molesworth is quoted from Gundelach 2002.

The Anne Knudsen quote is from her book: *Her går det godt – send flere penge (Things are good here – send more money)* (1996: 12-13).

Quote about Jante's Law in Denmark from Gundelach et al 2008: 41) and also (Reddy 1998: 36) is of the same opinion. Notes about praise: (Yüksekkaya 2007: 40) and Reddy (Reddy 1998: 37).

Quote about Poul Schlüter: (Sharma 2008: 22).

Ulla Holm Fadel (1999) ”Skik følge eller land fly. Danske forståelser af kulturel forskellighed” (When in Denmark, do as the Danes. Danish understanding of cultural differences). In: Peter Hervik (ed.) *The embarrassing difference – Danish answers to rising multiculturalism.* Hans Reitzels Forlag (Publishers).

That Denmark has the lowest income differences of all OECD countries (measured using the Gini coefficient) was confirmed most recently in a report in 2010 from the OECD.

*Trust*
Gert T. Svendsen and Gunnar L. H. Svendsen (2006) *Social Kapital – En introduktion (Social Capital – an Introduction).* Copenhagen: Hans Reitzels Forlag (Publishers).

About Danish associations (Gundelach et al, 2008: 123-24).

*Formalities*
Generally regarding formal and informal societies and where they are typically found: Richard Gesteland (2006) *Cross-Cultural Business Behavior.*

The point about polite phrases as especially adapted to life among strangers is from Frederik Stjernfelt's and Jens Martin Eriksen's *Adskillelsens Politik (The Politics of Separation)* (2008: 353).

Regarding the lack of a Danish word for "please": W. Glyn Jones and Kirsten Gade (1993) *Colloquial Danish.* Routledge, p. 73-4.

Regarding "tak" as creating equality and the general lack of polite phrases: Jenkins (2011: 42-46).

Regarding Danes' informal conversations in meetings: Fivelsdal og Schramm-Nielsen 1993: 31-32.

Erving Goffman (1967) *Interaction Ritual. Essays on Face-to-Face Behavior.* Allen Lane: The Penguin Press.

Another good book about politeness / formalities which compares Denmark with a number of other European countries is: Ulla Gjedde Palmgren (2007) *Håndbog i høflighed – kulturelle koder i 11 lande (Politeness Handbook – cultural codes in 11 countries).* Multivers.

Another is Torben Steno's critical look at the lack of Danish politeness in *Længsel efter faste former (Longing for fixed etiquette)* (2011) Multivers.

*Independence*
The article about Danish disobedience on the Øresund Bridge is from *Installatør Horisont (Installer*

*Horizon)* by Anette Lykke Rasmussen 19.3.2009.

The figures from the European study of independence: (Gundelach 2004: 153).

The figures of ideal upbringing: (Gundelach et al, 2008: 202).

The figures for influence in the workplace (Gundelach et al 2008: 210).

Hofstede's figures for uncertainty avoidance from: (Hofstede and Hofstede 2005: 169).

The example from India is borrowed from cultural consultant Line Mark Rugholt from consulting firm Culturewise.

*Punctuality*
Gesteland 2006: 291 and Reddy 1998: 50-51.

*Openness, privacy and individualism*
About collectively-oriented individualism: (Gundelach et al, 2008: 195).

The study of other countries' levels of freedom: (Gundelach 2004: 291).

Reddy's experiences in Hvilsager: (Reddy 1993: 23) and the story about the apples (Reddy 1998: 44) and about the home and neighbourliness (Ibid. 170).

Triloki Nath Sharma is one of the people from abroad who considers Danish individualism to be like a "drop of indifference and a bit of uncertainty" and is concerned about our tendency to loneliness. (Sharma 2008: 215-22).

The quotes from Tone Saugstad Gabrielsen and Maria Pilar Lorenzo are from: (Saugstad and Séférian 1991: 30-38  p. 103 respectively).

The study of how many Danes have friends at work was undertaken by Randstad, Blauw Research and Survey Sampling International and is described in an article on the website of 3F (a Danish Trade Union) on 9 July 2012.

The study of Denmark as a place to work by Oxford Research and Copenhagen Post (2007): *The Expat Study 2006 – Udenlandske videnarbejdere i Danmark (Foreign knowledge workers in Denmark).*

Data about Danes' increase in spending time with their children is from the Rockwool Foundation's studies (Jensen and Tranæs 2011).

The study about foreign students' problems making contact with Danes was published by CIRIUS in March 2009.

*Handling conflicts*
Quote from Agi Csonka: Yüksekkaya 2007: 67.

Kuttner, R. 2008. "The Copenhagen Consensus." *Foreign Affairs*, 87 (2): 78-95.

Salamon, Karen Lisa G. (1992): "I grunden er vi enige" ("Fundamentally, we agree"). En ekskursion i skandinavisk foreningsliv" ("An excursion into Scandinavian associations"), in: Tidsskriftet *Antropologi (Anthropology Newsletter)* 25. Copenhagen.

About public schools and conflict management: (Jenkins 2011: 201).

Sharma's general observations about Danish reserve about conflicts (Sharma 2008: 61) and the example from the silent section of the train (Ibid. 135).

Steno (2011) also describes the phenomenon and speculates whether Danes' lack of polite forms of address is the reason we don't approach each other. We only know the "inner" and "eye-level" ways of communicating and regard phrases of politeness as artificial and distant. That is also why we avoid conflict, especially with strangers, as we do not master the "meta-language" which we *could* choose to have the conflict in. Instead, we sometimes choose jovial irony...

Yüksekkaya's example of a culture of complaining and being reserved about conflict (Yüksekkaya 2007: 43).

*Humour*
Sources: (Sharma 2008: 53-56)

Study of Danes' views on their own superiority in humour was undertaken by the Jyllands-Posten newspaper and Rambøll/Analyse Danmark and was published on 26.7.2009.

The Catinét study and Halima El Abassi's reaction can be seen at: http://forsiden.3f.dk/ article/20050622/ MENNESKER/50622010.

Not all the results of the study on gelotophobia have yet been published but the University of Zurich has guaranteed that Denmark really *does* come at the bottom of the list of 72 countries surveyed: Mette Dahlgaard "Danskerne skammer sig ikke" ("Danes have no shame") in *Berlingske Tidende newspaper,* 15.11.2010.

*Religion*
The main source for this section is of course Phil Zuckerman's book *Society without God* (2010). NYU Press.

The figures for how many Danes believe in God can be determined in different ways and vary from study to study. 51% of people in Denmark believe in God according to a study by Ulla Bondeson (2003) *Nordic Moral Climates*. Transaction Publishers, and the large European values study have, however, set the number slightly higher, at 62% (Gundelach et al 2008: 139). In 2010, Gallup also did a study and got a figure of 48%. Therefore I write that about half the population believes in God.

Membership numbers for the National Church are given on the website of the Ministry of Ecclesiastical Affairs as 80.9% in January 2010.

Regarding Danes' cultural Christianity and relationship to the National Church (Gundelach et al 2008: 143-152).

The study of how great a role God play in Danes' lives: (Andersen, P. B. and Ole Riis "Religionen bliver privat" ("Religion stays private") 2002: 88 in: Gundelach (ed.) 2002.

About the flowering of religious interest with reference to Islam (Gundelach et al 2008: 137, see also Stig Hjarvad *En verden af medier (A world of Media)*, 2008: 173-177).

About Danes' religious sympathies being centrist: Højsgaard, M.T. and H. R. Iversen (2005) "Gudstro med forbehold" ("Believing in God with reservations") in: "Højsgaard, M.T. and H. R. Iversen (ed.) *Gudstro i Danmark (Belief in God in Denmark)*. Anis.

Quote "the world's weakest monopoly church" (Gundelach et al 2008: 143).

Phil Zuckerman's explanations of why belief is so weak: (Zuckerman 2008: 128-146) quote from Jokum (Ibid. 118) and about belief as a taboo in Denmark (Ibid. 93-94; 115-117).

Ina Rosen 2009. *I'm a believer— but I'll be damned if I'm religious. Belief and religion in the Greater Copenhagen Area. A focus group study.* Doctoral thesis, Centre for Theology and Religious Science, University of Lund.

*Self-image*

Jens Smærup Sørensen's quote from: Pia Fris Laneth, "Det danske fantasteri" ("The Danish Fantastery"), in *Information newspaper.*

Study of how proud we are of ourselves (Gundelach et al. 2008: 179).

Quote and points about Danish self-satisfaction also from (Gundelach et al. 2008; 190-92).

Gundelach's study from Dansk Sociologi (Danish Sociology) Gundelach, Peter. (2001) "National identitet i en globaliseringstid" ("National identity in times of globalisation") in: *Dansk Sociologi (Danish Sociology)*. (1) p. 64-80.

Qutoes from Bertel Haarder's *Den Bløde Kynisme (Soft Cynicism)* (1997) Gyldendal. About inferiority complexes and self-overvaluation (Ibid. 16) about "åndelig stormagt" (great spiritual power) (Ibid. 18) the example from the Parliament (Ibid. 19-20).

See also several examples of names with "Dan" in them on the very funny Facebook page "Dan this, dan that": http://www.facebook.com/group.php?gid=105485402833836&ref=ts.

About what is "not Danish" see (Lundgreen-Nielsen 1992: 12).

Richard Jenkins (1998). *Fra Amalienborg til Kvickly: Dannebrog i dansk dagligliv (From Amalienborg to Kvickly: The Danish flag in daily life)*. Skive: Skive Museum.

And Danes' attitudes to flag-burning during the Mohammed cartoon crisis: Jenkins 2011: 147.

The characteristics of Germans and Brazilians respectively are taken from an interview undertaken with two of Living Institute's course participants in a Master's thesis at the University of Lund: Anne-Mari Fagerström and Elias Mellander (2010) *Striking a Balance – a cultural analytical study of a Cross-Cultural Consultancy*. University of Lund.

## 5. Can countries be compared?
Geert Hofstede (2001) *Cultures Consequences – 2nd edition*. Sage Publications.

Geert Hofstede and Gert Jan Hofstede (2005). *Cultures and Organizations. Software of the mind*. McGraw-Hill.

And the website: www.geert-hofstede.com.

Fons Trompenaars and Charles Hampden-Turner (1998) *Riding the Waves of Culture*.

Shalom H. Schwartz (1992). Universals in the Content and Structure of Values: Theoretical Advances and Empirical Tests in 20 Countries. In: *Advances in Experimental Social Psychology*. M. Zanna. San Diego, Academic Press.

Edward T. Hall (1959) *The Silent Language*. Doubleday & Company.

Edward T. Hall and Mildred Reed Hall (1990) *Understanding Cultural Differences*. Intercultural Press.

Robert J. House et al 2004. *Culture, leadership, and organizations: The Globe study of 62 societies*. Sage Publications.

Richard Gesteland (2006). *Cross-Cultural Business Behavior*. Copenhagen Business School.

Richard D. Lewis (2006) *When Cultures Collide*. Nicholas Brealey International.

Web resource: http://www.world-valuessurvey.org/.

## 6. Some are more equal than others...
The example with the Egyptian is from (Gesteland 2006: 48-49).

About attributed and attained status: There is also a correlation between Hofstede's high PDI and the societies which Trompenaars and Hampden-Turner give as countries with attributed status (Smoterman and Kooros 2001: 15).

Per Meilstrup describes the situation surrounding COP 15 and the lack of cultural intelligence of the Danish leadership with lots of examples in *Kampen om klimaet* (Battle for the climate) (2010). People's Press – and the quote from the Indian Environment Minister: p. 171.

## 7. The ones we know and those we don't know so well
About Guanxi: Ambrose Yeo-chi King (1991): "Kuan-hsi and Network Building: A Sociological Interpretation". In: *Daedalus*, Vol. 120, No. 2, p. 63-84.

About telemarketing in Asia (Gesteland 2006: 22).

The figures in the table are from Gert Tinggard Svendsen and Gunner Lind Haase Svendsen who combined figures from the World Values Survey and their own SoCap study to give a measurement of "General Trust". All figures from the 86 countries in total and more details about social capital and trust can be found in their book *Social Kapital* (2006) Hans Reitzels Forlag (publishers).

Circle models about specific and diffuse relationships from Trompenaars and Hampden-Turner 1998: 84, which also borrowed them from social psychologist Kurt Lewin's book about the difference between American and German social spheres.

Example of the French director: Nathalie Ostrynski (2009) "Jeg har følt, at folk er ligeglade med én" ("I felt that people didn't care about me") in *Berlingske Tidende newspaper*, 16.4.2009.

A specific analysis of the difference in context between Denmark, Germany and the UK which is the basis for where they are placed on the line: Malene Djursaa (1994) "North European Business Cultures: Britain vs. Denmark and Germany", in *European Management Journal* vol. 12 no. 2 pp 138-146, June 1994.

## 8. For my sake, or the group's?

Richard E. Nisbett 2003. *The Geography of Thought*. Free Press. New York.

The example with the pens is also from there, as is the in-group out-group model and the studies of the animals and the aquarium.

Data about individualist and collectivist working patterns is from Hofstede and Hofstede 2005: 100-101. As is the explanation of the term "filótimo" (p. 90).

The Norwegian anthropologist Unni Wikan has described the mechanisms behind honour killings in her book *Ære og drab (Honour and Killing): Fadime – a case for thought* (2004) Copenhagen: Gyldendal.

The example with universal vs. particular rules in the study of the traffic accident can be found in Trompenaars and Hampden-Turner 1998: 33-35.

About Americans and American individualism, nothing beats: R. N. Bellah et al. (1996) *Habits of the Heart – Individualism and Commitment in American Life*. University of California Press.

In fact, it can today be measured that brain activity in American and Asian brains is simply different when they have to undertake tasks which require an understanding of the whole rather than tasks which focus on individual details: Trey Hedden et al. 2008. "Cultural Influences on Neural Substrates of Attentional Control", In: *Psychological Science*, 2008, 19 (1), p. 12-17.

It is an exciting area which is called "Cultural Neuroscience" and which has been giving lots of interesting results the past few years.

About the problems of saying "no" in Asian cultures see Gesteland 2006: 35-45 for an even more thorough study of the relationship between dishonesty, lying and harmony, particularly in China, se Verner Worm (1997). s. 111-13.

The dialogue between Sumitra and Brigitte can be found in: Craig Storti: *Speaking of India – Bridging the communication gap when working with Indians*, 2007, p. 48.

The history of the Walkman as a cultural product: Marieke de Mooij (2009) *Global Marketing and Advertising: Understanding Cultural Paradoxes*, p. 5.

The internal Scandinavian differences: Kirsten Weiss 2006 and the quote from Søren Milner, p. 24.

The example from Japan is from Lisbeth Clausen (2006), *Intercultural Organizational Communication*. Copenhagen Business School, p. 99.

About the difference between in-group collectivism and institutional collectivism and country placement within these parameters see Robert J. House and Mansour Javidan "Overview of GLOBE" in: Robert J. House et al. (2004) *Culture, Leadership, and Organizations – the GLOBE study of 62 Societies.*

## 9. How much change is allowed?

About flexibility in Chinese culture see Verner Worm (1997).

The example with the trains is from British sociologist Peter Lawrence who has also called the German attention to maintaining standards and generally very conservative and controlling attitude "organisational impudence" in his book from 1980: *Managers and management in West Germany.* London: Croom Helm.

The ranking of European countries in Shalom Schwartz's study is taken from "Basic Values in Europe" from the ESS Launch Conference, Brussels, 25 November 2003.

There is also a strong correlation between Schwartz's results by country and Hofstede's (according to Dahl, S. (2004). Intercultural research: The current state of knowledge. Middlesex. University Business School Working Paper).

According to Hofstede, uncertainty avoidance also correlates with indications of neurotic behaviour (Hofstede and Hofstede 2005:. 172).

Considerations about Norway come from Thomas Hylland Eriksen's *Typisk Norsk (Typically Norwegian)* (1993) C. Huitfeldt Forlag (publishers), Oslo.

Quote from Anita Ekwall from Kirsten Weiss 2006: 66.

About Putin's popularity and Russians' craving for stability see among others Sergei Kovalev "Why Putin Wins" In: *New York Review of Books*, vol. 54, no. 18, November 2007, not least also Anna Libak's excellent contemplations about this special people from her time as correspondent in: *Rusland på røde plader (Russia on Red Plates)* (2004) Lindhardt and Ringhof and the quote about the carwash is on p. 38.

About Japanese loyalty to a company (and more details about such relationships) see: Fiona Graham (2003) *Inside the Japanese Company.*

Malinowski's observations from the Trobriands: Bronislaw Malinowski, (1965) "The Role of Magic and Religion," from *Reader in Comparative Religion: An Anthropological Approach*, red. William A. Lessa and Evon 2.Vogt. New York.

## 10. Gorilla or mother hen?

The description of the fundamental characteristics of masculine and feminine societies are from Hofstede and Hofstede 2005.

George Lakoff describes the difference between maternal morals and paternal morals in his masterly: *Moral Politics – How liberals and conservatives think* (1996).

Gallup's survey can be read at: Andreas Luth, "Mænd er så kloge – synes de selv" (Men are so clever – that's what they think) in *Berlingske Tidende newspaper*, 14.11.2010.

About Japanese women and the way they change society. Blaine Harden "Japanese Women Shy From Dual Mommy Role" in *the Washington Post*, 28.8.2008 and about the same situations in Italy: Mads Frese "Italienske mødre skal ofre alt" (Italien mothers have to sacrifice everything) in *Information newspaper*, 1.10.2008.

Anne Knudsen 1996: 53-54.

A provocative book about the subject, which to a great extent shows how masculine behaviour creates a number of problems for young men with muslim backgrounds and shows how this behaviour is learned at an early age is described in Nicolai Sennel's (2009) *Blandt kriminelle muslimer – en psykologs erfaringer fra Københavns Kommune (Among criminal Muslims – a psychologist's experiences in the City of Copenhagen)*.

The same thing has been written very well by Naser Khader in (2006) "Ære og Skam" (Honour and Shame).

The quotes from the case of Thor Pedersen and Barsebäck are from: Lars Lemche "Bildt kræver undskyldning af Schlüter" (Bildt demands apology from Schlüter) in *B.T. newspaper* on 6.1.1993 and Jens Holsøe "Humør-krig over sundet" (Humour war across the Øresund Strait) from *Politiken newspaper*, on 7.1.1993.

Other points about the differences between Denmark and Sweden: Weiss 2006.

## 11. May I show my feelings?
The introductory example is inspired by a similar case from Gesteland 2006: 71.

About the Chinese *Mianzi*, Verner Worm 1997: 50.

The model for conversation patters is from Nancy J. Adler (1986) *International Dimensions of Organizational Behavior*. Kent Publishing Company.

Excellent summary of how much contact there is in the two types of society in Gesteland 2006 and also Trompenaars and Hampden-Turner 1998: 70-82.

## 12. Is time a limited resource?
The theory about polychronic and monochronic cultures and their division across countries is primarily from Edward T. Hall 1990 and Trompenaars and Hampden-Turner 1998, who use the terms "synchronic" and "sequential" for what Halls calls polychronic and monochronic.

Another thorough, well-researched and entertaining book about this field is Robert Levine's "The Geography of Time" (2006).

The African story: Louise Windfeld-Høeberg. "Frøken Tracys fornemmelse for tid" (Miss Tracy's perception of time). I *Weekendavisen newspaper* no. 19, 2008.

Richard Gesteland, quotes and observations about time and especially how things are in the South in Gesteland 2006: 59-67.

Max Weber's famous thesis about protestantism's culture, which gave rise to capitalism, is described in the book: *The Protestant Ethic and the Spirit of Capitalism* from 1904.

About work morals in the Middle East and their connection with fatalism, see: Raphael Patai: 2007, *The Arab Mind*. Hatherleigh Press, New York, but I should also mention that other reserachers believe that this fatalistic element in the Arab world can also quickly be emphasised too much: Yusuf M. Sidani and Jon Thornberry (2009): *The Current Arab Work Ethic*. In "Journal of Business Ethics" 91: 35-49.

The report about in which countries you cover 60 feet (18.3 metres) fastest is from a study by Professor Richard Wiseman and The British Council in 2006 and can be found at: www.paceoflife.co.uk and in Wiseman's book (2008) *Quirkology – the Curious Science of Everyday Lives.*

About Japanese switching between linear and circular time perception see: Yohko Tsuji (2006) "Railway Time and Rubber Time: The paradox in the Japanese conception of time" in *Time & Society,* vol.15; p. 177-195.

The Chinese and time from Richard D. Lewis 2006: 58-59.

## 13. Use cultural knowledge in the right way

The division between prejudices and stereotypes is from Rolf Kuschel and Faezeh Zand's *Fordomme & Stereotyper* (Prejudices & Stereotypes). Frydenlund publishers (2007). Parts of the theory about stereotypes presented here is also from there.

The studies done about how Americans, Germans and Frenchmen are perceived and which stereotypes they have about each other was undertaken by a number of different researchers and is compared to Kuschel and Zand 2007: 74-78.

In 2012 (6.8.2012), Metroexpress and YouGov did a survey of 1011 Danes' prejudices about other Europeans which correlates highly with the prejudices in the table.

Fredrik Barth developed his theory about borders' meaning for "ethnicity" in his classic "Ethnic Groups and Boundaries: The Social organization of cultural differences (1969). Boston: Little Brown. And the theory was further developed and elaborated by among others Richard Jenkins in (1997) *Rethinking Ethnicity – Arguments and Explorations*. London: Sage Publications.

The cognitive cycle was developed from the model in: Ulric Neisser (1976) Cognition and reality: principles and implications of cognitive psychology. *WH Freeman.*

Examples of the question full of prejudices is from (among other sources) Plum: 2007.

Alex Ahrendtsen (2009), *Når danskerne bøjer af,* (When Danes Yield) Trykkefrihedsselskabets Bibliotek, publishers.

## 14. How to choose your cultural battles

The Amartya Sen quote is from his own book (2006) *Identity and Violence*. The New Republic.

Theory of identity in modern and traditional societies.

Craig Calhoun (1997) *Nationalism* Minneapolis: University of Minnesota Press and Rogers Brubaker and Frederick Cooper (2000) "Beyond 'Identity'" in *Theory and Society,* vol. 29 (1), p. 1-47.

E. E. Evans-Prichard: "The Nuer of Southern Sudan", in M. Fortes and E.E. Evans-Pritchard (eds.): *African Political Systems*. Oxford: Oxford University Press 1962 (1940), 272-296.

Of globalisation as a force which creates more diversity and "glocalisation" just as much see: Robertson, Roland. 1995. "Glocalization: Time-Space and Homogeneity-Heterogeneity." P. 25-44 in M. Featherstone, S. Lash, and R. Robertson (eds.), *Global Modernities*. London: Sage.

On brothership in certain Danish professions: Henrik Dahl (1997) *Hvis din nabo var en bil (If your neighbour were a car)*. Akademisk Forlag, publishers.

That we believe people from other races look the same as each other has been confirmed by several psychological experiments. Most recently: Corenblum, B., Meissner, C. (2006). Recognition of faces of ingroup and outgroup children and adults. *Journal of Experimental Child Psychology, 93*(3), 187-206.

"Scandinavian Dream Management" is from Weiss: 2006: 103.

A good, research-based study of what actually works when people are to be integrated into another culture, and which a large part of this chapter's various "assertions" are built on, can be found at: Young Yun Kim (2004) "Long-term Cross-Cultural Adaptation" in Dan Landis et al. *Handbook of intercultural training*. Sage Publications, pp. 337-362.

About diversity management:
Susanne Nour & Lars Nellemann Thisted (2005): *Mangfoldighed i arbejdslivet – når vi er lige men ikke ens. (Diversity at work – when we are equal but not identical).* Copenhagen: Børsens Forlag (publishers) (and the specific quote is from p. 20).

Sine Nørholm Just and Mikkel Bülow Skovborg (2008): *Mangfoldighedsmanifestet – principper og praksisser for mangfoldighedsledelse (The Diversity Manifesto – principles and practice for diversity management)*. Danmarks ErhvervsforskningsAkademi.

The story about Korean Air and David Greenberg's work to get them back on their feet again is described in: Malcolm Gladwell (2009) *Outliers: The Story of Success*. The comparison of plane crashes with the PDI parameter (as well as a number of other parameters) is elaborated on further in Hofstede 2001: 115.

## 15. What everyone should know about cultural encounters with the Danes

The quote about independence from Oxford Research *Expat Study,* p. 60 and on the same page there are also the figures for the evaluation of decision-making processes among Danes.

Cases from Susanne Ekman are from the article "Hvad forventes jeg at lave? (What am I expected to do?) from *Weekendavisen newspaper*. No. 23, 2010. And the overall conclusions are available in her thesis: Ekman, Susanne (2010). *Authority and autonomy – paradoxes of modern knowledge work*. Copenhagen Business School.

The quote from director Torben Møller is from: (Yüksekkaya 2007: 102).

The study of to what extent people expect managers to be able to answer specific questions about staff's work is from: André Laurent "The Cultural Diversity of Western Conceptions of Management" in *International Studies of Management & Organization*, Vol. 13, No. 1/2, Cross-Cultural Management: II. Empirical Studies (Spring – Summer, 1983), pp. 75-96.

The study of Danish work ethics and willingness to go to work without being paid, compared to other countries: Svallfors, S, J Goul Andersen & K Halvorsen (2001) "Work orientations in Scandinavia: A Comparison of Denmark, Norway and Sweden" in *Acta Sociologica*, Vol 44, pp 139-56.

About the modern and western tendency to seek identity through work: Sennett, Richard (1998): *The Corrosion of Character – The Personal Consequences of Work in the New Capitalism*, W.W. Norton & Company, New York London.

Together with the creative director at Living Institute, Heidi Rottbøll Andersen, I have myself elaborated on the reflections about Danes, the modern "nomads" of expats and what we can expect from integration from them in a comment in *Berlingske newspaper* 14.10.2012.

The article about Ib Ravn's results in the study of Danish meeting culture, where there is also a reference to the study from other countries. Bjørn Themsen (2007) "Dårlige møder koster penge og vrede ansatte" (Poor meetings cost money and angry staff). In *Nordjyske Stiftstidende newspaper*, 21.10.2007.

And the good advice which came out of the research project can be read here: Ib Ravn (2005) "Bedre møder gennem facilitering" (Better meetings through facilitation) in *Controlleren (The Controller)*, by P. N. Bukh (ed.), Børsens Forlag (publisher), from where the quote also comes (p. 1).

Reflections about Danish and Swedish meeting culture from: (Weiss 2006: 42-44).

That we have an especially time-bound "window of opportunity" for learning languages as children, which later closes so that we can no longer learn a foreign language as well as the first one we learn is called "The Hypothesis about the Critical Period" and has been studied and confirmed by experiments several times. Sources: Robert M. DeKeyser (2000). "The Robustness of Critical Period Effects in Second Language Acquisition". In: *Studies in Second Language Acquisition*, 22:4: 499-533, Cambridge University Press and in Steven Pinker (1994) *The Language Instinct*. Morrow.

Mie Femø Nielsen. 2002. "Nå! En skiftemarkør med mange funktioner (So! A change marker with many functions)". *Årsberetning for Selskab for Nordisk Filologi (Annual Report for the Society of Nordic Philology)*, 2000-2001.

The calculation of vocal sounds in Danish is from linguist Dr. Ruben Schachtenhaufen's blog about phonetics and phonology: http://schwa.dk/vokaler/hvor-mange-vokallyde-er-der-i-dansk/.

That Danish is a difficult language to learn because of a large number of reasons I mention is confirmed by a number of language researchers in this article: "Dansk, et flippersprog du ikke kan nå" (Danish, a hippie language you can't manage) in *Information newspaper*, 4.4.2003.

The significance of language for integration in Denmark can also be read in the Expat in Denmark survey. There is a strong correlation between language and cultural integration. Oxford Research: *The Expat Study 2010* p. 66. What determines what is of course difficult to say anything precisely about, but other studies also confirm that knowledge of the language where you are moving to is crucial for feeling that you understand the other cultural codes in the society. Sharing language means to a great extent that you get the feeling of sharing the world, and so language integration is thus such an essential element in feeling at home in another culture: Milton J. Bennett and Ida Castiglioni. 2004. "Embodied Ethnocentrism and the Feeling of Culture" in Dan Landis et al. *Handbook of Cultural Training*. Sage Publications.

Studies of Danish leadership abroad and the existence of "German-Danes" and a more autocratic management style, when we are no longer in Denmark, is documented and described in:

Bjørn, L. B. 1997. *Managing Uncertainty in Transnational Headquarters-Subsidiary Interfaces*. Aarhus University, Aarhus.

Lauring, Jakob and Selmer, Jan (2008). "Globalizing Denmark: Open-minded while Self-sufficient?". Not yet published, but available at http://www.asb.dk/fileexplorer/fetchfile.aspx?file=7603.

Lauring, J., Bjerregaard, T., and Søderberg, A. 2008. "Intercultural Encounters in an English Subsidiary: An Ethnographic Field Study", *EURAM Conference*. Ljubljana.

And an article about the term "German Danes": Marcinkowski, Victoria (2008) "Danske ledere fejler i udlandet" (Danish managers fail abroad) : *Børsen newspaper*, 19.12.2008.

Reflections about Danish versus southern alcohol culture are from Anne Knudsen and Lisanne Wilkens (1993) *Kulturelle Verdener (Cultural Worlds)*, Columbus, (p. 120-21).

The OECD's list of diligent nations can be found here: http://www.bizaims.com/articles/social/meet procent20worlds procent20hardest-working procent20countries.

## 16. Communications and negotiation

Coordinated Management of Meaning has been especially developed by W. Barnett Pearce and its description can be found at:

W. Barnett Pearce. 2008. *Making Social Worlds: A Communication Perspective*. Wiley-Blackwell.

The Pakistani Prunes story is distributed by: R. J. Lewicki, B. Barry and D. M. Saunders (2006) "Negotiation – readings, exercises, and cases". McGraw & Hill.

There are also lots of advice, checklists and exercises to find in the following books:

Richard W. Brislin and Tomoko Yoshida. 1994. *Intercultural communication training: An introduction*. Sage Publications.

Dan Landis et al. 2004. *Handbook of intercultural training*. Sage Publications.

Lee Gardenswartz and Anita Rowe 1994. *The Managing Diversity Survival Guide*. Irwin Professional Publishing.

# About Living Institute

Living Institute was founded in April 2004, originally to solve Danish companies' challenges with attracting and retaining key foreign staff. Very quickly, the focus was expanded to also give *Danish* staff a global outlook.

Living Institute works with cultural intelligence in some of Denmark's largest companies.

Dennis Nørmark joined in 2007 and is now a partner, the chief consultant and the head of training.

# Thanks to the informants

An anthropologist is worth nothing without informants, and in my
years of work with cultural understanding my most valuable source
of information about Denmark and the Danes has most definitely
been all the fantastic and capable expats I have taught, trained and
most of all listened to. They have become thousands of good
sources, and I want to thank all of them.

That these encounters between them and me were at all possible
is of course due to the founder of Living Institute, Heidi Rottbøll
Andersen. I also owe her my thanks for her useful input and for
introducing me to all the fascinating people who have been sources
of inspiration for this book. Among them are the specialist consultants I have worked in partnership with over the years. Several of
them are mentioned in this book, and some merely "between the
lines". Thanks to Victoria Vorting, Line Mark Rugholt, Mads
Fuglede, Sidsel Rastrup Magnussen, Anne Mette Lundtofte, Tom
Hale, Anette Villemoes, Kirsten Weiss and Hanna Leanderdal.

For the English edition, I also owe special thanks to Sofka Ane
Brændgaard and Helle Katholm Knutsen.